TESTING FOR
TEACHER CERTIFICATION

Edited by

William P. Gorth
and
Michael L. Chernoff

National Evaluation Systems, Inc.

LEA LAWRENCE ERLBAUM ASSOCIATES, PUBLISHERS
1985   Hillsdale, New Jersey   London

Lawrence Erlbaum Associates, Inc., Publishers
365 Broadway
Hillsdale, New Jersey 07642

Library of Congress Cataloging-in-Publication Data
Main entry under title:

Testing for teacher certification.

Includes bibliographies.
1. Teachers—Certification—United States—
Addresses, essays, lectures. I. Gorth, William P.
II. Chernoff, Michael L.
LB1771.T47 1986   379.1'57   85-20628
ISBN 0-89859-758-7

Printed in the United States of America
10 9 8 7 6 5 4 3 2 1

PREFACE

Testing for Teacher Certification is a compilation of papers, none of which have been previously published, on a topic that has emerged as one of the most challenging of this decade. The subject matter ranges across the technical and legal issues surrounding teacher certification testing, program administration, and the history and future of certification testing.

The book will be of interest to state education department staff, deans and faculty of colleges and departments of education, state legislators with an interest in educational issues, classroom teachers and school administrators, and boards of education on both the state and district levels.

Testing for Teacher Certification is comprehensive and current. We hope it serves as an introduction to this critical area for those who have not encountered it in the past and as an update of the field for those with more direct experience.

The staff at National Evaluation Systems, Inc. (NES) hope that the book meets its goal of furthering the intelligent discussion of this topic.

ACKNOWLEDGMENTS

Our first thanks go to the authors who contributed chapters to this book and then generously tolerated our editorial manipulations. We also wish to acknowledge Jack Burton and his staff at Lawrence Erlbaum Associates, who were quick to see the value of this book and were supportive during the editing and production process.

Laura Tills, Maureen Horak, and Carolyn Ayers at National Evaluation Systems did the bulk of the copyediting and proofreading on the individual chapters, instilling some degree of consistency without violating the substance of any of the chapters. Special thanks also to Julie Collins, the NES Production Manager, Cait Whittle, Manager of Word Processing/Typesetting, Bunny Chamberlain, typesetter, and Kay Delli Bovi, graphic artist, for their help in turning the chapters into production-ready materials.

—Michael Chernoff for NES

CONTENTS

INTRODUCTION

Overview of Teacher Certification

Few developments in recent educational history have generated as much interest as the use of tests in the certification process for prospective teachers. By the end of 1984, approximately 38 states had begun using some kind of test as part of their certification procedures. Although a few states remain that do not use tests, it is fair to say that every education department in the country has seriously considered implementing such a program.

The topic is familiar to those in professional education circles, especially those who specialize in teacher education. Among classroom teachers, the use of tests has aroused considerable controversy. Teacher certification testing has also generated interest in the professional measurement community, which follows credentialing programs and techniques regardless of field.

Although the public at large typically does not pay attention to debates on educational policy, the topic of teacher testing has attracted significant public attention. Indeed, it was public pressure that helped launch several teacher certification testing programs. Public concern about teacher skills arose at times because of grammatical and other errors in notes or reports teachers wrote to parents. This concern sparked a demand for stricter standards. Highly visible and well-publicized incidents involving public pressure were not, however, the only incentive for teacher certification testing.

PURPOSE OF THIS BOOK

This volume contains chapters that review teacher certification testing from a number of different perspectives. The discussions include technical, legal, logistical, and administrative views of the topic. The material presented should be of value to several audiences:

1. *State education department staff.* Personnel directly involved in teacher certification issues will find much of interest in this volume, as will personnel at the policy-

making levels. The responsibility for establishing a policy and a set of fundamental guidelines for testing programs often rests with individuals at the state commissioner and associate commissioner levels. This book should prove valuable to those in the testing and evaluation bureau who may or may not have direct responsibility for a certification program, but who often have an opportunity to participate in the design and implementation of such an effort.

2. *Faculty and deans of teacher education institutions.* As one of the chapters in this volume points out, a population most directly affected by teacher certification testing programs is the faculties of colleges and universities that educate prospective teachers. Although the introduction of a testing program in a given state is by no means an indictment of teacher preparation, the testing programs are often viewed as a further incursion into the independent right of schools to certify their graduates to teach in the classroom. On the other hand, there is no doubt that in individual states, a concern for the quality of teacher preparation in at least some institutions has helped convince state policymakers that a statewide testing initiative is required.

Regardless of the reasons for beginning teacher certification testing, these programs have direct effects on teacher educators. And teacher educators have been among the most vocal participants in the discussion about the merits of teacher certification testing.

3. *Professional measurement specialists.* Academicians and others involved in the measurement of mental abilities and knowledge have played a prominent role in designing and providing expert consultation in the development of many teacher certification testing programs. The tests seek to measure some stated characteristics or attributes of individual candidates. This objective brings up the traditional issues of concern in test development: the statistical analyses of results, the validity and reliability of individual items and of tests as a whole, and so on. Members of this professional community should, therefore, find many of the chapters in this book of interest, particularly those dealing with technical issues.

4. *Classroom teachers.* Although the programs covered by this book do not test practicing classroom teachers (indeed, that policy is rare), classroom teachers and their professional organizations (e.g., The American Federation of Teachers, The National Education Association) initially were among the populations most apprehensive about certification testing. Recently, both organizations have discussed the value of a national examination for teachers. And, at least with the customized, criterion-referenced programs that are a focus in this volume, teachers are active participants in both test design and development.

5. *Lay public.* These chapters were not written for the general public. Nonetheless, with rare exception, they are accessible to the interested general reader. Because of the wide range of topics discussed in this book, including the history of certification practices as well as some of the more direct policy issues, citizens can obtain a useful introduction to teacher certification testing. It is ordinary citizens, after all, who pay the taxes that support education in their states and whose children are directly affected by teacher quality.

ACCOUNTABILITY

In general, as accountability in education becomes more important, the impetus for testing prospective teachers grows. There is heightened sensitivity across the country to the results of classroom instruction and to the various components that determine its quality. As a result, there has been a reawakening of interest in student testing as a means of verifying that effective instruction has taken place. All elements of school budgets are receiving greater scrutiny. And teachers, as the critical ingredient in instruction, are the focus of attention to accountability that results from competency testing.

BEYOND REGULATION

It is common to think of teacher certification testing programs as existing primarily for regulatory purposes. State agencies, including departments of education, have an obligation to protect the interests and welfare of the citizens in their jurisdictions. In the case of education, this includes the responsibility to ensure that all teachers in the classroom have the requisite skills and knowledge to perform adequately. The state's responsibility to license teachers is not in question. The tests are a fairly recent and increasingly important aspect of that licensing process, but they are by no means the only criterion by which prospective teachers are evaluated.

On the other hand, there is much that teacher certification testing programs can do to move beyond simple regulatory functions. In many of the programs discussed in this book, the test development process includes an explicit definition of the content taught in the classrooms of a given state. This content definition process provides personnel in the state education department and teacher training institutions with a tremendous amount of information about the objectives that a curriculum should include in order to prepare teachers for their jobs. By carefully reviewing the content of classroom instruction and the aggregate test results of their graduates, teacher training institutions can bring their own teacher training programs into closer alignment with classroom practices throughout the state. Through the test development process, state education departments have a vehicle for evaluating whether state-mandated curricula are, in fact, being taught in the classroom. In short, the test development process and the scores achieved individually and in aggregate by examinees offer a large amount of detailed information to a state interested in reviewing its educational practices and policies.

This theme is explored in more detail in several of the chapters in this volume, and it reflects a mature attitude toward teacher certification testing, one that extends far beyond the mere classification of candidates into "pass" or "fail" categories.

TRENDS FOR THE FUTURE

Current Options

At present, a state initiating a teacher certification testing program has three options for obtaining the tests.

CUSTOM DEVELOPMENT
An agency can contract to have tests developed on a custom basis. This entails a set of test questions keyed to objectives validated through a job analysis survey conducted in the state. Moreover,

all of the objectives and test items would be written new for that agency. This approach is represented to a large extent by the programs described in the chapters of this book.

OFF-THE-SHELF TESTS

A state agency can make arrangements for an off-the-shelf testing program to be administered to its candidates. In this situation, the agency accepts the tests and test administration policies as given; there is no opportunity for modification or control by the state. The National Teacher Examination (NTE), offered by the Educational Testing Service, is an example of this approach.

MODIFIED CUSTOMIZATION

In this approach, a state agency works with existing test materials but has the ability to modify, adapt, or augment those tests at the item and/or objective level. Also, modified customization typically allows the agency to control the policies governing test administration. The approach combines elements of customization with the use of existing test materials.

The Shift to Modified Customization

Based on a review of states considering teacher certification testing programs, there appears to be increasing interest in the modified customization approach. While the specifics vary from state to state, agency staff cite several reasons.

REGULATORY ISSUES

As licensing examinations, tests for initial certification invoke governmental and professional standards and regulations. To be legally defensible, a test should be based on a job analysis of incumbent teachers in a given state and only those items judged to be content valid should be used. The job analysis identifies those objectives that classroom instruction requires in the state. The modified customization approach often includes a job analysis whereas the off-the-shelf approach does not. The ability to modify test items can create a more content valid test reflective of the state's certification laws.

IMPROVEMENT OF TEACHING QUALITY

Certification testing occurs in a context of other policies designed to improve education in general. To the extent a program is customized, it is more likely to serve these other policies and goals. Again, this approach is more similar to that taken in fully customized programs as opposed to off-the-shelf products.

FUNDING

The funding issue has two sides.

1. *Initial expense*—Modified customization provides a state with a program at a cost less than that of customized development.

2. *Use of examinees' fees*—Modified customization gives the state control over the fees collected as a part of test administration. In an off-the-shelf program, where all fees go to the vendor, these fees are not available to the agency for other activities. The revenues generated in a modified customization program can be used to fund development in low incidence fields, to create support materials for examinees and teacher education institutions, and to pursue other goals.

POLICY CONTROL

As in a custom program, modified customization gives the agency control over all policies governing the administration of the tests, including dates, size and nature of the fees, sites, score report formats, use of test data for research, and security. This is in contrast to off-the-shelf programs.

There seems to be a trend toward the use of the modified customization approach in testing programs for the initial certification of teachers. The approach appears to be appealing to state education agencies because it includes the several benefits of a fully customized approach but without the initial test development expense.

TCT PROGRAM TYPES

Different states give teacher certification tests at various points in an individual's career. The variety of types of tests given is reflected in the content of this book.

TIMING

Tests are generally required twice in an individual's career. The first is at entry to a teacher education program. Here the test typically is one in the basic skill areas of reading, writing, and mathematics. Second, tests are often required upon completion of one's training but before the award of a certificate. The professional and content area skills and knowledge tests normally fall into this category.

CONTENT MEASURED

The tests used in teacher certification also vary in content. The major categories are as follows:

1. *Basic skills.* Many states test applicants for teacher education programs in the basic skills of reading, writing, and mathematics. Successful performance in these areas is considered a prerequisite to adequate participation in the teacher education program. The writing test usually involves a writing sample and less often multiple-choice questions about writing mechanics. The mathematics and reading tests are normally multiple-choice in format.

2. *Content areas.* Although most observers would agree that knowledge of subject matter alone is not a sufficient prerequisite for effective classroom teaching, it is certainly a necessary one. Therefore, at the point of certification, many states test individuals on their content knowledge of the field for which they seek a certificate.

   Typically, the content areas tested reflect the structure of the certificates awarded by a state. This is especially true for those states that have developed their own custom programs. In these states, such as Oklahoma, tests are prepared for certificate areas. Oklahoma currently offers 79 different tests in such areas as elementary education, science, home economics, industrial arts, and journalism. The program in Oklahoma and the one under development in Texas are among the most extensive.

States that have adopted the National Teacher Examination (offered by the Educational Testing Service) are limited, of course, to the approximately 28 content tests offered in that program.

It should be noted that several states use these content area tests for teachers who are already certified and are seeking additional certificates.

3. *Professional skills.* Teacher education programs convey a set of professional skills that transcend the differences among individual academic areas. Consequently, many states test certification candidates, at the conclusion of their college experience, in the professional skills deemed necessary for classroom performance. These skills include familiarity with standard reference and information sources, lesson planning, classroom management techniques, learning theories, and other general pedagogical topics.

4. *Other (e.g., general knowledge).* A smaller number of states test graduates in their general knowledge and background in the liberal arts. The purpose of these tests is often worded vaguely; for example, the purpose may be presented as trying to ensure that the teacher is a "well-educated" individual. Despite the difficulties in defining the content base for such a test, several states do assess teaching candidates' general knowledge.

The kinds of tests mentioned above are all precertification events, that is, tests to be passed as a part of becoming a licensed teacher. Testing certified, practicing teachers is a very different matter, one that has been attempted in only a handful of states. Some states (e.g., Arkansas) have recently implemented programs to test current teachers in the basic skills of reading, writing, and mathematics. This program is distinguished by the fact that real penalties will occur for teachers who do not eventually pass the examination. A number of other states, notably Texas, are beginning programs with similar characteristics. These highly controversial initiatives are too new for much, if any, reflective experience to have accumulated. They are therefore only indirectly covered by the chapters in this volume.

A number of states are considering the use of their content tests as a part of career ladder programs for teachers. These programs offer professional advancement opportunities to a teacher who meets a number of criteria, including passing a content test in his or her subject field. Again, since career ladder testing components are so new, they are not dealt with in this book.

CLINICAL ASSESSMENT

States also require student teaching experience as a condition of certification. Moreover, some states have extensive clinical classroom assessment procedures with beginning teachers. The Georgia program, under the direction of Lester Solomon, is quite advanced in this regard. Beginning teachers are closely supervised and provided support and counseling on a regular basis and in a variety of formats. Readers interested in more information should contact the Georgia State Department of Education.

DIFFERENT COMBINATIONS

Individual states vary in the number and types of tests they use in their certification programs. The most common are the basic skills tests used for admission to a teacher training program, the content knowledge tests administered at the point of certification, and the professional skills tests also given at the point of certification. The most common testing scenario includes, therefore, a basic skills test to enter a teacher education program and both a professional skills and content field test at exit, that is, at the point of certification.

SOURCES OF TESTS

From a psychometric perspective, there are two types of tests used in teacher certification programs. The first is norm-referenced tests, which are typically used as a way of comparing one candidate with another in an admission situation. These tests are not normally tied to specific learning objectives and therefore yield only a total test score for examinees. The most widespread example of this type of test is the National Teacher Examination (NTE), a set of tests prepared and administered by the Educational Testing Service (ETS).

The NTE provides no breakdown of test content into subareas of any kind. The tests were prepared by ETS for use on a national basis, and their content reflects the content of teacher training programs across the country. States that adopt the NTE are obliged to validate the tests against state standards and to attempt to establish the job relatedness of the instrument for classroom requirements in the state. The NTE, a "shelf" product, is never altered to reflect the specific concerns or needs of a given state.

In contrast, many states use criterion-referenced instruments, which are most valuable for comparing an individual against a specified standard of performance or knowledge. These tests are tied to specifically defined learning objectives and therefore yield detailed subtest scores and other diagnostic information. Members of both the legal and measurement professions generally agree that criterion-referenced tests are more appropriate for credentialing situations. Indeed, criterion-referenced tests along with their benefits are the themes of many of the chapters in this volume.

Many of the criterion-referenced programs are developed and administered by National Evaluation Systems (NES) of Amherst, Massachusetts. The tests and programs developed by NES are customized to the policies and certificate areas of the individual states. The tests yield detailed subarea scores and diagnostic information for individual examinees and the institutions that train them. In order to establish a valid basis for test development, the test instruments are based on a review of curriculum materials used in classrooms in the state and on job analysis surveys of practicing teachers.

Source of Materials

The chapters in this book were originally presented as papers at two major conferences. The first and more important was a conference entitled "Testing for Teacher Certification," sponsored by National Evaluation Systems in 1985 and held in Chicago. This presentational conference brought together state education department staff and technical experts in relevant fields. The second conference was a National Council on Measurement in Education

(NCME) symposium sponsored by NES in 1983 and held in conjunction with the annual meeting of the American Educational Research Association (AERA) and NCME. The authors of the chapters include state education department staff members who are involved in teacher certification testing programs, technical experts in given fields (some academically based, others practicing professionals), and NES staff members directly involved in designing and running these testing programs in cooperation with state education department personnel.

Structure of the Book

This volume is divided into four sections. The chapters cover all major aspects of the teacher certification domain. As the brief descriptions that follow demonstrate, both design and technical issues are included as well as discussions of the context in which these testing programs are developed and implemented.

OVERVIEW OF TEACHER CERTIFICATION TESTING

The two chapters in this section contain a history of teacher credentialing and a discussion of the commonalities among teacher certification testing programs in various states.

FUNDAMENTAL ISSUES AND PROGRAM DESIGN

The five chapters in this section deal with planning teacher certification testing programs. They discuss the political, legal, and administrative issues that surround these programs and create an argument for an early consideration of these issues. The authors argue that early attention to significant issues helps create programs that meet goals, are legally defensible, and are sensitive to the general educational context in which they exist.

CRITICAL TECHNICAL ISSUES

Creating a valid, job-related, reliable program also entails consideration of several testing issues (e.g., establishing a passing score for the test). The six chapters included in this section deal with a variety of technical issues. Each of the issues discussed in this section has important implications for the effectiveness and quality of the testing program.

BEYOND REGULATION

The three chapters in this section argue that programs may meet their regulatory goals and simultaneously support the general improvement of educational programs in a given state. These chapters explore how the testing programs reach beyond the testing situation itself to provide support to teacher training institutions, the state department of education, and individual teacher candidates.

National Evaluation Systems

National Evaluation Systems (NES) was founded in 1972. Since that time, it has focused almost exclusively on the development of criterion-referenced tests for educational purposes. This work includes a large amount of activity in student assessment and teacher certification testing. Located in Amherst, Massachusetts, with an office in Palo Alto, California, NES's large, predominantly professional staff offers custom, full-service capabilities in program design, materials development and production, and program administration.

In the mid-1970s, NES worked with the Georgia State Department of Education to pioneer the first customized, criterion-referenced teacher certification testing program in the country. That program involved the development of tests matched to certificate areas in the state and was based on extensive job analysis surveys of practicing teachers in the certificate fields. Moreover, hundreds of Georgia classroom teachers and teacher educators participated in committees for each content area to review topic outlines and objectives, review job analysis survey results, select objectives for the test, review draft test items, and periodically update test materials.

The Georgia program provided a model for other states desiring a criterion-referenced program over which they could maintain policy control. Subsequently, NES has developed programs with the states of Alabama, Oklahoma, West Virginia, and Connecticut.

NES was awarded the contract for the largest teacher certification testing program ever designed, the Examination for the Certification of Educators in Texas program.

SERVICES

National Evaluation Systems provides states with a complete range of services related to criterion-referenced testing programs, including:

- *design* of the testing program, the flow of work, the procedures to be used for quality control, and the maintenance of security;
- *development* of the tests and all related support materials, including conducting the job analysis surveys, advisory committee meetings, content definition, item writing, and field testing; and
- *administration* of the program, including preparation of policies and materials for examinee registration and test administration, actual test administration, test scoring, and complete diagnostic reporting.

Services offered by NES support the individual state completely in the effort to design and implement a program that will meet the state's needs and unique requirements. The size and composition of NES staff enables it to provide these customized services and materials to many clients simultaneously.

OVERVIEW OF TEACHER CERTIFICATION TESTING

The last twenty years or so have witnessed a significant change in the procedures and requirements for obtaining a teaching certificate in most states. In general, the trend has been toward more rigorous control and more exacting standards on the profession. Two major aspects of this movement are the implementation of "approved programs" in the colleges and universities that prepare teachers and the introduction of tests as a part of the requirements for certification.

The two chapters in this section deal with the general history and current status of teacher certification testing. Rubinstein, McDonough, & Allan offer a historical review of teacher certification requirements through to the present day. Vorwerk & Gorth stress the commonalities that exist across programs in various states. While teacher certification requirements are enacted on a state-by-state basis, there are many similarities in the form that these requirements take.

The Changing Nature of Teacher Certification Programs

Sherry A. Rubinstein
Matthew W. McDonough
Richard G. Allan

Introduction

Early in the 19th century, the sole criterion required of public school teachers was basic proficiency in reading, writing, and arithmetic. With the advent of mass compulsory education later in the century, the states became interested in extending this requirement to include proficiency in professional techniques and specific subject-matter knowledge. These three domains of competence—possession of basic skills, proficiency in teaching techniques, and knowledge of subject matter to be taught—have continued to the present as the mainstays of teacher assessment systems.

This characterization suggests considerable continuity in and consensus about the important aspects of teacher evaluation. This consistency notwithstanding, the last decade has been marked by dramatic change in approaches to certifying public school teachers. The change has been not so much in the domains of competence that are subject to scrutiny, but in the degree of emphasis accorded each domain, the manner in which they are characterized, and the way in which they are assessed.

Richard Allan is Vice President for Instructional Development, National Evaluation Systems. Sherry Rubinstein is the former Director of the Division of Project Services, National Evaluation Systems. Matt McDonough is a former Project Manager at National Evaluation Systems.

EVIDENCE OF CHANGE

The nature of the change in credentialing practice is shown by the significant increase in efforts to reexamine and modify state-level programs that have the responsibility for licensing teachers. *Licensure* is the "process by which an agency of the government grants permission to an individual to engage in a given occupation upon finding that the applicant has attained the minimal degree of competency required to ensure that the public health, safety, and welfare will be reasonably well protected" (U.S. Department of Health, Education, & Welfare, 1977). An individual without a teaching license from a particular state is legally barred from the practice of public school teaching in that state. The closely related process of *certification* grants the use of a title (e.g., "teacher") to an individual who has met a predetermined set of standards or qualifications set by a credentialing agency (Shimburg, 1981). Although this distinction is real, the commonly used referent *teacher certification program* will denote individual state government policies and procedures regarding the granting of teacher licenses.

EARLY POLICIES

Before the late 1960s, most states certified prospective teachers on the basis of successful completion of a teacher education program of study. Only a few states even required accreditation or approval of such programs, and only a few others took the additional measure of requiring entrants into the teaching field to pass any kind of examination. These policies remained unchanged for a considerable length of time, which suggests that certification programs were fulfilling their purpose. The lack of controversy implied satisfaction with the adequacy of training programs to ensure that unqualified individuals were excluded from teaching and that all qualified applicants had fair and unbiased access to the profession.

THE 1970s

The 1970s stand in marked contrast to the preceding century. During this decade, teacher certification programs were criticized by a variety of interest groups concerned with the quality of teaching in the nation's schools; state departments of education encountered strong and often contradictory demands for change.

As a result, many teacher certification programs were reviewed and modified extensively. The purpose of this chapter is to characterize these changes—particularly those related to tests— and to reflect on the factors that propelled, or at least influenced, the direction of those changes. In doing so, the authors first call upon empirical evidence to document the extent of alterations and then to identify the significant features of the changes, which include: (a) new and different emphases in the testing of the skills and knowledge that prospective teachers should possess and (b) increasing adoption of criterion-referenced measures to assess the skills and knowledge so described.

The chapter then analyzes the changes in terms of events and factors in three separate spheres: (a) the general political environment, (b) the legal and regulatory environment, and (c) the educational and measurement environment.

Evidence of Change

Substantiating claims of change in teacher certification programs is not difficult. That change was in the air is revealed in a study by Pittman (1975), which showed that between 1970 and 1975 every state in the country had considered modifying teacher certification practices to incorporate the then new principles of competency-based education. This spate of activity took a variety of forms, including appointment of study panels, commissioning of position papers, hosting of conferences, and review of concrete proposals. All this, at a minimum, suggests an interest in reanalyzing teacher certification requirements; in a significant number of cases, this interest was followed by action. A number of states made significant modifications to their existing certification programs; others designed totally new programs to replace existing ones. Changes were effected on the policies and practices in all four phases of teacher certification programs: (a) upon admission to teacher training programs, (b) on completion of such a program (initial certification), (c) during the first year of incumbency in a teaching position, and (d) during later incumbency (certification renewal).

TIGHTER STANDARDS

One major form of revision ended the automatic granting of certification to a graduate of any teacher education program. From 1970 to 1975, 26 states implemented systems of approving teacher education programs (Pittman, 1975). By far the most dramatic action, or at least the most publicly visible one, was to require that graduates of teacher education programs pass a state-sponsored test to obtain a license to teach. Between 1977 and 1981, 16 states enacted legislation or state board of education policies of this sort. More states have joined the trend of late. In fact, keeping track of policy and legislative initiatives and changes in teacher certification testing requires full-time attention. Only four or five states remain that have neither a testing program nor serious plans to test. The move toward more widespread adoption of the approved-program model reflects the imposition of more stringent requirements in an effort to upgrade programs and improve the quality of professionals. Both the gradual expansion of testing across states and the increase in types of tests used (e.g., basic skills, content) indicate the movement toward more rigorous standards.

Nature of Testing-Related Changes

More significant for the discussion here are those requirements that involve changes in testing practices: (a) the testing of prospective program entrants and (b) the testing of program graduates as eligible, prospective license holders. Examples of the former are Alabama's English Language Proficiency Test, which assesses basic skills in reading, writing, language skills, and listening, and Connecticut's Competency Examination for Prospective Teachers, which assesses reading, writing, and mathematics. Tests such as these reveal a heightened emphasis on the basics in the screening of prospective teachers. The trend is mirrored in end-of-program testing. An increasing number of states are including a basic skills test as one component of end-of-program initial certification requirements; Florida's program is a prime example.

The fact that more and more states require a test over and above fulfillment of course and program requirements is evidence of increased stringency in certification programs. This evidence is less compelling, however, than the changing character of the tests themselves. In the past the most common test was a standardized norm-referenced one—the National Teacher Examination (NTE)—either unvalidated or validated to local requirements. More recently, criterion-referenced tests (CRTs) have come into common use for end-of-program testing. This trend complements increasing specificity in the description of the skills and knowledge that entering teachers should possess, specificity characteristic of objective-referenced assessment.

Another significant feature of the change in initial certification testing is an increased emphasis on content-oriented tests. Although some states have traditionally used the NTE Specialty Area Examinations, more and more states are funding the development of criterion-referenced tests in these and other areas. South Carolina legislation, for example, called for customized development of CRTs in teaching areas not covered by the NTE (including trades and industries, distributive education, German, Latin, earth science, psychology, speech and drama, and health). Georgia has a program comprising only CRTs that assess prospective teachers' knowledge in a variety of subject areas (e.g., agriculture, music, early childhood, middle childhood, communicative arts, business, home economics, industrial arts, French, and Spanish), with a 19th field (health) currently under development. Oklahoma's program encompasses more than 75 separate certificate areas, each with a criterion-referenced instrument.

Even the foregoing recitation, along with other examples one could cite, underplays the range of content areas being assessed by CRTs. Special education receives considerable attention. South Carolina has four separate special education area exams, Georgia has three, and Oklahoma has seven. There are also tests for other pupil personnel service positions such as psychologist, school counselor, speech pathologist, psychometrist, reading specialist, audiovisual specialist, and librarian. In addition, there are CRT certification exams for administrators (e.g., Georgia's Administration and Supervision test and Oklahoma's three separate tests for superintendents, elementary principals, and secondary school principals).

The development and implementation of these tests are strong indications of the increasing emphasis on content-area (subject-matter) tests and the increasing adoption of criterion-referenced approaches to measurement. Other changes have come hand in

hand with these. The developmental process for teacher certification tests has been increasingly characterized by a strong
validation effort. Examples are the local validation process to which
the NTE is being subjected in some states and the full-scale job
analyses (e.g., in Georgia and Oklahoma) that, as an early step
in the development of CRTs, identify the knowledge and skills
viewed by job incumbents (i.e., teachers of the specific subject
matter) as frequently used and important in their work.

There is little doubt that recent developments in the nature
and the types of tests in use represent a significant change in teacher
certification policy. These trends, however, did not develop in a
vacuum. They have their sources in, or at least were influenced
by, three other factors: the general political environment, the legal
and regulatory environment, and the education and measurement
environment.

The General Political Environment

Political environment denotes here the set of factors that,
taken together, constitute the sociopsychological and socio-
economic fabric of our collective lives. Thus we are referring to
factors that appear to be out of the purview or control of any single
individual, group, agency, or institution. The indicators of the
general political environment are often perceptible, and over the
past decade, one of the most obvious was an alarmingly pervasive
dissatisfaction with the outcomes of public education. This
dissatisfaction, voiced and also fueled by the national media,
included educators' frustration with a decline in SAT scores,
parents' reports of functionally illiterate high school graduates,
and business leaders' complaints about the lack of even minimally
qualified entrants into the work force.

In the early 1970s parents and other critics alike began
demanding a return to basics as a means of assuring the accountability of local school systems. Accountability became a byword,
if not a bona fide movement, and it targeted all tangible features
and products of the schools. First, the spotlight was turned to
students themselves; public pressure led legislatures and state

departments of education to institute minimum competency test programs in the 1970s. These programs, though diverse in design, had the common purpose of reflecting the school systems' success or failure at teaching certain predefined basics to each student. These programs imposed consequences on students who failed to perform at minimally acceptable levels.

An equally harsh light was cast on school curricula, not only at the traditional "three Rs," but social studies, science, and a host of other subjects. Public pressure was exerted to increase the utility of what was taught to students, a continuation of the demand for relevance heard earlier in the 1960s. In response, educators began modifying curricula in form and substance to focus on skills and knowledge useful to students in their economic, political, and social lives. The emphasis moved from what students should know to what students should be able to do, the latter emphasis being more observable and allowing for greater accountability.

Throughout the decade the mass media and the popular press devoted substantial coverage to the "crisis in education" and the system's ability to educate the nation's youth. It should come as no surprise, then, that the focus broadened to include an appraisal of the agents of instruction—teachers themselves. The public demanded assurances that teachers were qualified to do their jobs—to such an extent that it was estimated that the teacher testing movement, the most visible of all certification-related activities, was supported by 85% of U.S. adults (*Time Magazine*, 1980).

The underlying cause of the demand for accountability might have been a common preoccupation with economic pressures. The 1970s were beset by rapid inflation and diminishing resources that turned the public's attention away from perceived luxuries in education and spawned the new back-to-basics movement. Similarly, as an extension of concern about personal budgetary constraints, the consumers of education were asking (and continue to ask) what value they were getting for their education tax dollars.

In the face of strong countervailing efforts by teachers' unions to "protect" incumbent teachers, the states' response to these consumer demands focused on the certification of prospective teachers, often by expanding and strengthening initial certification testing components.

The Legal and Regulatory Environment

As public pressure was brought to bear on teacher certification programs, a number of legal and regulatory precedents influenced the direction of the movement. These were an outgrowth of Title VII of the Civil Rights Act and the Equal Employment Opportunity Commission (EEOC) Guidelines on Employee Selection Procedures. In addition, the development of the 1974 version of the Standards for Educational and Psychological Tests (APA, AERA, NCME, 1974) had an effect. The promulgation of these regulations and standards reflected increasing legislative, judicial, and professional concern with fair employment practices both in and out of education.

LEGISLATION, REGULATIONS, AND THE COURTS

Stated simply, Title VII of the Civil Rights Act of 1964 outlawed employment discrimination on the basis of sex, race, color, religion, or national origin, and empowered the EEOC to enforce the law. The 1970 EEOC Guidelines, a revision of the original 1966 version, included a set of stipulations founded on the premise that standardization and proper validation in employee selection procedures would build a foundation for the non-discriminatory personnel practices required by Title VII. These stipulations (EEOC, 1970) included the following:

- Empirical data should be made available to establish the *predictive validity* of a test, that is, the correlation of test performance with job-relevant work behaviors; such data should be collected according to generally accepted procedures for establishing criterion-related validity.

- Where predictive validity is not feasible, evidence of *content validity* (in the case of job knowledge or proficiency tests) may suffice as long as appropriate information relating test content to job requirements is supplied.

- Where validity cannot otherwise be established, evidence of a test's validity can be claimed on the basis of validation in other organizations as long as the jobs are shown to be comparable and there are no major differences in context or sample composition.

- Differential failure rates (with consequent adverse effects on hiring) for members of groups protected by Title VII constitute discrimination unless the test has been proven valid (as defined above) and alternative procedures for selection are not available.

- Differential failure rates must have a job-relevant basis and, where possible, data on such rates must be reported separately for minority and nonminority groups.

As a result of Title VII and the EEOC Guidelines, many concepts, which were previously in the private domain of psychometricians, took on important legal ramifications. In the first major challenge to employment tests (*Griggs v. Duke Power Company,* 1971), the Supreme Court unanimously interpreted Title VII as prohibiting "not only overt discrimination but also practices that are fair in form, but discriminatory in operation." This decision decreed that absence of intent to discriminate was insufficient to justify the use of a test that had a disproportionate impact on protected minorities; even the employer with the best of intentions bore the responsibility of demonstrating "that any given requirement . . . (bears) a manifest relationship to the employment in question." The Court further commented that the tenets of the EEOC Guidelines were "entitled to great deference" because they were drafted by the enforcing agency for Title VII. It was in this way that the concept of job relatedness came to be incorporated into the law of employment testing (Bersoff, 1981) and virtually came to have the effect of law (Rebell, 1976).

Two other early cases are worth noting. In *Chance v. Board of Examiners* (1972), the New York licensing exams for principals and other administrators were declared invalid for lack of job relevance. Later, in *Albermarle Paper Company v. Moody* (1975), the court invoked EEOC and, in effect, established criteria to be used in proving whether employers' tests were job-related. Specifically, the court made reference to the importance of analyzing "the attributes of, or the particular skills needed in" a given job as a basis for creating a job-relevant test.

Most significant for teacher certification programs was passage of a 1972 amendment (Public Law 92-261) to the Civil Rights Act that struck out the exemption for educational personnel in public institutions, which extended the provisions of EEOC beyond private industry to state and local government agencies. Before the amendment, court challenges against public employers (e.g., *Chance v. Board of Examiners,* 1972) were initially brought on equal protection grounds under the Fourteenth Amendment, which required only that employers demonstrate a rational basis for use of a test. The 1972 amendment paved the way for later litigation (e.g., *United States v. State of North Carolina,* 1975) that successfully challenged the NTE as a teacher selection test. For an excellent review of these early cases and an overview of the law and teacher certification, see *Licensing and Accreditation in Education: The Law and the State Interest* (Levitov, 1976).

Throughout the decade the concepts in the 1970 EEOC Guidelines were refined through litigation and resulting court opinion. Concurrently, various federal agencies were debating related issues. This debate culminated in the publication of the 1978 Uniform Guidelines (EEOC, CSC, U.S. Department of Labor, & U.S. Department of Justice, 1978), a document that contained "specific statements in most sections, in contrast to the more general statements of the 1970 Guidelines" (Novick, 1981). The intent was made clear: A test must be a representative measure of the actual domain of skills used on the job and must be validated for its intended purpose.

PROFESSIONAL STANDARDS

A discussion of the regulatory environment cannot exclude the process through which professionals and practitioners regulate themselves. An example of this self-regulation is reflected in the publication of the *Standards for Educational and Psychological Tests* (APA, AERA, & NCME, 1974). Unlike earlier documents of its kind that stressed the obligations of test producers, the 1974 Standards addressed competency in testing practice and test use (Novick, 1981). Novick reviews the evolution in professional standards over the last three-quarters of a century, but most revealing is his comment that this first document on test use "might not have happened, had it not been for the emergence of the social questions to which the EEOC Guidelines clearly responded, and the concomitant civil rights pressure of numerous advocacy groups" (p. 1043).

The 1974 Standards display many similarities to the EEOC Guidelines and, in fact, both the 1974 document and its 1966 precursor were cited in numerous court cases to bolster the credibility and importance of the EEOC Guidelines themselves

(Bersoff, 1981). Beyond the emphasis on validation strategies, however, the 1974 Standards stressed the requirement to investigate potential bias in the measures and to report results for separate subsamples (i.e., minority groups). Further, the 1974 Standards specified that any pass-fail scores used should be accompanied by "a rationale, justification, or explanation" for their adoption. Provisions such as these were taken seriously by the designers and implementers of the newer teacher certification programs.

THE COMBINED EFFECT

Taken together, Title VII, the EEOC Guidelines, resulting court challenges, and the 1974 Standards can be seen as catalysts and guides to the restructuring of teacher certification programs. Their influence is shown in several ways:

1. Since it has not been feasible to conduct predictive validity studies (primarily because of difficulties in obtaining reliable and valid measures of the criterion), the response has been to incorporate other validation efforts more fully. Increased attention is being paid to the validity of certification tests, almost exclusively to content validity.

2. The focus on content validity has greatly expanded the involvement of incumbent teachers and subject-matter specialists in the test development process, both through committee review work and participation in job analyses. Through these methods the test development process relates the specific attributes of a job and the test's relevance to those job features.

3. There is increased awareness of potential differential impact, with expanded efforts to include diverse interest groups in the test development process and to report test results separately for relevant minorities.

4. Finally, there has a been a shift toward the use of criterion-referenced, as opposed to norm-referenced, models of standard setting; a variety of methods incorporating expert judgments about the test items themselves are coming into wider use.

These trends reflect the significance of the legal and regulatory environment on the design of teacher certification programs.

The Education and Measurement Environment

In this final context, the education and measurement environment, the discussion focuses on factors within the purview of educators and psychometricians, rather than on factors external to the domain of education. Two distinct themes are theory development in relation to teacher education practice: the growth of competency-based teacher education (CBTE); and advances in measurement theory and in statistical techniques relevant to criterion-referenced tests.

CBTE

The early 1970s saw the start of the CBTE movement, a newly conceived pedagogy for teacher education programs based initially on the established concept of mastery learning. Among 14 defining and ancillary features of CBTE, Hall and Houston (1981) included six that have at least a surface relationship to the characteristics of the newer teacher certification programs:

1. Instruction focused on learner outcomes rather than on time in attendance.
2. A priori description of the intended learner outcomes.
3. Introduction of subcompetency and competency statements.
4. Emphasis on mastery, at least to some minimum level of identified learning.
5. De-emphasis on how well a student performs relative to other students in favor of emphasis on demonstration of desired outcomes.
6. Clear and public communication of minimum levels of success with continual feedback on performance.

From the start, there were optimistic predictions that CBTE would result in "new measures of teacher behavior" and "new criteria for certification" (Hall & Houston, 1981). The basic tenet that instruction be objective based was most influential. As CBTE spread to teacher training institutions, educators rarely completely understood or adopted the pedagogy. But even if only superficially incorporated, it included a focus on establishing objectives for learning. The debate surrounding CBTE therefore included in-depth examination and discussion of the skills and competencies teachers needed to develop. One product of this debate was performance-based standards against which teacher competency could be judged. CBTE provided the testing movement with the criteria necessary to develop clear, valid, job-relevant certification tests.

TESTS, MEASURES, AND STATISTICS

As CBTE provided the criteria to measure, the measurement community responded with more appropriate tools and instruments. It became clear that existing, standardized, norm-referenced tests could not fulfill the demand for content validity, for tailored job relevance, for specification of objectives, or for scoring in comparison to preset criteria rather than in terms of group norms.

Although we cannot provide details in this chapter, the growth of CBTE supported (and, in turn, was supported by) research on and development of new criterion-referenced measurement techniques. We have witnessed refinements in methods of defining domains (Popham, 1980), ways of generating statements of learning objectives (Popham, 1978), strategies for developing test items (Hambleton & Eignor, 1979), and methods of setting cut scores (Nassif, 1978; Hambleton, 1980). Significant advances in CRT-relevant statistics include indices of reliability (Subkoviak, 1980), application of latent trait models (Cook, Eignor & Hutten, 1979), new approaches to item analysis (Berk, 1980), and new methods of investigating test item bias (Merz & Grossen, 1979). These technical developments enabled increased rigor in criterion-referenced testing conducted for public policy reasons. Also, the communication between researchers and practitioners and the need for a stringent and legally defensible system for certifying teachers fueled support for continuing technical refinements.

Summary and Conclusions

Earlier the authors suggested a bandwagon effect in the increasing adoption of CRT-based teacher certification programs. In doing so, we did not intend to suggest automatically that "the band is playing the right tune," although the many CRT supporters in the professional community would like to think so. Yet, it can be argued that the recent increasing rigor in the teacher certification process is associated with a variety of positive effects:

1. The visibility of the change has increased the involvement of educators and special interest groups in the debate over what teachers should know. This debate fends off any complacency that might thwart growth in our knowledge base about the constitutive elements of effective teaching.

2. The movement has substantially increased discussion about what tests measure, a trend that enhances the meaningfulness of test scores. This contrasts with the traditional score interpretations of norm-referenced tests, which diverted attention from test content to person-to-group comparisons.

3. The objective-based construction of the tests enables test takers to learn in advance the expectations set for them, a condition that contributes to maximum performance according to recent research.

4. The newer certification programs entail expanded feedback to examinees on their performance, including indications of strengths and weaknesses in regard to specified domains on the tests.

5. The objective-based approach has also increased the utility of feedback to institutions about the performance of their graduates. The optimists among us (Hall & Houston, 1981) anticipate that "teacher education programs will start preparing their students to a sufficient level of mastery of each test criterion" (p. 25). In essence this would constitute the upgrading of teacher education programs that was the initial intention of CBTE.

6. The legal implications have heightened the impetus to incorporate sophisticated approaches in the measurement of the competencies of prospective teachers. The increased technical rigor can only serve to protect further the test takers.

7. The visibility of all these developments has turned a spotlight on the role of the public school teacher in American

society. State education departments have, in turn, increased their outreach efforts to explain or justify policies and practices. These efforts have, at a minimum, increased information and heightened public awareness of state efforts to fulfill accountability demands.

IMPLICATIONS FOR FURTHER STUDY

Notwithstanding these positive effects, aspects of the testing movement remain that deserve serious study. The first concerns teacher supply. With more stringent criteria for certification, fewer prospective teachers are likely to receive licenses, and school systems are likely to have increasing difficulty staffing certain positions. Even if teaching institutions upgrade the skills of their graduates, there is little doubt that a significant time lapse will exist. In the meantime, state departments of education are likely to experience substantial pressure to implement politically expedient solutions to the supply problem.

Second, reporting test results for examinees on an institution-by-institution basis has already engendered political pressure to reward or punish institutions on the basis of their "performance." Where failure rates are excessive, for example, threats of loss of accreditation may be heard. In the face of these pressures, it may be difficult to ward off simplistic solutions to what are, in fact, complex problems.

Third, and finally, the differential passing rates for minority groups have direct consequences for the proportion of minority group teachers in the nation's schools. Although the testing programs and the tests themselves may be held to be valid, the implications of their use must be considered from the larger cultural and sociological perspective.

We raise these issues as caveats to testing practitioners to emphasize that testing for public policy purposes must be conceived and implemented in a manner that is both professionally and socially responsible.

References

Albermarle Paper Co. v. Moody, 95 S CT. 2362 (1975).

American Psychological Association, American Educational Association, and National Council on Measurement in Education. (1974). *Standards for educational and psychological tests and manuals.* Washington, DC: American Psychological Association.

Berk, R. A. (1980). *Criterion-referenced measurement: The state of the art.* Baltimore: Johns Hopkins University Press.

Bersoff, D. (1981). Testing and the law. *American Psychologist, 36,* 1047-1056.

Chance v. Board of Examiners, F. Supp. 203 (S.D. N.Y. 1971), Aff'd 458 F.2d 1167 (2D Cir. 1972).

Cook, L. L., Eignor, D. R., & Hutten, L. R. (1979). *Considerations in the application of latent trait theory to objectives-based criterion-referenced tests.* (Laboratory of psychometric and evaluative research report). Amherst: University of Massachusetts, School of Education.

Equal Employment Opportunity Commission (1970). Guidelines on employee selection procedures. *Federal Register, 35,* 12333-12336.

Equal Employment Opportunity Commission, Civil Service Commission, U.S. Department of Labor, & U.S. Department of Justice (1978). Adoption by four agencies of uniform guidelines on employee selection procedures. *Federal Register, 43,* 38290-38315.

Griggs v. Duke Power Company, 401 U.S. 424 (1971).

Hall, G., & Houston, R. (1981). Competency-based teacher education: Where is it now? *New York University Quarterly, 3,* 20-28.

Hambleton, R. K. (1980). Test score validity and standard-setting methods. In R. A. Berk (Ed.), *Criterion-referenced measurement: The state of the art* (pp. 80-123). Baltimore, MD: Johns Hopkins University Press.

Hambleton, R., & Eignor, D. (1979). *A practitioner's guide to criterion-referenced test development, validation, and usage.* (Laboratory of psychometric and evaluative research report No. 70.) Amherst: University of Massachusetts, School of Education (2nd ed.).

Help! teacher can't teach! (1980, June 16). *Time Magazine.*

Levitov, B. (1976). *Licensing and accreditation in education: The law and the state interest.* Lincoln: University of Nebraska.

Merz, W. R., & Grossen, N. E. (1979). *An empirical investigation of six methods for examining test item bias* (Final report grant NIE—6-78-0067). Sacramento: Foundation of California University.

Nassif, P.M. (1978, March). *Standard-setting for criterion-referenced teacher licensing tests.* Paper presented at the annual meeting of the National Council on Measurement in Education, Toronto.

Novick, M. (1981). Federal guidelines and professional standards. *American Psychologist, 36,* 1036-1047.

Pittman, J. (1975, February). *Actions taken by state departments of education in developing CBTE certification systems.* Paper delivered at the Association of Teacher Educators Annual Conference, New Orleans, LA.

Popham, J. (1978). *Criterion-referenced measurement.* Englewood Cliffs, NJ: Prentice-Hall.

Popham, J. (1980). Domain specification strategies. In R.A. Berk (Ed.), *Criterion-referenced testing: The state of the art* (pp. 15-31). Baltimore, MD: Johns Hopkins University Press.

Rebell, M. (1976). The law, the courts, and teacher credentialing reform. In B. Levitov (Ed.), *Licensing and accreditation in education: The law and the state interest* (pp. 1-25). Lincoln: University of Nebraska.

Shimberg, B. (1981). Testing for licensing and certification. *American Psychologist, 36,* 1138-1146.

Subkoviak, M. J. (1980). Decision-consistency approaches. In R. A. Berk (Ed.), *Criterion-referenced measurement: The state of the art* (pp. 129-185). Baltimore, MD: Johns Hopkins University Press.

U.S. Department of Health, Education, and Welfare, Public Health Services. (1977, July). Credentialing health manpower (DHEW Publication No. (05) 77-50057). Washington, DC: Author.

United States v. State of North Carolina Civil, No. 4476 (E.D.N., CAR., 1975).

Common Themes in Teacher Certification Testing Program Development and Implementation

Katherine E. Vorwerk
William Phillip Gorth

Teacher competency training and testing programs prior to certification are not new. Yet confusion still exists about the intended purpose and outcomes of such programs, particularly teacher certification testing programs. For example, it has been said that teacher certification testing programs will either:

- improve the quality of education *or* lower the teaching profession's standards because of their emphasis on minimal knowledge;

- serve to define what a good teacher is *or* end up being nothing more than a "search for victims" and a "hollow means of judging the efficacy of teachers" (Cole, 1979, p. 233); or

- test for content that is an absolute necessity *or* test for content that is unrelated to successful teaching.

Like all occupational licensing laws, the primary purpose of teacher certification laws and their testing component is to protect the public health, safety, and welfare by ensuring that only individuals who are competent in a subject are allowed to teach it. In most cases, certification testing programs do effectively emphasize minimum content knowledge, they can result in improvement in

William Gorth is President of National Evaluation Systems. Katherine Vorwerk is a former Project Director at National Evaluation Systems.

the quality of education, and they may end up being *part* of a definition of what a good teacher is and what content knowledge is absolutely necessary. But these are secondary outcomes of such programs. The primary outcome that every program is designed to achieve is the protection of the public from incompetence.

PUBLIC CONCERN

The public is clearly concerned about teacher competence. For example, more than 85 % of those surveyed in recent national polls agree that teachers should be required to pass examinations in their subject areas. Teacher incompetence is frequently used by parents and legislators as a partial explanation for the decline in students' test scores witnessed over the past 15 years. Moreover, the large number of states that require or will soon require a teacher certification testing program (almost 40), or are considering doing so, is further testimony to the desire of the public to protect its children from incompetent teachers.

A systematically developed teacher certification program can prevent persons who lack competence in critical subjects from entering the teaching profession. This chapter presents a general model for developing the testing component of a certification program. The model applies only to the formal testing components of a teacher certification program, such as structured observation or a paper-and-pencil content test. It does not apply to other parts of the certification process, such as course requirements or student teaching.

DEVELOPMENT MODEL

The model consists of five components (see Figure 1):

(a)   developing certification requirements;

(b)   deciding how to assess requirements;

(c)   defining measurement strategies and instruments;

(d)   handling logistical issues of assessment; and

(e)   communicating and using assessment results.

Figure 1

TEACHER CERTIFICATION TESTING
PROCESS MODEL

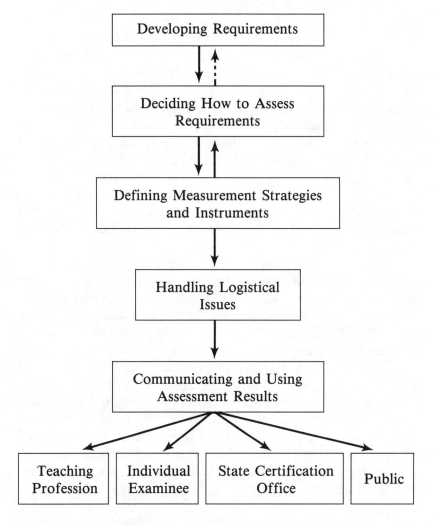

The components are roughly sequential, although several overlap.
Each component is discussed separately in the sections that follow.

Developing
Certification Requirements

Requirements mandating teacher certification testing generally come either from state boards of education or from state legislatures. For example, the authority for Alabama's testing program comes from the State Board of Education; the authority for Florida's program comes from the legislature. Occasionally, developing certification requirements is a joint effort. After the requirements are developed, they are generally passed on to the state's department of education for further definition and implementation. Ideally, the department of education would have provided input during the development of the mandated requirements, and therefore would be at least familiar with, and perhaps have influenced, their content. Departments not involved in creating the program often confront a mandate that does not specify the mode of implementation or a mandate that has features they do not like.

Other constituencies that should participate in developing certification requirements are the state's teacher training institutions, teachers, and the general public. The requirements will affect each of these groups. Their input during the initial program definition will help ensure that the requirements are both workable and acceptable.

At this stage, some states contact other state departments of education for advice and background on their certification programs, or they engage the services of consultants who can also provide information about existing certification testing programs and provide psychometric consultation. The benefits of sound planning and broad political support are felt throughout the life of a program; likewise, problems built in at this stage will continue to plague activities.

Deciding How to
Assess Requirements

Generally, the state department of education is responsible for deciding how the requirements will be assessed. Requirements, of course, vary widely. Some merely specify the use of a particular test or series of tests. For example, Arkansas's regulations require persons applying for initial certification to satisfactorily complete "an existing teachers' examination" or other similar examination. Then the state department of education moves on to the next component of the model. In other states, the requirements specify a more comprehensive and detailed testing program which can include entrance examinations to teacher education programs, exit examinations covering basic skills and specific content knowledge, and other nonexamination requirements (e.g., practice teaching and inservice training for certified teachers and administrators).

Deciding how to assess requirements heavily affects the measurement strategies that will be used as well as the type of results that will be produced. For example, deciding to assess teaching skills using an on-the-job observation procedure will result in a very different type of measurement instrument than deciding to assess the content knowledge of teachers in the subject or subjects they aspire to teach.

KEY ISSUES

Several key issues must be considered in reaching a decision. First, budgetary constraints must be realistically evaluated because assessment strategies vary in cost. The cost will be borne partly by the state (for start-up costs) and partly by the individual examinee (for operating costs). Second, time considerations are critical. Mandated requirements often include an implementation date. The development of a certification testing program tailored to the state's curriculum requirements involves more time than does adoption of an existing test. If a testing program must be produced within three to five months, custom test development may be precluded. Third, the state must ask which assessment strategy will best protect the public. For example, should systematic observation of teachers on the job and paper-and-pencil tests of content knowledge both be used, or is one sufficient? Clearly, some combination of observation, paper-and-pencil tests, and preservice evaluation is preferable, but given time and budgetary constraints, is this possible? If not, which approach is actually going to meet the needs of the state in the most satisfactory manner?

Defining Measurement Strategies and Instruments

This component is closely tied to the previous one; deciding how to assess requirements does, in effect, define measurement strategies. The actual creation of assessment instruments, however, involves additional technical work.

Defining measurement strategies and instruments is critical, and it generally consumes most of the start-up resources expended on the testing program. In this phase the actual testing instruments are developed. Professional and legal guidelines for tests used for certification purposes apply here and must be clearly understood and followed. Major issues covered by these guidelines include the need for job relatedness of the measurement instruments, test validity, test reliability, and the establishment of passing scores or standards. Specific technical considerations involved in each of these are discussed elsewhere in this volume.

INVOLVEMENT

Beyond adherence to professional and legal guidelines for test development and use, the department of education must take care to involve members of the teaching profession—both practicing teachers and teacher educators—in preparing the assessment instruments. These individuals play a critical role in assuring the appropriateness of the test instrument to the state. Clearly, teaching professionals should be involved in a job analysis procedure to establish the job relatedness of the content of a particular examination. Oklahoma, for example, surveyed more than 4,500 teachers as part of establishing the job relatedness of its certification tests.

In addition, teachers and teacher educators should participate in all other steps at this stage, particularly if a customized paper-and-pencil test or other measurement instrument is being developed. For example, committees of teachers and teacher educators should be formed to review the domain of knowledge or skills to be included on the test, to review the results of the job analysis procedure and make judgments on how those results are to be used, and, finally, to review the actual test items appearing on the test. Such reviews by teaching professionals are typical of the testing programs in Georgia and Alabama.

Handling Logistical Issues of Assessment

Registering candidates for testing assessment and actually carrying out the assessment, the two major parts of this component, are logistically demanding. Depending on the program, this component can vary from two or three administrations of one test at several sites distributed across a state, to a sequence of preservice and inservice evaluations coordinated with a test of content knowledge given several times a year.

It is important that the registration procedures provide certification applicants with complete information about testing program requirements, administration procedures, and results reporting. This notification is best accomplished through a detailed registration bulletin that clearly specifies the state's certification laws and regulations and explains to the applicants their responsibilities and rights during the testing program. The bulletins should be widely distributed in the state through teacher education institutions and the department's certification office. Other information may also be available. For example, if a test is developed from a set of content objectives, the department should make the content objectives available to students through libraries or teacher education programs, so the students can use the objectives to prepare for the test.

Registration procedures should be as simple as possible to avoid mistakes and confusion. Information about registration procedures, deadlines, fees, and testing locations should be presented in the registration bulletin. Regardless of how the registration materials are delivered to examinees, it is important that the materials be provided in advance of their administration so that students have sufficient time to peruse them, send in registration forms, and still have time to change their registration if they choose.

Test administrations should be standardized and secure so that all applicants perform under the same conditions. Also, administrations should occur several times during a year to provide ample opportunity for taking the examinations, which should be spaced so that the results of one administration are reported to the candidate before the registration deadline for the next administration. In Oklahoma, for example, testing sessions are held four times per year, and students may take up to eight tests at each 2-day session.

Communicating and Using Assessment Results

At a minimum, examination results should be reported to four parties. First, results should go to individual examinees. In addition to information on whether examinees passed or failed the test, the reports should provide diagnostic information; that is, score reports should include information on how individual students performed on each of the major content areas covered by the examination. This diagnostic profile of strengths and weaknesses can serve as a springboard for additional growth or remediation. For example, a score report for a test in health and physical education might provide feedback on questions related to elementary physical education, physical development, and mental health, among other possible domains.

Second, results should be reported to the colleges and universities the certification applicants attended. These results provide institutions with two types of useful information: (a) the performance of each of their students on the test and (b) the performance of their respective teacher training programs. Content areas in which students in the aggregate show consistent strength or weakness may indicate corresponding areas of strength and weakness in the instructional programs themselves. This information can stimulate curriculum modification and the strengthening of the training programs.

Third, the state should receive results to determine whether certification should be granted or denied. Statewide data also provide information about how the total group of students has performed and allow for comparison among subgroups within the sample, for example, men versus women.

Fourth, and finally, aggregate results should be reported to the public. Results demonstrate to the public that certification is limited to teachers who are found to be competent in those areas determined necessary for classroom performance. Hence children are protected from incompetent applicants to the teaching profession.

Conclusion

Teacher certification testing programs do not solve all the problems of American education or even the smaller cluster of problems related specifically to teacher competency. This chapter has not discussed many of the important details involved in the definition and implementation of teacher certification testing programs. These programs are, however, able to identify people who can and cannot demonstrate, in a relevant testing situation, the competencies that the state feels they should be able to demonstrate. The model presented here provides a general description of the steps in the development and implementation of such a teacher certification testing program and the issues that must be considered.

References

Cole, R. W. (1979, December). Minimum-competency tests for teachers: Confusion compounded. *Phi Delta Kappan, 61*(4), 233.

FUNDAMENTAL ISSUES
IN PROGRAM DESIGN

Any state initiating a teacher certification testing program faces a number of design issues. The nature of the tests, the legal requirements that must be met, the role of state-mandated curricula—all play a role in forming the program in a given state. Each chapter in this section addresses some aspect of program design.

Folks's discussion centers on the political context from which a teacher certification testing program emerges. He focuses on the stakes that various educational constituencies have in a testing program and how their perspectives affect the roles they play. Rebell's chapter deals with the significant and critical legal aspects of teacher certification tests. As licensing instruments, they are subject to a variety of federal and professional standards, guidelines, and requirements. Moreover, a body of legal precedents is rapidly developing that will undoubtedly color the nature of testing programs in the future.

The Gabrys chapter describes how the West Virginia program was developed using the various state-required learning competencies for public school students. Similar sets of required classroom activities organized by subject area exist in many other states as well (Texas is another state with such requirements). The teacher certification testing program must take these requirements into account, as they define the content that teachers will teach.

Solomon's chapter deals with the issue of passing rates on examinations. He argues in favor of the calculation of a cumulative passing rate that considers the retake experiences of individuals who do not pass an examination on their initial attempt.

Finally, the Pecheone, Tomala, & Forgione chapter describes the process by which a basic skills test for entry into teacher training programs was developed in Connecticut. Besides describing that process, the authors offer some guidelines for other states that may be undertaking similar efforts.

Stakeholders in Teacher Certification Testing

John Folks

In most states, establishing a testing program for prospective teachers is a complex and often perplexing task. In addition to the technical and logistical issues that surround such tests, the testing programs are born in a highly charged political climate. Launching a teacher certification testing program involves a number of constituencies and political powers. This chapter explores the teacher testing process as it evolved in Oklahoma.

As many observers of teacher testing activity can attest, efforts to undertake programs in many states were delayed or defeated because of the conflicts among the various populations that are stakeholders in such a program. Obviously, the exact perspective individuals and groups bring to the teacher testing process varies from state to state. Moreover, anyone's viewpoint can change over time. Because testing programs generally take time to emerge, shifting coalitions of stakeholders are not uncommon. Maintaining at least civil relationships with everyone becomes important— yesterday's adversary in the process may be today's supporter.

To declare the foregoing is merely to point out the political backdrop that surrounds teacher testing programs. The issues in testing may be argued in terms of improving education, but the more traditional political concerns of control and authority are very relevant. That is not to say that those involved in the discussions are unconcerned with the quality of education provided in their state—far from it. The point is simply that to ignore the stakeholders from a political perspective is to take an unrealistic view of events.

John Folks is Superintendent of the Oklahoma State Department of Education.

The Stakeholders

Before the teacher testing program as it evolved in Oklahoma is discussed, it is worth identifying the stakeholders in the situation:

1. The Oklahoma State Department of Education: As implementors of the teacher certification testing program and educational activities in general, the department had a large stake in what happened.

2. The state legislature: Besides providing the funding for the program, legislators have an obligation to work for educational improvement.

3. The Oklahoma State Board of Education: As in most states, the Oklahoma board had a significant interest in the program.

4. Local school district administrators: Because the testing program influenced the type and quantity of job applicants school districts received, local administrators were quite concerned.

5. Incumbent teachers: Even though the Oklahoma program tests only those seeking initial certificates (or an additional endorsement area), current teachers were very much involved in the dicussions.

6. Deans of schools of education: Probably no single group had as much at stake as did this group.

Of course, everyone has a stake in education, even if indirectly. This paper limits itself to discussing groups that had a more direct stake in the teacher testing program and that, indeed, played a role in shaping the program.

The Legislation

Oklahoma was fortunate to have good legislation upon which to base the program. But the legislation itself represented the end product of what seemed at the time to be an endless process. What were the origins of the legislation? Why did Oklahoma get involved in teacher certification testing? There are several answers.

First, Oklahoma became involved in testing teachers because all the opinion polls taken in the state and on the national level showed that people were concerned about the quality of teachers in the classroom. The polls also indicated concern about the quality of people entering the teaching profession.

Second, and more locally, a regional magazine published in Texas printed an article entitled "Why Teachers Can't Teach" (Lyons, 1980). That article received much attention and generated heated debate in Oklahoma.

Last, the State Regents for Higher Education conducted a survey and found that people entering teacher education programs in Oklahoma had the lowest ACT scores, on the average, and the lowest grade point averages of any other students within the university system. That finding was of serious concern to state legislators.

As a result of these three factors and other concerns, the legislature introduced House Bill 1706, subsequently enacted as the Teacher Education Reform Act of 1980. The first meeting the legislature held on H. B. 1706 involved the author and several other staff people from the department of education in a virtual all-night review session, reviewing the legislation word for word and line by line. At that particular meeting, more than 105 amendments were offered; 35 were eventually adopted. The detail of review at that one meeting gives some sense of the level of debate and discussion the topic engendered.

LEGISLATIVE PROCESS

The eventual passage of the bill occurred after it had gone to the House Education and House Appropriations Committees, to the House floor, to the Senate Education Committee, to the Senate Appropriations Committee, to the Senate floor, into joint conference, back to both floors of the legislature, and ultimately to the governor. Members of the State Department of Education lost track of the number of times the bill was amended, but the result reflected considerable compromise.

Passage took so long partly because the teacher certification issue was only one part of a more general educational reform initiative; a large number of topics were covered by the legislation. One topic, for example, concerned increasing admission standards for teacher education programs in Oklahoma colleges and universities. The argument was that by tightening admission standards, schools would strengthen their programs in the schools and colleges of education.

TESTS

The bill also called for the testing of prospective teachers. It specified that there was to be a test for every area in which the state offered certification and for every area in which a person received a teaching credential. The legislation required candidates to take a test in those areas in which they wanted to receive teaching credentials: algebra, geometry, trigonometry, elementary analysis, or calculus, for example.

Faced with this rather large and frightening task, the department of education formulated a program that included 79 different certification tests. The department was fortunate to know of Georgia's experience in creating a customized, criterion-referenced program and received considerable valuable information from that state. The department of education in Georgia suggested we speak to National Evaluation Systems for help in developing these particular examinations.

INTERN AND STAFF
DEVELOPMENT PROGRAMS

The Oklahoma legislation also called for an intern program. The first year of teaching is called an "Entry-year Assistance Program." The bill also stipulated additional staff development. The details of these provisions are not discussed in this chapter, although each of these areas legitimately merits considerable time and discussion.

INTERACTIONS

When a state implements a multifaceted testing program of this sort, there are many interactions among the various components. There are questions to be asked when one considers the legislative and educational stakeholders in this type of program. One major question is: What will the state policy be and what is the relationship between teacher preparation and teacher certification in the state? These are two separate aspects of a general educational goal. One might say that they come hand in hand, but they are conceptually distinct. The distinction is especially noticeable in terms of who is responsible for the preparation of the individual candidate and who is responsible for passing judgment on that preparation. Indeed, it is the attempt to separate the function of preparation (held by the colleges and universities) from that of certification (held by the department of education) that underlies much of the initiative for teacher certification testing. In the past the state would accept a candidate for certification on the basis of the word of the institution that trained that individual. That is no longer the case.

Who is responsible for developing and implementing these new policies? This is a very controversial issue. Everyone has a stake in what happens and how policies are implemented, and everyone pushes a perspective that serves individual ends at least to some extent.

The schools that prepare teachers have a long tradition of independence and consequently oppose efforts to control what they do. The battle over approved programs in many states during the past several decades is evidence of this. Now teacher education schools are being told that their fundamental product, the teaching candidate, will be tested to make sure the schools have done a good enough job. The State Department of Education has been given a legislative mandate to test for initial certification. It almost does not matter if the department supports the policy or not; it must implement it. In Oklahoma, the department of education was very supportive of teacher certification testing. Nevertheless, the program puts the colleges and universities and the state education department in somewhat different camps, even though both would endorse better educational programs in a global sense.

The schools that prepare teachers and the department of education are not the only groups with their own perspectives. The professional associations say that they represent the profession and they should be deciding what happens in these programs. The legislatures, on the other hand, argue that they have the public welfare to consider and the right to require standards in the practice of a profession that affects a large and generally unprotected segment of the population. The situation can verge on chaos.

In the midst of conflicting tendencies, someone has to be the focal point and take responsibility. Who that should be is infinitely less important than that *someone* has to assume the role. It may be that the outcome of the questions, especially in the details of a program and its implementation, is affected by who takes control. In the case of Oklahoma, it was the State Department of Education that assumed the leadership role. The department of education staff worked exceptionally hard to involve all the relevant parties in discussions and thus minimize the antagonisms. But the important thing is that the department made the decisions about what would be done.

Effects on the Stakeholders

It is now appropriate to ask the question "What is the effect of these policies on each one of the stakeholders?" What follows reflects a personal judgment and evaluation, but it is the perspective of one very deeply involved in all aspects of program design and implementation.

What is most amazing to this author is that though the legislation came into effect out of a concern for the quality of teachers, as the effects and policies of the program were debated, virtually no one was interested in the quality of teachers per se. People were concerned about the effect the legislation was going to have on them, their programs, their interests, and so on. Every group seemed to lose sight of what the total package would be, and what its goals were. It was forgotten that the legislation called for a range of educational reforms, not only teacher certification testing. The main concern was, as usual, who would win and who would lose. As any reader with experience in politics knows, politicians do not want any losers. Politicians want everybody to be a winner.

LOCUS OF CONTROL

The discussions and negotiations that followed occurred in a context in which it is the legislators and the State Board that set educational policy. The locus of control is not held by teachers, not even through their professional associations; it is not held by local schools; and it is not held by colleges of education. Other interested parties, therefore, work within the context of domination by the legislators and the State Board.

FUNDING

The other factor that influences policy design is availability of funds. Funding is the biggest problem many states have in designing their programs and one of the few factors working against the wider use of customized, criterion-referenced tests. Luckily, the Oklahoma program got off the ground at a time when oil revenues were high; Oklahoma had a lot of money. Oklahoma probably could not now afford the type of program it has if it had to start all over again. But at the time of the project, the state of Oklahoma had the money to do the things it needed to do. In some respects, the availability of funds gave more power to the legislature; it could back its desires with money and use funding as a "carrot" to encourage other changes.

THE LEGISLATORS

In Oklahoma and elsewhere, legislators want to be able to go back home and say to constituents, "Look what I did for education." Most legislators also want good schools and quality programs. But their top priority is getting reelected, and they want to be able to go home and point to particular things they have done for education.

Legislators are also susceptible to accountability issues. As previously mentioned, money was abundant at the time the program was initiated, and there were several proposals for salary increases for teachers. At the same time, however, public confidence in the quality of teaching and the resultant quality of education for school children was waning. Legislators wanted to say to the public: We are increasing teacher salaries and making big expenditures in education, but at the same time, we are beefing up standards—we are increasing the requirements at the college level, we are putting in a testing program, we are adding an internship, and we are also requiring staff development on the part of incumbent teachers.

THE STATE BOARD OF EDUCATION

In Oklahoma, the State Board is the governing body of the State Department of Education, setting rules, regulations, and policies for all public schools. As this author sees it, reputation was at stake for the Board as much as anything else. Faced with a legislative directive to achieve certain ends, it had to be able to take pride in the rules and regulations in order to implement the legislation. It had to be in control. It wanted to be out front saying, "We're leading the reform."

And, of course, the State Board knew it was going to be closely watched by local school districts to see if the board took the side of the legislature or of the local boards of education. There were definitely sides to be taken. The board had to hold the line for the legislature but in a way that would not alienate the local schools.

THE STATE DEPARTMENT OF EDUCATION

The department of education had to provide the leadership to set the policy in place and convince local boards of education that everything being done was for the improvement of education. At the same time, the department had to demonstrate to the legislature that it had a strong commitment to implement the policies that the legislature had required. Also, would the State Department of Education ever again get the responsibility for a major program if it did not properly implement the teacher certification testing program? The department's professional reputation was at stake.

INSTITUTIONS OF HIGHER EDUCATION

In general, teacher education is the stepchild in most of our universities. The legislation was a step in the direction of saying to the college and university presidents of Oklahoma's private and public institutions, "Are you willing to make a commitment to teacher education?" The ability of the college presidents to respond was at stake as well as their reputations. More important, so was their funding.

DEANS OF COLLEGES OF EDUCATION

If there was any group that had a stake in the implementation of the testing program, it was the deans of Oklahoma's colleges of education and, in general, their staff and faculty. The deans had more at stake than anybody else because they were the ones who were being criticized: they were being told that their programs were the reason that the testing program was being instituted. "You have not adequately prepared teachers," was the implied message.

The colleges of education were in a difficult situation. Historically, they had controlled their own programs. Their "stamp" was all the approval a certificate candidate needed. Increasingly, they were not attracting the better students. This is a situation that has affected teacher education programs across the country. Yet the teacher preparation institutions bear the most obvious responsibility for the quality of the teachers entering the classroom. It is their job to train these people for their tasks. They wanted control of their own programs, and they were being criticized for the product they were providing.

In fact, the department of education staff, and this author in particular, spent considerable time defending the colleges and schools of education. We met weekly then, and still meet monthly, with the Oklahoma Association of Colleges of Teacher Education (the AACTE affiliate), and we continue to discuss a number of these issues.

In the end, the department of education had to say that the schools were not going to have control, but that the department was going to work with them, listen to them, and take all the suggestions possible from them and put the suggestions in place. The pride and professionalism of the schools were at stake. Their commitment to and involvement in teacher education were at stake. The schools of education wanted control of the testing program, but the department of education was obliged to say no.

In general, the situation is now much improved after the initial anxiety and even antagonism that characterized early discussions of the program. It is probably the case, however, that schools of teacher education can never rest easy with a testing program because that kind of program threatens them. Every examinee who fails to measure up to the state's standards becomes a problem for the schools. The spotlight shines quite clearly on the institutions.

What helped in our case was that many teacher education faculty members were involved in developing and reviewing materials for the tests. They were consulted as a part of the program design. They were treated as participants in the general effort to improve the quality of teachers in public schools, not as impediments to be overcome.

Many observers think the attention focused on education schools and departments as accountable for teacher preparation in content areas is misplaced. It is really the faculty in arts and sciences that provide the instruction in the content fields. But the brunt of the criticism falls on the schools of education.

TEACHERS

Oklahoma teachers also had a stake in the testing program. Their stake was primarily money. The testing program was part of an educational reform bill that called for many changes, including higher salaries for teachers. The legislature was not going to put money into teachers' pockets if the teachers did not go along with the other aspects of the legislation. That assertation may seem harsh, but reality dictates that people need some motivation for supporting an activity that does not initially appeal to them. The teachers did buy into it because they wanted the money.

On the other hand, the teachers could go to the negotiating table with the state legislature and say, "We have agreed with all of these things, so you're going to have to give us our money." Hence, the teachers came out winners also.

Summary

As was established at the beginning, everybody had a stake in this legislation. Every group had something to gain and something to lose. The department of education worked hard to identify what each group had to win, then tried to incorporate it into the overall educational reform. The teachers had the money to gain, the administrators had clout to gain, and the deans of the schools of education had their reputations to regain.

Essentially it fell to the department of education to sell the program, which it did largely through the involvement of people (although, of course, the legislature's mandate precluded other options). The legislature, in fact, was more interested in the certification testing component of the entire program because it was something the legislature could put a finger on.

The department of education involved everybody it could: not just the Oklahoma Education Association and the American Federation of Teachers, but also the Oklahoma Council of Teachers of Mathematics and similar professional groups. There were more than 400 people on advisory committees and more than 4,500 who were involved in the job analysis surveys. The department of education found that these participants were excellent ambassadors for the program, returning to their home districts and talking positively about what was happening. Although this level of participation helped, the most important ingredient was the attitude and leadership taken by the Oklahoma State Department of Education and the State Board of Education in dealing with the program in its early stages. They had to be the agents of change working with the various parties to obtain their trust and involvement.

One cannot take the position that a program can successfully be forced upon anyone. Nor can one take a position that defies the legislature in terms of implementation. Success requires a middle-of-the-road approach and considerable sensitivity to the politics of the situation. One has to define carefully the stake that each constituent group has in the program and its outcomes and work from there.

References

Lyons, G. (1980). Why teachers can't teach. *Phi Delta Kappan, 62,* 108-112.

Recent Legal Issues
in Competency Testing
for Teachers

Michael A. Rebell, Esq.

In the wake of the recent wave of commission reports on educational improvement,[1] many states have enhanced their teacher certification requirements. According to a recent 50-state overview survey, 17 states now require that some or all teacher education candidates pass a state prescribed basic skills test before entering a teacher education program, and 22 states have established a testing requirement for entry-level certification.[2]

Moreover, the trend toward expanded teacher certification requirements—and more specifically toward more extensive testing requirements—appears to be accelerating. For example, Albert Shanker (1985), president of the American Federation for Teachers, recently called for a national entry-level teacher competency examination to measure fundamental skills well beyond the minimum competency level.

From a lawyer's perspective, this proliferation of testing requirements will have one predictable result: a dramatic increase in litigation. It has become a virtual truism in contemporary America that disgruntled individuals and, in fact, society at large bring their grievances and their public policy disputes to the courthouse door. Consequently, it can be expected that those individuals and groups who fail the examinations and are denied teaching certification will commence individual or class action litigations. Indeed, several major class action suits are already pending.

Michael Rebell is a Founding Partner of Rebell & Krieger of New York.

PRIOR EXPERIENCES

The courts had some experience with teacher certification examinations a decade or so ago when challenges were raised in many southern states about the use of the National Teacher Examination (NTE) as a certification device. Judges had little difficulty invalidating the use of the NTE for this purpose, because the Educational Testing Service, the developer of the test, admitted that it had not been validated for certification purposes.[3] Nevertheless, these cases do not provide direct precedent for legal challenges to more recent customized tests that have been developed with a specific awareness of the need for validation for certification purposes in each particular locale. Moreover, in recent years test makers in general have become more responsive to the legal requirements for test validation set forth in Title VII of the 1964 Civil Rights Act and in the Uniform Guidelines on Employee Selection Procedures adopted by the Equal Employment Opportunity Commission (EEOC) and other federal agencies in 1978.

Mention of Title VII and the EEOC Guidelines may lead to an assumption that future decisions in cases challenging teacher certification practices should be relatively straightforward: all the court need do is apply the statute and the EEOC Guidelines to the testing practices at issue and determine whether they pass muster. Nevertheless, the situation is not that simple. As a matter of law, there is an unresolved technical issue whether Title VII and the EEOC Guidelines apply to licensing or credentialing examinations at all.[4] Moreover, even if the assumption is made that the law and the EEOC Guidelines do apply, a further question arises—precisely how validation standards, which were created largely in the context of individual employer job selection tests, should be implemented in the conceptually distinct licensing or credentialing context.[5]

PUBLIC POLICY AND CANDIDATE SELECTION

Licensing and certification examinations adopted as a matter of fundamental public policy by a state legislature or agency to exercise its Constitutional responsibilities to protect the public welfare present a substantially different legal context than job selection devices adopted by a single employer to choose candidates most likely to be successful on the job. Whether these differences should elicit more or less exacting judicial scrutiny is debatable. On one hand, the fact that failure to pass a licensing examination will preclude a candidate from obtaining any employment opportunity in the field might induce a court to apply more exacting standards to licensing examinations than to individual job selection tests. On the other hand, because licensing examinations usually test for minimal entry-level knowledge and skills for jobs that responsible state officials have deemed to be critical to the public welfare, judges might tend to defer broadly to the state's goals and procedures.

From a technical, psychometric point of view, licensing examinations also present special validation problems, because the range of potential job settings covered by the examinations may be so broad that undertaking a meaningful job analysis and defining specific content domains become difficult. To use as an example the author's profession, it is unlikely that any adequate analysis of the "job" of a lawyer has been undertaken that would reasonably cover the very different skills exhibited for instance by litigators and labor negotiators. Thus far, courts considering challenges to bar examinations (all of which, to the author's knowledge, have been upheld) have not yet addressed these substantive validation issues.

COMING LITIGATION

The professional bodies involved in the test construction and psychometric fields, however, have shown a growing awareness of this problem. For instance, the 1985 Standards for Educational and Psychological Testing, jointly adopted by the American Educational Research Association, the American Psychological Association, and the National Council on Measurement in Education, have set forth a separate new section on Professional and Occupational Licensure and Certification. The introductory background discussion and comments contained in that section show a sensitivity to the distinctions between licensing and employment selection tests, although the five specific standards articulated in the section provide little guidance on how to implement these distinctions. It is likely that the courts will be called on to apply the general conceptual distinctions in particular factual settings and to develop a case law on these issues in the next few years. Teacher certification testing may become the prime context for doctrinal development on licensing matters because adverse impact on the large number of minority candidates in the field is likely to compel substantive judicial responses.

Although more focused judicial attention in this area can be anticipated, there is no reason to expect any change from the marked trend in recent Title VII testing litigation toward judicial deference to state officials and testing consultants who in good faith have undertaken validation techniques that fall within a very broad range of "professional judgment." Of course, in situations where tests have been shown to have adverse impact on minority candidates, courts will place the burden of justification on the test developers and test users. Nevertheless, the courts have clearly recognized "the need to modify rigid technical conclusions [because] . . . if this view guided interpretation of Title VII, then at the current stage of the technology of testing, no test that produces a disparate racial impact could be used . . . ."[6]

VALIDATION ISSUES

Within this general framework, we shall briefly consider two specific validation issues that have emerged from recent attempts to apply legal standards developed in other contexts to teacher certification testing. These two issues are (1) the extent to which job elements contained in state law or regulations, but not reflected in empirical job surveys, should be included in the content domain upon which a test is constructed, and (2) whether a validation process that has incorporated a suitable job-related content domain must be supplemented by evidence that the job-related knowledge and skills have, in fact, been taught to graduates of teacher training institutions in the particular state.

Job Analysis

Undertaking a job analysis as part of a content validation process for a teacher certification examination presents a basic conceptual issue because some of the professional standards set down in the applicable state law or regulations may not be reflected in an empirical analysis of what incumbents actually do on the job. This problem could arise either because the state standards involved have been newly promulgated and have not yet been implemented in the field, or because long-standing state mandates have been ignored by many practitioners.

Most of the discussions in the literature on content validation and job analyses emphasize the importance of including in a job description only those job elements that represent or directly relate to actual job behaviors. In the typical job selection setting, this is appropriate. If an empirical job analysis indicates that specific elements of a purported job description are not related to any actual on-the-job requirements, there is no valid reason to continue to include the elements in the job description. Under such circumstances an insistence on testing candidates for knowledge or abilities that are not job related would be an indication of arbitrariness at best or intentional discrimination at worst.

With licensing and certification examinations, however, the situation is entirely different. Here, both the state and the immediate employer (e.g., the local school district) have a legitimate interest in defining the job elements. Therefore, the fact that the employer may accept performance that omits certain elements does not mean that the state's additional—and supervening—interests can be ignored. Simply stated, any disparity between legislative mandates and actual on-the-job practice requires, as a matter of law, that the job practice, and not the job description, be changed. In addition, in a changing regulatory environment, certification tests must reflect emerging regulatory standards; therefore, the fact that a new requirement is not yet fully reflected in field practice is not a justification for omitting it from a test domain.

In sum, then, where there is a disparity between job-related objectives (as revealed by survey or observational evidence of actual classroom practice) and stated essential elements set forth in applicable state law or regulations, a teacher certification test should include items based on the legally mandated objectives. To put the matter bluntly, where state law mandates that certain essential elements be taught and an empirical job survey demonstrates that the essential elements are not being taught, the survey indicates, in essence, that the law is being violated. And, certainly, a certification test should not reflect or condone illegal practices.

In most situations, of course, the problem will not arise so starkly. One can reasonably presume that a thorough empirical analysis will reveal that most of the essential elements set forth in state law and regulations are being taught in most classrooms. A disparity between law and practice will typically occur in only a few discrete areas. Consequently, incorporation of objectives and test items to reflect these disparate legal matters would not require a fundamental reorientation of the test. Furthermore, since state laws and regulations mandating essential elements typically allow local school districts to add additional elements or to exceed minimum requirements as long as the defined essentials are not omitted, test makers can give added emphasis—and often substantial added emphasis—to those elements that are more heavily stressed in actual practice. In short, although each of the minimum essential elements required by state law must be given some weight in the test construction process, those elements shown to be more important in classroom practice may correspondingly be emphasized on the test.

Instructional Validity

If one assumes that a proper job analysis has established a domain that reflects the knowledge and skills necessary for appropriate performance in the classroom, a further issue to consider is whether an additional element of "curricular validity" or "instructional validity" must be demonstrated. Applied to teacher certification testing, these concepts would require a demonstration not only that the test objectives are job related but also that they are included in the curriculum at teacher training institutions in the state (curricular validity) or that students attending those institutions were actually taught the specific objectives (instructional validity).[7]

The concepts of "curricular validity" and "instructional validity" (often used in a confused, interchangeable manner) were given significant judicial imprimatur in the context of student minimum competency testing by the ruling of the United States Court of Appeals for the Fifth Circuit in *Debra P. v. Turlington* (1979), the case involving the Florida functional literacy examination.

The court found in *Debra P.* that initial administration of the state student assessment test resulted in substantial adverse impact on minority students: 78% of the black students failed one or both sections of the first administration, compared with 25% of the white students. In light of these statistics, the district court judge scrutinized the test closely. He determined that it had adequate content and construct validity. However, he also determined that given the history of *de jure* school segregation in Florida, it would be unfair to penalize black students who had been forced to attend segregated schools during part of their public school career by denying them a diploma for failure to pass this test. For this reason, the state was enjoined from implementing the diploma denial sanction for a period of 4 years.

CURRICULAR VALIDITY

The appeals court accepted the lower court's findings concerning the basic validity of the examination and specifically affirmed the trial court's holding that the test items were not biased. Nevertheless, the appeals court also held that for competency tests an additional element should be required, which would call upon the state to prove that "the test covered things actually taught in the classrooms." The court labeled this requirement "curricular validity" and remanded the case for further proceedings at the trial court level to determine whether this newly articulated standard had been met.

The *Debra P.* (1979) court's application of the doctrine of curricular validity in 1981 has generated substantial interest in psychometric circles[8] and has apparently led to widespread assumptions that curricular validity has now become an established judicial requirement for student competency testing programs and also, perhaps, for related fields such as teacher certification testing. This perception is highly overblown; the actual legal significance of *Debra P.* is much more modest than most psychometricians seem to realize.

QUALIFICATIONS

Although much attention has been given to the court's initial succinct endorsement of curricular validity in 1981, much less attention has been paid to the courts' qualifications and clear retreat from thoroughgoing application of the doctrine two years later. Having compiled a record of the practical problems involved in assessing curricular validity in the remand hearings, both the district court and the appeals court judges were markedly more circumspect in their approach to the issue. Other courts in related testing contexts have declined to adopt or extend the doctrine,[9] and this author, therefore, sees little likelihood that the doctrine will be applied to teacher certification testing.

FAIRNESS

The concept of curricular validity had initially appealed to the *Debra P.* (1979) court's sense of "fundamental fairness." There was obvious common sense plausibility to the notion that it would be unfair to penalize students who may not have been taught many of the items tested on the minimum competency examination because they had been compelled to attend inferior, racially segregated schools. But the remand hearing showed that any actual attempt to determine what a particular student had actually been taught is an undertaking fraught with overwhelming, perhaps insuperable, logistical difficulties. In order to establish that every student in the state had actually been taught (or even had a fair opportunity to learn) each of the myriad basic objectives covered by an examination, the actual practices of every school district—and indeed of every school and every classroom—in the entire state over the 12-year span of a child's public school education would theoretically need to be analyzed. Moreover, as noted by one of the Fifth Circuit judges in *Debra P.,* additional questions about how well each child was taught (and how much or how recently) also inevitably arise. And even if courts were to accept approximations about the learning experiences of millions of students (an approach that is problematic for a legal system rooted in concepts of individual justice), the methods for making such general inferences as have been suggested to date (including various techniques of classroom observations, teacher self-reports, student self-reports, development of individual pupil cumulative record cards, etc.) are clearly too cumbersome and too costly. As one observer aptly noted, "Attempts to assess curricular validity on a statewide basis will lead to debilitating bureaucracy, costly administration, and a stifling of education innovation"[10] (Venezky, 1983, p. 193).

The *Debra P.* (1979) remand decision directly considered these practical implementation problems. In response to the first appeals court decision, the state of Florida retained a consulting firm to undertake an extensive four-part validation study: A teacher survey was sent to 65,000 teachers, 47,000 of whom responded; a detailed survey was undertaken in all 67 Florida school districts and four university laboratories; site visit teams were sent to each of the districts as a follow up; and student surveys were completed by 3,200 students. Despite this comprehensive range of data, the plaintiffs strongly argued that the validation study remained fundamentally flawed for three major reasons: (a) the survey was constructed so that it invited positive responses from the teachers; (b) the survey covered only one year, rather than the full 12 years of a student's educational experience; and (c) the survey provided insufficient evidence of what actually goes on in the classroom. The district court's frustrated response to these arguments was, "But, absent viewing a video tape of every student's school career, how can we know what has really happened to each child?"

Because of this difficulty, the district court upheld the examinations on a significantly more limited "curricular validity" basis than on the broad "instructional validity" grounds that were the clear basis for the court of appeals' earlier decision.[11] After weighing the various factors involved, the court emphasized that, "what is required is that the skills be included in the official curriculum and that the majority of the teachers recognize them as being something they should teach." In other words, as long as the curriculum included the basic objectives and teachers were aware of them, the court would not insist on the more difficult instructional validity requirement of showing that all or most students actually received instruction in each of the requisite objectives.

The three-judge appeals court panel that affirmed this holding also seemed less committed to the instructional validity concept than did their predecessors in 1981. They specifically noted that "the experts conceded that there are no accepted educational standards for determining whether a test is instructionally valid." Their decision was a carefully qualified affirmance of the district court's findings of fact as not being "clearly erroneous," and they specifically eschewed the difficult task of establishing a clear legal standard to apply in this area. One gets the distinct impression that the appeals court, having studied the complex record of the remand proceedings and realizing the complexities involved, sought to limit the prior holding, rather than to reaffirm or extend it.

APPLICATION TO TEACHER CERTIFICATION TESTING

Given the difficulties experienced by the courts in attempting to implement a concept of instructional validity in the student‧ testing context, it appears unlikely that other courts would attempt to apply the doctrine to the teacher certification testing process where its suitability is even more tenuous. In contrast to student tests that have their roots in instructional assessment, a licensing examination purports to assess job-related skills, rather than any abstract body of knowledge, however they may be acquired.[12] Moreover, an exam oriented to the instruction offered at particular state institutions might well be subject to legal challenge from out-of-state candidates, who would be unfairly disadvantaged.

Stated in more specific legal terms, it is significant that in *Debra P.* (1979), the court's decision was based largely on its holding that high school students have a "legitimate expectation" to receive a high school diploma if they passed all their courses and otherwise met standards in effect before implementation of the competency testing requirement. Whatever legitimate expectation a student might have to a diploma,[13] candidates for teacher certification have no similar legitimate expectation to a license to teach young children. Indeed, the concept of state certification is based on the proposition that the public must be protected against incompetent practitioners and that, therefore, no one has a right to enter the teaching profession without demonstrating the requisite degree of competency.

CONCLUSION

The foregoing analysis has indicated that strict job-relatedness requirements, as applied in the employee selection context, and strict instructional validity, as developed in the student testing context, cannot be directly applied to licensing or certification situations. The experiences in these other areas are, however, not without significance. Even if not logically compatible with the psychometric realities of the teacher testing setting, the strong equity concerns that motivated the court in *Debra P.* (1979) are also relevant to many teacher certification situations. Clearly, the courts will not be oblivious to the plight of minority candidates who may have been denied fair opportunities to prepare for enhanced certification requirements, especially if the case arises in a state with a history of *de jure* segregation. In such situations courts will undoubtedly be inclined to apply some fundamental fairness or due process doctrines.

For these reasons, I believe it will be the due process doctrine, emphasizing reasonable notice and a fair phase-in period, rather than the tenuous instructional validity concept, that will constitute the enduring precedential significance of *Debra P.* (1979) for future teacher certification litigations. Even if a test can be shown to be fully job related and to constitute a reasonable public policy instrument for assuring that only individuals who demonstrate some level of competence are permitted to teach, the courts are likely to insist that fair notice be provided to teacher candidates and that candidates be afforded reasonable notice of changed standards and adequate time to prepare for any new tests.

In *Debra P.* (1979) the court mandated a 4-year waiting period to insure that such adequate notice had been provided. Whether a 4-year phase-in period would be required in another situation depends, of course, on the particular facts and issues involved. For example, if new state regulatory standards or the specific objectives underlying a new certification examination had previously been widely disseminated within the profession, a court might accept a shorter phase-in period. Also, one expects that the more opportunities that are provided for unsuccessful candidates to obtain remediation assistance, to retake the examinations, or to have their shortcomings assessed at an early stage in the training process, the less stringent would be the notice requirements.

In conclusion, although it is impossible to predict in advance how judicial judgment will be applied to any particular circumstance—especially in a rapidly developing area like teacher certification testing—there is every reason to anticipate that teacher certification tests, if developed in good faith with appropriate professional judgment and implemented with fair notice, will, by and large, be upheld by the courts.

Footnotes

1. *See, e.g.,* National Commission on Excellence in Education (1983), Recommendation No. D-1: "Persons preparing to teach should be required to meet high educational standards...and to demonstrate competence in an academic discipline."

2. Goertz, Ekstrom, & Coley (1984). In 14 states applicants for certification are tested in basic skills, in nine states for general knowledge, in 12 states for professional knowledge, and in 14 states for knowledge of the teacher's specialty areas.

3. *See, e.g., Baker* (1971). *Walston* (1973); *United States v. State of North Carolina* (1975), *Georgia Association* (1976). In United States v. South Carolina (1977), where an attempt had been made to validate the test for certification purposes in the state of South Carolina, the test was upheld by the courts. This case is discussed in more detail below.

4. *See, e.g., Tyler* (1975); *Delgato* (1977); *Vanguard Justice Society* (1979); South Carolina, *supra* note 3, at 1110.

5. Generally, "licensure" and "certification" are considered distinct concepts, the former referring to a method for government to assure itself that a candidate has attained a minimal degree of competency necessary to protect the public welfare, and the latter connoting a designation of a level of professional performance that is not a prerequisite for entry into the field. For a discussion of these distinctions, *see* Shimberg (1981). In the teaching field, however, certification is virtually synonymous with licensing, and, therefore, the terms will be used interchangeably in this paper.

6. *Guardians Association of New York City* (1980). *See also* the deferential approach to professional judgment reflected in *Washington* (1976); *South Carolina* (1977); and *Contreras* (1981).

7. These terms originated in the context of student ability tested. "Curricular validity" was defined there as "a measure of how well test items represent the objectives of the curriculum to which the test takers have been exposed." "Instructional validity," by way of contrast, measures whether or not the school districts translated stated objectives into topics actually taught in the classroom. *See* M. McClung (1977). *See also* McClung (1979).

8. Note in this regard that Standard 8.7 of the newly adopted "Standards for Educational and Pyschological Testing" states:

> "When a test is used to make decisions about student promotion or graduation, there should be evidence that the test covers only the specific or generalized knowledge, skills and abilities that students have had the opportunity to learn."

9. *See, Bester* (1984) (court declines to apply the instructional validation doctrine to a school district's policy of requiring mínimum reading standards for promotion). *Cf. Anderson* (1982) ("curricular validity" upheld on the basis of educational authorities' testimony, without empirical field evidences). *See also Brookhart* (1983); *Board of Education of Northport Union Free School District* (1982) (handicapped students denied diplomas for failure to pass minimum competency tests covering areas not included in their IEPs).

10. R. Venezky (1983). The Madaus volume contains a series of articles that wrestle with the problems of developing suitable techniques for establishing curricular validity. Significantly, the articles were all written in response to the 1981 Debra P. decision, and tend to assume a legal climate that may no longer exist in light of the courts' 1983/84 decisions.

11. Note that although the 1981 Appeals Court decision had used the term "curricular validity," it clearly meant to impose a requirement for "instructional validity" since it required a showing that test objectives "covered things *actually taught* in the classrooms." The Court's confusion on the terms is an indication of its lack of full awareness of what the seemingly straightforward psychometric concepts it was endorsing really meant in practice.

12. Validation of the local teacher training college curriculum was upheld by the court in the United States v. South Carolina, supra note 4, but the court did so on a record that offered nonstandardized program approval practices which the court considered highly undesirable, as the only alternative. *See* 445 F. Supp. (*Debra P.,* 1979) at 1115-1116. If the current state of the art now can provide a job-related certification examination as an acceptable alternative, it is reasonable to assume that the courts would endorse this preferred approach. In that context, South Carolina would not provide precedent for adding an additional, and inconsistent, curriculum validity requirement to an otherwise acceptable job-related examination. *Cf. Ensley Branch of NAACP* (1980) (training program validation suitable only for tests of minimum reading and verbal skills).

13. The Debra P. court's holding on this point was strongly attacked by Judge Tjoflat, who in dissenting from the Fifth Circuit's denial of a reconsideration *en banc* of the 1981 ruling, argued that the panel opinion had misapplied relevant Supreme Court precedent. 654 F.2d at 1081.

References

American Psychological Association, American Educational Research Association, National Council on Research in Education. *Standards for educational and psychological tests.* Washington, DC: Author. Forthcoming.

Anderson v. Banks, 540 F. Supp. 761 (S.D. Ga. 1982).

Baker v. Columbus Municipal Separate School District, 329 F. Supp. 706 (N.D. Miss. 1971), *aff'd* 462 F.2d 1112 (5th Cir. 1972).

Bester v. Tuscaloosa City Board of Education, 722 F.2d 1514 (11th Cir. 1984).

Board of Education of Northport Union Free School District v. Ambach, 60 N.Y. 2d 758 (1982).

Brookhart v. Illinois State Board of Education, 697 F.2d 179 (7th Cir. 1983).

Civil Rights Act of 1964, Title VII, Section 703(h).

Contreras v. City of Los Angeles, 656 F.2d 1267 (9th Cir. 1981).

Debra P. v. Turlington, 474 F. Supp. 244 (M.D. Fla. 1979), *aff'd in part and rev'd in part* 664 F.2d 397 (5th Cir. 1981), *on remand* 564 F. Supp. 177 (M.D. Fla. 1983), *aff'd* 730 F.2d 1405 (11th Cir. 1984).

Delgato v. McTighe, 442 F. Supp. 725, 730 (E.D. Pa. 1977).

Ensley Branch of NAACP v. Seibels, 616 F.2d 812, 819 n. 17 (5th Cir. 1980), *cert. den.* 449 U.S. 1061.

Equal Employment Opportunity Commission, Civil Service Commission, U. S. Department of Labor, & U. S. Department of Justice. (1978). Adoption by four agencies of uniform guidelines on employee selection procedures. *Federal Register, 43,* 38290-38315.

Georgia Association v. Nix, 407 F. Supp. 1102 (N.D. Ga. 1976).

Goertz, Ekstrom, & Coley. (1984). *The impact of state policy on entrance into the teaching profession* (Final report, N.I.E. Grant No. G83-0073 9).

Guardians Association of New York City v. Civil Service Commission, 630 F.2d 79, 89 (2nd Cir. 1980).

McClung, M. (1979, September). Competency testing: Potential for discrimination. *Clearinghouse Rev., 439, 446.*

McClung, M. (1979). Competency testing programs: Legal and educational issues. *Ford. L. Rev., 47, 651, 682-683.*

National Commission on Excellence in Education. (1983). *A nation at risk: The imperative for educational reform.* Washington, DC: U. S. Government Printing Office.

Shanker, A. (1985, January 30). Address at National Press Club, Washington, DC.

Shimberg. (1981). Testing for licensure and certification. *Am. Psych., 36,* 1138.

Tyler v. Vickery, 517 F.2d 1089, 1097 (5th Cir. 1975).

United States v. State of North Carolina, 400 F. Supp. 343 (E.D. N.C. 1975), *vacated* 425 F. Supp. 789 (1977).

United States v. State of South Carolina, 445 F. Supp. 1094 (D. S.C. 1977), *aff'd* 434 U.S. 1026 (1978).

Vanguard Justice Society v. Hughes, 471 F. Supp. 670, 696 (D. Md. 1979).

Venezky, R. (1983). Curricular validity: The case for structure and process. In G. Madaus (Ed.), *The courts, validity and competency testing* (pp. 183-193). Hingham, MA: Kluwer-Nijhoff Publishing Co.

Walston v. County School Board of Nasemond County, 492 F.2d 919 (4th Cir. 1973).

Washington v. Davis, 426 U.S. 229 (1976).

The Use of State-Mandated Competencies in Building the Teacher Certification Testing Program

Robert Gabrys

CONTEXT

The context in which West Virginia has approached teacher certification testing is critical to understanding the goals of the program. This context has several dimensions:

1. It is learner focused.
2. It is public school curriculum based.
3. It recognizes the essential role of institutions of higher education in teacher education.
4. It recognizes the realistic limits of testing.
5. It allows for ease of movement of teachers and other professional personnel across state lines.

Learner Focused

West Virginia recognizes its people, especially children, as its greatest resource. This resource must be nurtured in the school system, through which the state meets its constitutional obligation to provide educational opportunity to every citizen.

Robert Gabrys is Director of the Office of Educational Personnel, Division of Teacher Certification and Development, West Virginia State Department of Education.

Recently the West Virginia educational system systematically developed a comprehensive education plan for West Virginia schools (involving the State Board of Education, State Board of Regents, State Department of Education, legislature, institutions of higher education, public school districts, lay citizenry, and even the courts). The plan reflects the learning needs of pupils as they move through the developmental learning stages of early childhood (K-4), middle childhood (5-8), and adolescence (9-12). West Virginia's adoption of this three-level framework modifies the basis of educational programming from a reliance on the traditional grade-level organizational patterns in elementary and secondary education to an emphasis on the developmental needs of the classroom pupil.

Public School Curriculum Based

Within the three-level learner focus, the state is developing (with the assistance of public school and higher education personnel task forces) curriculum guidelines that describe the learning outcomes expected of public school learners. In July 1983 the State Board of Education adopted such outcomes for K-12 art, science, mathematics, and reading. Draft outcomes exist in all other areas at this time and are being validated before adoption. These outcomes are tentatively scheduled for adoption in July 1985, with a public school implementation date of 1986-87.

In addition, in April 1982 the State Board of Education adopted Policy 5100 as a means of assuring the quality of educational personnel. This policy mandated a direct link between higher education teacher training and public education; Policy 5100 called for the expiration of approval of all higher education programs on August 31, 1985. Programs for every type of endorsement had to be revamped and submitted for approval between March and May 1985. Teacher education programs must now include four components:

1. Preprofessional skills in reading, writing, speaking, listening, mathematical computation, and computer literacy at a proficiency level necessary for an educator. (This professional literacy component is measured by the

National Teacher Examination Preprofessional Skills Test, the American College Testing COMP Tests, and individual college assessment.)

2. General education defined operationally as that which a liberally educated person would know. (Each institution assesses this component.)

3. Content specialization defined as the knowledge level necessary to deliver the public school curriculum in a given content area. (Standardized criterion-referenced tests, developed under contract by National Evaluation Systems, assess this component.)

4. Professional education based on state-adopted objectives at each developmental level and in each content area for which certification is sought. (Individual institutions assess this component, but it will eventually become part of the state's testing program.)

Teacher Education and the Essential Role of Institutions of Higher Education

While the public school system defines its expectations, the education department's Office of Educational Personnel Development is reviewing its standards for both initial and ongoing teacher education and personnel development programs in West Virginia's colleges and universities. This review is predicated on the belief that the changes forecast for public school curricula provide the primary direction for educational personnel preparation programs. Therefore, state board policies and the resultant educational program directions of the public schools become major factors in determining teacher education curriculum. Recent research developments, traditional bodies of knowledge, and the existing college curricula serve as supporting factors.

West Virginia has long advocated the state-approved teacher education program approach to certification as the most workable system for training and licensing personnel. A related emphasis is on a systematic program of training verified by an accredited institution. For these reasons the state does not award certificates based upon the random accumulation of hours at multiple institutions.

West Virginia is a participant with some 30 other states in the Interstate Certification Compact (ICC) and operates on the basis of the required five-year program approval process. Between 1975 and 1980 the state's 17 institutions of higher education underwent on-site evaluations of their teacher education programs. The rigor of the review is verified by the fact that on initial consideration not one of the institutions received full approval for all of its programs. On the other hand, by 1980, as a result of institutional and external technical assistance efforts, all 17 institutions had received full approval for all programs.

The West Virginia Advisory Council on Professional Development of Educational Personnel undertook a needs assessment related to future teacher education directions. The results clearly indicated that if colleges were going to assist public schools in their improvement effort and if the institutions themselves were going to grow, some flexibility in state process standards was necessary. The state agreed and moved to establish an outcome-based rather than a process-based system for program approval. Outcome-based came to mean "job-related," and standardized testing became the vehicle for assuring common outcomes from various institutions. The state decided that the relationship between teacher characteristics and styles and student performance was complex; it no longer appeared feasible to pursue a single definition of effective teaching. At the same time, however, a body of teacher education knowledge and a definition of the teaching profession were emerging. Accountability became as valued as flexibility in delivery of teacher education programs.

West Virginia has chosen to provide institutions with a high degree of process flexibility on one hand, but to institute a testing program that measures common outcome expectations on the other. No individual can complete a state-approved teacher education program, regardless of the degree granted, without obtaining the requisite cut score within the testing program. This position is crucial to West Virginia's responsibility to avoid encouraging individuals to go to other states to become teachers if they cannot meet in-state certification requirements.

Realistic Recognition of the Limits of Testing

As previously noted, the education department has operated since 1974 on the assumption that credit counts based upon transcript analysis are an alternative to state-approved college teacher preparation programs. This same philosophy holds true as the department moves to a testing program. Although the department recognizes that tests may reliably and validly measure the outcomes of a program, tests are no substitute for teacher preparation programs. Specifically, the department recognizes that (a) all that defines effective teaching is not currently known, let alone measurable; (b) test items reflect only a sample of the population of objectives; (c) tests, being time bound, cannot expand to cover the entire range of appropriate content; and (d) test objectives are based upon a job analysis and therefore tend to reflect what *is* rather than what *should be*.

JOB ANALYSIS

A major criticism of the job-related objective verification system is that it seeks verification from current practitioners and is therefore subject to their expertise or lack of expertise. Test verification processes are increasingly criticized for emphasizing legal defensibility over state-of-the-art research findings. It is difficult for some to believe that high standards can derive from a system that relies heavily on current employees. This is especially true given difficult teacher working conditions, nonoutcome-based staff development, and the dearth of research on effective teaching. In addition, there is rising criticism of teacher preparation course work because it is not immediately relevant to classroom behavior with a specific class of pupils.

LOCAL FACTORS

It is difficult for a state testing program to encompass situational variables that reflect local needs and job criteria. A testing program, as part of the licensure process, may well raise the quality of entrants by ensuring that learning did occur. The same testing program, however, will not identify the "best" qualified individual, only those who are qualified above the threshold. Therefore, local employment criteria and personnel review processes will still be critical aspects of hiring and subsequent employment.

In fact, there are many factors that keep schools from hiring the "best" qualified. Many districts use standardized recruitment and selection processes in filling positions. Many teachers are hired on the same day a resignation was received, especially in August, or are hired because they happened to walk into the building or district office at the right time. Many teachers are hired not only because they meet the short-term goals of covering a third grade class or five periods of English, but also because they are viewed as contributors to the overall long-range goals of the district or because they demonstrate leadership potential.

In short, a testing program will upgrade the quality of personnel to some extent, but it must not be mistaken for a panacea for all major educational problems. It is also unrealistic to expect that colleges will adjust their programs to reflect only job-related test objectives, no matter how valid the objectives may be. It is a function of higher education to contribute to the body of knowledge in a field and to experiment with diversity. The tension between academic freedom and state-prescribed standards is healthy, and, indeed, one must hope that higher education will never relinquish its expansive role in research and experimentation. Higher education must ensure that training does not become a "bag of tricks" or a response to the immediate with little concern for the theoretical underpinnings of the body of knowledge that is an essential attribute of any profession.

Testing programs can help strengthen the perception of teaching as a true profession, but they are only one factor. A systematic program of educational reform, not isolated significant changes, is what is needed to attain educational excellence.

Movement of Teachers and Other Professional Personnel Across State Lines

Perhaps one of the more critical issues to be resolved as a result of the "decision to test" relates to personnel trained beyond state boundaries. This issue must address two distinct populations: trained but inexperienced teachers from other states and experienced teachers from other states.

INEXPERIENCED TEACHERS

The current West Virginia position is that the testing program is part of the state-approved program structure and is therefore not applicable to every out-of-state applicant for a license. This position is not a new one because West Virginia has been a participant in the ICC since the 1960s. An underlying premise of that contract is that states that have and monitor standards for teacher preparation institutions are much more alike than different. Such states recognize that their differences are not significant to the licensure process or to the success of an entry-level teacher in the receiving state.

The testing component of the West Virginia-approved program, though more politically sensitive, is really no different from previous state requirements for a specific number of credits in specific courses that the ICC contract addressed. Although West Virginia now incorporates testing as part of its process, the state has not taken the position that testing is a *sine qua non* for licensure. Tests are not required of out-of-state applicants who bear a certificate. The West Virginia approach for individuals without teaching experience is based upon the inference that completion of a state-approved program and recommendation by the institution merit a license.

EXPERIENCED TEACHERS

The second group of people potentially affected by testing programs is experienced teachers from other states. Here again, West Virginia does not require tests of such individuals. Once teachers have established an employment record, the testing program becomes even less salient from West Virginia's perspective. Why test teachers' knowledge base when their behavior with pupils and interactions with colleagues in the same field have been established? Although one could argue that tests provide additional assurance, tests appear to be more appropriate for staff development rather than for licensure purposes. Moreover, in an era of shortages in some fields, it is neither politic nor good business to test experienced teachers; such testing could make West Virginia less attractive to teachers. There must be a time in a teacher's professional life when the cloud of "licensure" is no longer over the teacher's head, and the teacher can get down to the business of the profession.

It is within the context of the above factors that the following description of the West Virginia content specialization and professional education testing program should be considered.[1]

GOALS OF THE STANDARDIZED TESTING PROGRAM FOR THE CONTENT SPECIALIZATIONS

The West Virginia standardized testing program for the content specializations has three primary goals:

1. To ensure that candidates for teacher certification meet established proficiency levels of cognitive information related to the specialization or specializations for which certification is sought.
2. To provide diagnostic information about candidates' strengths and weaknesses to the teacher certification candidates and to the institutions in which they are enrolled.
3. To provide precise information to the institutions and their Educational Personnel Preparation Advisory Committees for evaluating their educational personnel preparation programs and facilitating the improvement of those programs.

Legal and Technical Requirements

The content specialization tests were developed in light of a number of legal and technical requirements that affected both design and implementation variables.

TESTING APPROACH

One of the first decisions that had to be made in the design of the content area testing program was to choose between criterion-referenced and norm-referenced tests. The testing program in West Virginia was enacted to ensure that individuals seeking certification meet a specified level of cognitive proficiency in reference to public school curriculum. Thus the testing program compares teacher candidates with a specified standard, and the content knowledge tests are criterion-referenced to the public school curriculum.

JOB RELATEDNESS

Guidelines developed by the federal Equal Employment Opportunity Commission (EEOC) govern the development of all tests used for certification purposes and call for job relatedness. Specifically, the EEOC Guidelines state that such an examination must satisfy three requirements:

1. The test must be composed of a representative sample of important work behaviors to be performed on the job for which candidates are to be evaluated.

2. The test must not result in *adverse impact* on any of certain protected groups.

3. If adverse impact does result, the test must be proven valid for the purpose for which it is used.

In other words a test must be demonstrably job related, and it must be fair and objective to ensure that it does not cause adverse impact. If the test is clearly job related but still results in adverse impact, then the user must prove the test is valid for its intended use.

To comply with the requirement that certification examinations be job related, a combination of expert judgment and empirical data must be applied during development. In West Virginia, job experts specified the domain of knowledge and skills to be included on the certification examination by judging the appropriateness of content objectives. These objectives were empirically validated through a job analysis survey of incumbent teachers. These respondents determined the extent to which the knowledge and skills identified were important to the job and indicated the frequency with which they were used on the job. The combination of expert judgment and empirical data ensures the job relatedness of the examination.

VALIDITY

The tests developed for the content specializations must be proven valid for the purpose of certifying teachers. One way to establish validity is to conduct a content validation study. A validation study demonstrates that the test content represents a sample of the knowledge and skills included in the subject area's domain. The content validation of teacher certification instruments generally has two components: (1) determining if the content of the test reflects significant aspects of the educator's job and (2) determining if the test items accurately measure that content. The content of each test, defined by objectives, derives from the job analysis discussed above. The second component—determining whether test items accurately measure the content—is established by expert judges who review the test items to verify that they accurately reflect the domain of knowledge and skills defined in the job analysis.

ESTABLISHING PROFICIENCY LEVELS

The standardized testing program is aimed at ensuring that only those individuals who meet specified proficiency levels are permitted to teach. The establishment of these proficiency levels is a critical issue. The levels established must clearly separate those candidates who meet an essential level of competency from those who do not. These levels are established through the use of expert judges drawn from educational personnel from the West Virginia Department of Education, public schools, and institutions of higher education. A panel of experts within each area of certification reviews the test items to determine the level of competency that must be achieved by candidates for certification. By having the levels established in this way, the meaning of proficiency will reflect the essential competencies necessary to practice in West Virginia schools.

Diagnostic Information

The second goal of the testing program is to provide diagnostic information about candidates' strengths and weaknesses to the candidates and to the teacher training institutions. Criterion-referenced tests measure specified objectives and domains of knowledge and skills. Score reporting for these tests can therefore provide not only information about the pass-fail decision for each candidate, but also specific information about performance on each domain of the test. This information can be used by candidates to improve their knowledge and skills in areas of weakness. Similarly, teacher training institutions can use the information on their candidates' strengths and weaknesses to determine areas in which emphasis in the curriculum may be needed. This diagnostic information can also be used to evaluate performance on a statewide basis.

TEST SCORING

The certification program is designed to provide information about the performance of candidates in relation to established standards of competency and to provide diagnostic information about candidates' strengths and weaknesses. The method of scoring the tests must be consistent with these goals.

Although a single standard (passing score) will be established for each examination, separate scores for each subarea will be provided to examinees for diagnostic purposes. Information on subarea performance will provide examinees with an indication of their strengths and weaknesses and will allow examinees to prepare for retesting if they fail to meet the specified standards. Candidates failing to meet the standards on the first attempt must retake the entire test. Candidates will be permitted to take the tests as often as the tests are offered.

WHO WILL BE ASSESSED

All candidates for professional certification will be required to attain the assessment requirements mandated by Policy 5100 (and subsequent policies and regulations). Educators currently holding valid professional certificates in West Virginia are not required to pass the tests in order to maintain their certification. However, individuals seeking additional endorsements must meet the state assessment requirements for each new area.

Method of Assessment

Content knowledge in each area will be assessed through paper-and-pencil tests. Each test will comprise three to six content subareas that reflect the major areas of content knowledge within the area of specialization.

Evaluation Design

One of the most important components of any educational program is an evaluation of its effectiveness in order to continue to improve the program. The evaluation of the certification testing program will draw information from a number of sources including: examinee score reports, institution score reports, statewide score reports, objective summary reports, retake analyses, teacher candidate surveys, institution surveys, and test development technical reports.

The various score reporting mechanisms will be the primary sources for evaluating the extent to which the testing program is meeting its stated objectives. In addition, a survey questionnaire will be administered to all teacher education program candidates. A sample of teacher candidates, both those meeting and failing to meet standards for certification, will be asked to complete a questionnaire covering their perceptions of the testing program. The education department will conduct the survey at the conclusion of the third year of the program to allow sufficient opportunity for the program to have an effect.

Perhaps the most critical component of the evaluation is whether the program produces better quality personnel to serve pupils in the public schools of West Virginia. The state has undertaken this entire effort as a step toward assuring the quality of educational personnel. The program's success, therefore, cannot be judged solely by the perceptions of test takers or by technical or legal experts. Obviously, such an evaluation will be extremely complex, seeking to assess variables that are difficult to measure and encompassing criteria that have not been previously used. The education department anticipates that a plan for this evaluation will be developed during the 1985-86 school year.

PROFESSIONAL EDUCATION PERFORMANCE ASSESSMENT

Equally as important as the content area test component in West Virginia's program is the professional education performance assessment. As a result of the framework of early, middle, and adolescent learning levels, the development of learning outcomes at these levels, and the current development of a criterion-referenced testing program for pupils based upon learning outcomes, it is crucial to interrelate professional education training with these concepts.

In March 1985, when institutions of higher education refiled their teacher education programs for approval, they did so in accordance with the state board policy[2] that implemented the testing program and the new certification patterns. In the professional education sequence at each institution, the performance of each candidate must be assessed relative to behavioral indicators that reflect state-adopted objectives developed in conjunction with National Evaluation Systems.

These performance assessments must relate to each endorsement being sought and be conducted at each level (early, middle, or adolescent) that will be included on the certificate. Also, the successful completion of the performance assessment must be verified by public school personnel, not just the college supervisor. Therefore, the college supervisor could conceivably recommend a passing grade for the student, but the public school teacher could refuse to recommend the individual for licensure. This significantly increases the direct professional input into the decision of who becomes a teacher.

The education department anticipates that efforts in the 1985-86 school year will be directed toward developing a standardized performance assessment. A major issue to be addressed is whether West Virginia should develop its own performance assessment, team with other states, or perhaps even join in efforts to develop a national performance assessment. After all, do the professional skills required of teachers differ as one crosses state boundaries?

Conclusion

West Virginia's testing efforts must be considered in the context of a comprehensive reform plan. Virtually every aspect of public education is being scrutinized in an effort to upgrade quality. Higher education has embarked on a comprehensive outcome-based system that stresses effective teaching skills and knowledge over process variables. Our staff development programs and our certification regulations are being reviewed to see if they assist professionals in achieving excellence or if they impede progress. Testing, both as criterion-referenced knowledge assessment and as job-related performance assessment, is one aspect of that reform movement. It is crucial to the total picture, but it is only a part of that picture. Testing will do its part and contribute to the overall quality of the movement, but it cannot constitute the total reform effort.

Footnotes

1. Special acknowledgment is made to Dr. Howard Kardatzke and Mrs. Noreita Shamblin of the Teacher Education Unit of the Office of Educational Personnel Development and to the National Evaluation Systems staff for their contribution to the program that is described in this chapter.

2. A copy of this policy (#5100) is available upon request.

Analysis of Candidates Who Retake the Teacher Tests

Lester M. Solomon

This chapter discusses the pattern of success and failure of examinees who take the Georgia Teacher Certification Tests. Georgia is one of many states that require passing a content knowledge test as a condition for initial certification. Working with National Evaluation Systems (NES), Georgia was the first state in the country to develop and administer a customized, criterion-referenced testing program.

The focus here is on one aspect of that program—the analysis of examinees who retake the certification test after initial failure. The state of Georgia has a policy of unlimited retakes; that is, it allows individuals to take the test as many times as they please in an attempt to obtain a certificate. Georgia believes retake analysis is an important part of any licensing project. Consequently, results of Georgia's retake analyses are included in this chapter in the hope that other states will undertake similar studies of their candidate populations. There is no formal attempt here to interpret the results of these analyses. Undoubtedly there are many interesting research questions embedded in the figures, but speculations about these questions are beyond the scope of this chapter.

RETAKE ANALYSIS: WHAT IS IT?

Most teacher certification programs offer examinees unlimited opportunities to take a given test. Failure on an initial attempt, therefore, in no way results in the termination of a person's

---

Lester Solomon is Director of Teacher Assessment, Georgia Department of Education.

candidacy. In fact, most people who fail on an initial attempt try again to pass the test. Our figures show that the number of people who make another effort always exceeds those who drop out after a given failure. One might, therefore, envision the career of an examinee, or group of examinees, as follows (see Table 1).

Table 1
Career of an Examinee

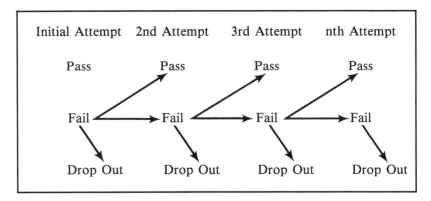

If one reviews a single administration of a test (i.e., the total population of people who take a test at any sitting on a given date at sites throughout Georgia), one can calculate the percentage of people who either passed or failed the test at that particular time. Normally it is this percentage that is presented in the media as the "passing rate." We do not dispute that this is a passing rate of sorts. Obviously it does convey the percentage of individuals who passed at a given administration.

Retake analysis, on the contrary, focuses on the "career" of an examinee who may fail initially but who may pass on a subsequent attempt. Retake analysis is concerned with the cumulative passing rate in an examination program. In other words, retake analysis has to do with how many individuals, out of all the individuals who initially take a test, pass, either on the initial or on some subsequent try. As Table 1 indicates, the only people who do not pass are those who, after a failure, elect not to retake the exam and who drop out. For some, the process is frustrating; they may take an exam four or even five times before passing or deciding to quit. But the point is that even if it takes someone several attempts to pass a test, that person is a passing candidate.

RETAKE ANALYSIS: WHY IS IT IMPORTANT?

The Georgia program believes retake analysis is an important undertaking because otherwise one gains a totally erroneous impression of the effects of the testing program on the candidate population. Simply looking at the percentage of people who fail a given examination sitting or an aggregate of such sittings presents a much more negative picture than is actually the case.

Many people make this mistake in reviewing test results. It is common in the field, and even leaders in the testing industry have contributed to the misconception. They forecast a bleak future for minority teachers because of the failure rates of minority candidates. Their figures are based on aggregate passing rate percentages and project that the minority teaching force in the United States could be almost half its current number by the year 2000.

Erroneous Approach

It is erroneous to treat the failure rate on tests as if each of the failures was an individual. Consider the person who passes the test on his or her fourth try. That person has failed three times. Those three failures are included in the overall pass-fail rate that many people consider to represent the true failure rate of the examination. But, actually, that individual is a passing candidate. It may have taken time, and it may have been frustrating. But the three times the individual failed are not, in fact, a part of the failure rate for the examination. The failure rate for an examination program should include only those people who, after a failure, do not take the test again.

Georgia believes it is much more accurate to describe the testing situation in a way that reflects its true complexity. At any given administration, some candidates are taking the test for the first time and some for the second, third, or other instance. The typical approach treats all these candidates as if they were part of the same testing population. Retake analysis, on the other hand, disaggregates these overall rates and yields a much more accurate picture.

The Georgia Case

Let us review the figures from Georgia that illustrate the point quite dramatically. Georgia has been giving its teacher certification tests for approximately 8 years. In that time (through May 1984), we have administered 34,629 examinations. Of those 34,629 testing events, our overall pass rate was approximately 70%. In other words, after all of those papers were scored, 70% were passes and approximately 30% were failures.

These 34,629 examinations do not represent 34,629 examinees. In fact, only 27,546 individuals account for the total number of tests; obviously, some people took the tests more than one time. Of the 27,546 individuals who have been a part of Georgia's testing program, 88% passed the examination—a substantially different figure from the 70% that would be noted under the other approach to calculating pass rates. The 88% figure is significant both in gross numerical terms and in the implications one draws from it. A program has a far different effect on the candidate population if almost nine out of ten individuals pass their examinations as compared with only seven out of ten.

CUMULATIVE PASS RATE

The 88% figure represents the cumulative pass rate. This is the rate at which individuals pass examinations, regardless of the number of attempts it may require. The dire predictions raised by some are greatly reduced in the face of the cumulative pass rates attained in the Georgia program. It is for this reason that the misconception that abounds in the media is so dangerous; the cumulative pass rate paints a very different picture of the prospects for candidates in general and minority candidates in particular. In fact, this chapter presents some dramatic instances of minority-dominated institutions whose initial pass rates are quite low but whose cumulative pass rates are very impressive.

Retake analysis is important because it provides a more accurate picture of what happens to individual candidates. The point is not to know what percentage of passes or failures are obtained at a given administration or over an aggregate of administrations. The important figure is the percentage of initial examinees who eventually pass a test.

RESEARCH CHALLENGE

National Evaluation Systems has been working with the Georgia State Department of Education for years to analyze retake patterns of our testing population. It would be highly appropriate for other jurisdictions to do so. In fact, we would challenge states that use the norm-referenced National Teacher Examination to calculate their figures. We doubt that their figures would compare favorably with ours. We believe that the objective-based nature of our tests, the availability of diagnostic information with test results, and other support provided to examinees in our program contribute in major ways to the eventual success of most of our teaching candidates.

RETAKE ANALYSIS IN GEORGIA

Table 2 (see next page) gives an overall picture of what is happening with examinees in the Georgia Teacher Certification Testing Program. The figures cover the period through May 1984.

Overall Cumulative Pass Rate

As noted in Table 2, the overall cumulative pass rate is 88%, and 11% of all examinees who take a test eventually stop trying after a failure. This table recalls the initial career graphic earlier in the chapter. We can see that after each administration, examinees are divided into four categories: (a) those who passed, (b) those who take the test subsequently and pass on that attempt, (c) those who take the test subsequently and fail, and make yet another attempt, and (d) those who fail the test and do not attempt to retake it.

This last category is the true "failure" population. Those are the individuals who are a part of the 11% we consider our failure rate in the Georgia program. They have essentially dropped out of the quest for a teaching certificate. Other individuals continue in their efforts.

Table 2
Georgia Department of Education
Georgia Teacher Certification Testing Program
Summary Results 1978-1984
All Fields
N = 27,546

STATUS	First Attempt	Second Attempt Cumulative	Third Attempt Cumulative	Fourth Attempt Cumulative	Five or More Attempts Cumulative
PASS	78.4%	84.5%	86.6%	87.4%	88.1%
FAIL	21.6%	8.4%	3.7%	1.7%	0.9%
NO RETAKE	N/A	7.1%	9.7%	10.9%	11%
RETAKE PASS RATE	N/A	42%	36%	31%	44%
CUMULATIVE	N/A	N/A	57%	62%	67%

Retake Pass Rates

It is also noted in Table 2 that the percentage of individuals who pass the test tends to decrease in subsequent attempts. Obviously, the less well prepared become an increasingly large proportion of the "failed on last attempt" population. Being less well prepared, they are less likely to pass the test, and as their percentage of the total test population increases, the passing rates go down.

On the other hand, of all individuals who fail the test the first time, two-thirds (67%) eventually pass. This is a striking figure—it says very clearly to our candidate population that initial failure on a test is by no means the same thing as failure in the long run. Most people who retake a test do eventually pass it. We believe there are several reasons for this. One is that the simple act of repeating a test may help an individual overcome the unfamiliarity with a testing situation that may contribute to failure on an initial effort.

SUPPORT FOR EXAMINEES

The Georgia program, like all the criterion-referenced programs developed by National Evaluation Systems, provides considerable support to examinees both before and after test taking. Objectives and sample questions are available to examinees preparing for a test. The examinees receive score reports that provide explicit information about the level of competence demonstrated in particular subareas of a teaching field. Using this information, an examinee who has failed can concentrate remediation efforts on the areas where performance was the weakest. The program has a major commitment to provide this sort of information to examinees.

In fact, Georgia is quite proud of the high success rate of the total population. We believe the standards set for the tests and the content itself reflect the requirements of sound performance in Georgia classrooms. We want as many qualified, certified teachers as possible. It pleases us, therefore, that the overwhelming majority of people (88%) eventually meet our rigorous standards. It benefits local educational systems throughout the state.

PARTICULAR CASES

As one looks at individual testing fields, the patterns obviously vary. Our initial passing rates for particular fields vary by as much as 15%. But the overall pattern is the same: the cumulative pass rate is substantially higher than the initial pass rate.

Early childhood education, one of our larger testing fields, is an example of this situation. Through May 1984, 6,839 individuals attempted this test. Eighty-four percent passed on the initial effort; the cumulative pass rate is 92%. In home economics, the initial pass rate is 79%, but the cumulative pass rate is 91%.

Interestingly, there are some fields in which the retake pass rate is higher than the pass rate on examinees' initial efforts. We find that to be the case, for instance, in administration and supervision. There are several possible explanations for this, and the department of education is holding discussions on this topic. It is important to us to understand what causes people to pass or fail the test on either initial or subsequent efforts. The variety of patterns across fields indicates that there may be characteristics of fields themselves that lead to the differences among pass rates.

INSTITUTIONAL SCORES

Likewise, the scores achieved by particular teacher preparation institutions vary. One interesting example comes from a predominantly black institution that has an initial pass rate of 33% across all testing fields. The retake pass rate for the institution is, on the other hand, 54%, culminating in a cumulative pass rate of 56%, which represents substantial improvement over the initial pass rate. Another example is shown by a small, private institution that has an initial pass rate of 65% but a retake pass rate of 81%, resulting in a cumulative pass rate of 84%, higher than that in one of our state universities. These examples illustrate the situation where the retake pass rate is higher than the initial one.

One more example provides particularly eloquent testimony about what can be done by individual schools. A predominantly black institution has an initial pass rate of 39% in the field of communicative arts (the test for English and speech teachers). The institution has made tremendous strides, however, and has a cumulative pass rate of 78%. The contrast between those two figures emphasizes most clearly the importance of considering cumulative pass rates in reviewing the effect of a program on the testing population in general and on minorities in particular. It would not give sufficient credit to the individuals in that program to focus on their initial rates as opposed to where they end up with their cumulative rates.

SUMMARY

Georgia has done a variety of analyses in conjunction with its teacher certification testing program. Even in the area of retake analysis, there have been a number of research studies. We have stratified examinees into cohorts by the year they first take the test and followed them as separate groups, and we have examined the figures for individual academic years.

The basic point of these studies and this discussion is that the situation in regard to teacher certification testing in Georgia is, in fact, a very positive one in terms of cumulative pass rates. Of all initial examinees, 88% eventually pass the test in the field of their choice. In this way, the program works; large numbers of examinees can attain the required levels of competence for classroom teaching. The use of passing rates that are based on the number of tests given as opposed to the individuals involved creates a misleading picture of certification testing programs. The Georgia Department of Education encourages all other states to undertake similar analyses. We believe this will go a long way in improving the public image of teacher certification testing programs and correcting serious misconceptions that might exist about them.

Building a Competency Test for Prospective Teachers

Raymond L. Pecheone
Gail Tomala
Pascal D. Forgione, Jr.

CONTEXT FOR TESTING

The quality of America's school teachers has been a hotly debated topic over the last several years. To meet the challenge, many states are quickly moving toward addressing quality through teacher testing. A recent report (Sandefur, 1985) found that seventeen states require some or all teacher candidates to pass a basic skills test before entering a teacher education program; 26 require a test for certification; 16 require both. Testing occurs in four areas: basic skills (34 states); professional skills (25 states); on-the-job analysis (13 states); content knowledge in the speciality area (26 states); 8 states test in all four areas.

The rush toward state prescribed tests is not merely a state education department choice; it is a choice that has substantial support nationwide. A recent Gallup poll (1984) found that the public support for teacher testing was overwhelmingly favorable (89%). In addition, the same poll found that the majority of practicing teachers surveyed favored state examinations for beginning teachers.

Raymond Pecheone is Educational Consultant, Office of Research and Evaluation, Connecticut State Department of Education. Gail Tomala is CONNCEPT Project Manager, Connecticut State Department of Education. Pascal Forgione, Jr. is Chief of the Office of Research and Evaluation, Connecticut State Department of Education.

When states adopt a testing model as a method for evaluating the capabilities of potential teachers, it is necessary to begin with a clear understanding of the purpose or purposes of the testing program. The most common response to the need for evaluation has been the initiation of policies that use competency tests, college entrance tests, or minimum grade point averages to control access to the teaching profession. By establishing these screens, states are, in effect, equating the testing plan with the goal of improving the quality of individuals entering the teaching profession. It can be argued, however, that testing policies alone are not sufficient for improving teaching and, ultimately, student learning. Clearly, to bring about change in these areas, a state must engage in a more comprehensive package of reform that goes well beyond testing.

The purpose of this chapter is to discuss issues related to building a competency examination for prospective teachers and to describe briefly Connecticut's approach to ensuring professional competence. The focus of the discussion is on the variety of decisions a state must make when considering the implementation of a teacher testing program. Particular emphasis is placed on providing advice to practitioners who are implementing a teacher testing program. The chapter addresses four major topics: (1) shared policy understandings; (2) general activities in designing a competency examination; (3) test selection or development; and (4) the conditions for establishing a testing program.

SHARED POLICY UNDERSTANDINGS

The decision to build a competency examination typically results either from legislation or from a state board of education initiative. The first major debate surrounding the examination usually begins when the state addresses its first major task: defining competencies. The manner in which a state defines teacher competencies will guide discussion about the state's testing program and will shape all analyses, interpretations, and recommendations that result from the program. A sharply focused definition of teacher competencies provides the foundation for a sharply focused test; clear definitions lead to a test with a specific purpose on which state department staff, higher education staff, practicing teachers, and local school districts can all agree.

Test Philosophy and Purpose: Issues and Cautions

Mutual understanding about the purpose of the examination and the goals of the testing program may revolve around a number of policy decisions made by the state education agency (SEA):

- The SEA must determine the scope of the examination. For example, should the examination include reading, writing, mathematics, speaking, or other content areas? Should the examination's focus be on basic skills (i.e., minimum competency) or on essential skills (i.e., job-related competencies)?
  Caution: Many of the competencies state education departments choose to assess are not those focused on in teacher education programs. As a result, accountability for student success or failure may be misplaced or misunderstood.

- The SEA must decide which type of test it will use: a criterion-referenced test or a norm-referenced test.
  Caution: In the development of either a criterion-referenced or norm-referenced test for licensure, the actual instrument must include only those competencies that have been validated as essential job-related skills for teacher education students or practicing teachers.

- The SEA must determine if remediation will be viewed as a responsibility of the higher education institutions.
  Caution: The SEA must determine whether funding for remediation will be made available to these institutions.
  Caution: If remediation is left to the discretion of each university, the availability and quality of remedial programs will vary. As a result, equity issues arise.

- The SEA must clearly establish the reference group that will form the basis for the test.
  Caution: If the test is used to screen out students who lack sufficient proficiency in essential skills required for teaching, it is a licensure examination, and, therefore, the examination is subject to Equal Employment Opportunity Commission (EEOC) Guidelines. With this focus, a state must concern itself with the legal implications of denying students access to the profession.

General Questions About the Test Framework

1. What is the purpose of the test?
2. What subject areas should be included in the skills examination?
3. What type of test will suit this purpose?
4. Who should be tested? When should they be tested? How often will the test be administered?
5. What criteria will be used to define competence?
6. What provisions, if any, will be made about the availability of remedial services?
7. What type of information will the student receive? Will diagnostic information be provided or simply a total test score?
8. What reference group will form the basis for the test?
9. Have EEOC Guidelines been met in the development and validation of the test?
10. What agencies will be held accountable for students' failures? What agencies will be credited for students' successes?

GENERAL ACTIVITIES IN DESIGNING A COMPETENCY EXAMINATION

To assist the SEA in implementing a testing program, the following activities should occur:

- Committees should be established including: (a) a policy committee—blue ribbon panel (10-15 members); (b) skill area committees (10-15 members in each committee); (c) a psychometric committee (10-15 members); (d) a committee to review test bias (10-15 members); and (e) a standard-setting committee for each skill area (10-15 members in each committee).

- SEA and higher education policy makers should become familiar with the EEOC Guidelines for validating a licensure examination.

- Legal services should be secured to advise the SEA in the implementation of a licensure examination.

- Every effort should be made by the SEA to work cooperatively with institutions of higher education and to keep them informed.

TEST SELECTION OR DEVELOPMENT

Competency tests can and should play a major role in improving the quality of teacher education programs. Low Scholastic Aptitude Test (SAT) scores coupled with public pressure to improve education have directly challenged states to address the competency question. In Connecticut, SAT scores for prospective teachers are well below those for almost all other disciplines. In 1984 the average combined SAT score for students enrolled in Connecticut's teacher education institutions was 817, compared with a state average of 904.

Competency examinations, if carefully developed and validated, can be a useful measure of the academic knowledge of prospective teachers. All tests have limitations, but within the framework of a paper-and-pencil test, competency tests can demonstrate the knowledge that prospective teachers have in essential skill areas. In addition, because these tests are administered statewide, they will provide a uniform measure for evaluating individuals and for offering feedback to institutions. Ultimately, it is essential to remember that many students may be denied career opportunities if they do not successfully pass these tests. In addition, education programs in institutions across the state may be threatened if their students consistently perform poorly on the test.

In the early stages of program planning, activities should revolve principally around one question: Should the state develop and validate its own examination or is it possible to purchase an existing test? Before making this decision, the state should identify the skill areas to be tested and have a clear understanding of the competencies to be assessed.

Choosing an Existing Test: Issues and Cautions

There are both advantages and disadvantages to selecting an existing instrument for use in a basic skills testing program linked with admission to a training program.

- The state realizes an economy of both cost and effort. *Caution:* Regardless of the purpose of the test, the match between state objectives and test objectives is critical. In a licensure examination, all items and objectives on the test must clearly measure competencies that the state has identified as essential.

- Test administration and test security systems may already be in place. *Caution:* In a licensure environment, test security is paramount. A SEA must ensure that proper procedures are in place to eliminate the risk that prospective candidates may have access to test questions before the test administration or that any materials may be lost during the process.

- Availability of normative information on a standardized test may be useful to the state.
  Caution: Because of many factors, few existing examinations have adequate norms. First, teacher tests are used for a variety of purposes such as admission, certification, and the diagnosis of strengths and weaknesses. Normative data are relevant only when the purpose of administration for the norming group matches the purpose of administration for subsequent groups who take the test. Second, teacher tests may not be nationally standardized but only normed on those states that adopted the particular test. This may greatly diminish the general applicability of the standardized norms.

Developing a Customized Test: Issues and Cautions

Similarly, there are advantages and disadvantages associated with preparing a customized program.

- The match between state objectives and test items can be carefully controlled by using well-conceived test development practices.
  Caution: The identification of competencies must be based on a thorough content validation of the proposed objectives. In licensure examinations, job analysis surveys should be performed to ensure that test objectives are both important and relevant to practicing teachers.
- Test development usually provides greater flexibility in designing the testing program.
  Caution: Any changes made to the examination over time must be accompanied by the proper validation of any new

objectives that might be included on the examination. States should consider developing criterion-referenced examinations that provide diagnostic information to candidates who do not pass the initial test administration. These data would be useful in structuring remedial assistance programs for those students who need them.

- The method of assessment can be completely determined by the state.
  Caution: In the selection of assessment methods, consideration must be given to how prospective teachers normally apply a particular skill. Novel assessment methods or experimental practices in assessment should be thoroughly researched before being included on a competency examination. On a licensure test, if the method of item presentation possibly interferes with the likelihood of passing the item, the validity of the item may be questioned.

- Test security and administration are controlled by the state.
  Caution: On a licensure examination, a special effort must be made by the state to guarantee test security as well as the integrity of the test administration process. The security practices are qualitatively different from those for typical statewide student tests. The state must not underestimate these differences.

General Questions About Test Selection or Development

These questions may help define the policy decision process for a state considering a teacher testing program.

1. Are the goals and objectives of the test content clearly understood and sharply focused?

2. Have the goals and objectives of the test content been validated both by content experts and a job analysis?

3. What existing instruments are available that measure the state's competency objectives for prospective teachers? How closely do they match competencies identified by the state?

4. What will be the cost of developing a state examination? Does the state have the fiscal and human resources to accomplish this task?

5. Who will make the decision to adopt a standardized test or to develop a state competency test? What will the criteria be for making this decision?

THE SCOPE AND CONDITIONS FOR ESTABLISHING A TESTING PROGRAM

It should be expected or predicted that the value of and need for teacher testing will be challenged in each state that considers the implementation of such a program. Of course, test scores do not guarantee that prospective teachers will be effective in the classroom. It is reasonable, however, to assume that teachers will not be effective if they lack a firm grounding in essential skills and a command of subject area knowledge. This rationale is analogous to a variety of government-regulated activities. For example, in order to receive a driver's license, an individual must pass a written examination and a performance test. Successful performance in these areas is regarded as a necessary but incomplete indication of actual driving ability. Thus, tests are useful in the sense that they can help to identify prospective drivers who may be a risk on the road, or in this particular instance, prospective teachers who may be a risk behind a desk.

Test Validity Issues

The state's goals for testing will serve, guide, and shape the state's development of a competency examination. Whether the state develops a customized competency examination or adopts an existing test, the validation of the examination for use with prospective teachers is essential. Tests that will be used for licensure decisions require additional steps to ensure that the tests meet the equity standards stated in the EEOC Guidelines.

- To ensure a high level of content validity, experts must examine the match between test content and competency objectives. The steps involved in establishing content validity include, but are not limited to: (a) examining commonly and currently used texts to identify competencies, (b) independently generating competency lists from experts in the content areas to be tested, (c) surveying constituent groups to rate the importance and relevance of the competencies selected, and (d) identifying a final list of competencies for inclusion on the examinations. If a state is adopting an existing test, it must also match test content with the judgments of a knowledgeable group of content experts.
  Caution: The selection of test objectives must reflect the goals and philosophy of the testing program. In a competency test for prospective teachers, objectives should represent essential skills that practicing teachers need in order to perform their job. The inclusion of objectives that teachers *should* acquire, whether they are currently receiving training in this area or not, is problematic. Inclusion of such objectives must be accompanied by a strong rationale, since it is these objectives that may be most challenged in court.

The validation procedures described below are intended as starting points and are not inclusive. It is strongly encouraged that states engaging in these practices become thoroughly knowledgeable of the options available. The following five issues should be carefully addressed to ensure the required test validity.

JOB ANALYSIS
Job analysis data will help the state to ensure that test objectives are both important and relevant to practicing teachers. A job analysis, as applied in this setting, is typically a process in which a representative sample of practicing teachers is surveyed to ensure that the competencies proposed for a teacher examination

are, in fact, essential and currently used by practicing teachers in their work. In addition, statewide textbook analyses are conducted to ensure that teachers, at a minimum, have had an opportunity to learn these competencies as part of their academic preparation. A job analysis goes beyond most traditional validation processes but is an essential step for validating a licensure examination whether the state develops or adopts an examination.

Consideration should be given to the timing and content of the job analysis. It is not recommended that a job analysis be performed to serve as the basis for the initial targeting of essential skills (i.e., administering the job analysis before the identification of content objectives). A job analysis is most valuable in confirming the judgments of experts or in adding to their judgments. A job analysis survey should not be misused as a "fishing expedition" for the initial targeting of skills.

ITEM SPECIFICATIONS

Item specifications should be developed to operationally define the scope and method to be used to assess a skill objective. This step is invaluable if test development procedures are planned. Criteria for the construction of the item stem and distractors and for difficulty level should be determined before the generation of test items. This ensures that item writers will stay on target and will create items that match the expectations of the state.

The quality of item specifications is directly related to the clarity of the content objectives. To the degree that the objectives are sharply focused, the item specification process will better reflect the intent and understandings of the content committees.

BIAS ANALYSIS

Performing a bias analysis is an essential step in determining whether any particular test item unduly favors a particular group or social class. Test items are examined for possible bias in a variety of areas: racial, ethnic, sex-role stereotyping, etc.

Examining test items for bias is both a judgmental and empirical process. Both procedures should be used. Because of the sensitivity of licensure testing, comprehensive documentation of this process is recommended.

PILOT TESTING

Pilot testing is used to examine the quality of test items by administering them to a representative sample as similar as possible to the eventual examinee population. In addition, pilot testing is often valuable for creating parallel forms of a test.

Finding a pilot sample for teacher testing is often difficult for a variety of reasons. First, higher education faculty members may be reluctant to mandate the test or give up class time to conduct the pilot. If the test is administered on a voluntary basis, it is difficult to motivate prospective teachers to cooperate with the testing plan. If practicing teachers are used for pilot testing, it may be extremely difficult to obtain their cooperation also. In addition, teacher unions may object to the proposal. Since practicing teachers and prospective teachers are the major reference populations for teacher testing, obtaining an adequate pilot sample typically requires considerable work and preparation. This is a task that is best started well before the pilot test is actually available for administration.

STANDARD SETTING

Standard setting defines the process of establishing a pass-fail score on a competency test. There are many models for setting standards on a competency examination (c.f. Angoff, 1971; Ebel, 1972; Jaeger, 1978; Nedelsky, 1954). The selection of a model is critical to the establishment of a standard because the use of different models may produce different standards. A precise understanding of the essential competencies that prospective teachers should possess will facilitate any standard-setting process. At all costs, setting standards solely on the basis of political pressures must be avoided. Prior litigation has indicated that such standards will not hold up in court.

General Questions About Test Validity

These questions are meant to guide SEA consideration of validity issues in test design.

1. Given the constraints of any particular test, what methods are available and what criteria should be used for estab-

lishing content validity, developing item specifications, constructing a job analysis survey, conducting a bias analysis, and setting standards?

2. What individuals and groups should be involved in the determination of content validity, item specifications, bias analyses, and standard setting?

3. When should these activities take place in order to best facilitate the process?

4. What is the most appropriate reference group for pilot testing the competency examination (e.g., university freshman, sophomores, juniors, practicing teachers)?

5. How will information about content validity, item specifications, job analyses, bias analyses, standard setting, and pilot testing be documented and reported to institutions of higher education, the SEA, prospective examinees, and the general public?

CONNECTICUT'S APPROACH TO COMPETENCY TESTING FOR PROSPECTIVE TEACHERS

In April 1982 the Connecticut State Board of Education adopted 25 recommendations for ensuring professional competence in the teaching profession. One recommendation endorsed the development of a competency examination for prospective teachers as a requirement for admission into a teacher education program. As an outgrowth of these recommendations, the Connecticut Competency Examination for Prospective Teachers (CONNCEPT) was implemented to ensure that Connecticut candidates for teacher preparation programs are competent in skills that are considered essential for teacher education candidates and practicing teachers.

The CONNCEPT consists of three tests: mathematics, reading, and writing. The mathematics test assesses a prospective teacher's performance in computational and problem-solving skills, conceptual understanding, and the ability to apply mathematical skills and concepts. The reading test assesses a prospective teacher's ability to read and comprehend a series of passages written at varying levels of difficulty. The writing test assesses a prospective teacher's ability to communicate a message effectively to an intended audience for a stated purpose. The total test battery is approximately three hours in length. The mathematics and reading tests are composed of multiple-choice items. The writing test requires a writing sample.

Recently approved legislation requires that, beginning July 1, 1986, all students who wish to be formally admitted to Connecticut teacher education programs pass the CONNCEPT. In addition, beginning May 1, 1987, all candidates for teacher certification will also be required to pass the CONNCEPT before being awarded a state teaching certificate.

For all examinees, the CONNCEPT score report will include an overall score for each of the three subtests and an indication of whether or not each subtest was passed. In addition, the score report will include scores on each of the five major subareas of the mathematics subtest. For examinees who fail the writing subtest, the report will also include a list of the writing characteristics in which weaknesses were identified.

Test results will be reported to the examinee and to the Connecticut State Department of Education. In addition, test results will be reported to the higher education institution the examinee is currently attending if the institution is located in Connecticut. Examinees who have failed one or more of the subtests must retake and pass the entire CONNCEPT at a later date. Those examinees who wish to retake the CONNCEPT may do so at any subsequent test administration.

Two alternatives to taking the CONNCEPT will be accepted as a prerequisite to formal admission into a teacher education program:

1. Official notification of a combined score of 1000 or more on the Scholastic Aptitude Test (SAT), with no less than 400 on either the verbal or the mathematics subtest, or

2. Official notification of a passing score on a comparable competency examination administered by another state and approved by the Connecticut State Department of Education.

The first test administration is scheduled for October 1985. Subsequent testing will occur twice each year—in the spring and fall.

References

Angoff, W. H. (1971). Scales, norms, and equivalent scores. In R. L. Thorndike (Ed.), *Educational Measurement* (2nd ed.) (pp. 508-600). Washington, DC: American Council on Education.

Ebel, R. L. (1972). *Essentials of educational measurement.* Englewood Cliffs, NJ: Prentice-Hall.

Jaeger, R. M. (1978). *A proposal for setting a standard on the North Carolina High School Competency Test.* Paper presented at the meeting of the North Carolina Association for Research in Education, Chapel Hill, NC.

Nedelsky, L. (1954). Absolute grading standards for objective tests. *Educational and Psychological Measurement, 14,* 3-19.

Sandefur, J. T. (1985). *State assessment trends.* Washington, DC: American Association of Colleges of Teacher Education.

CRITICAL TECHNICAL ISSUES

Whereas the previous section dealt with overall design considerations, this section addresses the more technical issues that are a part of teacher certification testing. Any testing program must address the issues considered here; indeed, the validity of the examinations rests to a large extent on how these concerns are met.

Nassif and Elliot, in separate chapters, provide an overview of the types of technical issues that confront the developers of teacher certification testing programs. They cover a wide range of areas and set the context for some of the more specific chapters that follow. The Veselka et al. chapter describes how, in the Texas program, the job analysis surveys were expanded to include other important constituencies, thus helping to improve the validity of the resulting test instruments.

Berk describes how item statistics and analyses for item and test bias play an important role in teacher certification testing. He describes the evaluative aspects of such statistics and how they provide feedback to test developers in regard to the validity and reliability of their instruments. Jaeger confronts the difficult issue of setting standards (passing scores) on licensing tests, including those used for teacher certification. Standard setting is a highly visible aspect of a testing program and one which has a clear and direct effect on examinees. Swaminathan discusses the role of Item Response Theory statistical techniques in building item banks for teacher certification testing programs. This discussion falls in the general area of test equating, i.e., the effort to insure that the tests examinees take are of equivalent difficulty from administration to administration.

In the final chapter in this section, Priestley discusses various approaches to assessment in general. While teacher certification testing has relied to a large extent on paper-and-pencil measures, there is diversity even within that category, not to mention other general approaches to evaluation.

Teacher Certification Testing Technical Challenges: Part I

Paula M. Nassif

Teacher certification testing programs present challenges to the practitioner in regard to several technical issues. This chapter focuses on standard setting and test equating; other contributions to this volume deal with validity and job analysis. This review delineates the methods currently in use and recommends alternatives where appropriate.

STANDARD SETTING

One of the most significant aspects of testing for employment decisions is setting the passing or cut score. This area of research is broad—replete with legal factors, technical concerns, and logistical considerations. Koffler (1980) and Hambleton and Eignor (1978), among others, have studied the various methods and examined their appropriateness, accuracy, and usefulness. Many methods of standard setting have been used in student competency assessment. These techniques include Nedelsky (1954), Angoff (1971), Ebel (1972), Jaeger (1978), and contrasting groups and borderline groups (Zieky & Livingston, 1977). A review of the methods used in setting cut scores for teacher certification testing reveals a much smaller list.

Paula Nassif is Vice President for Research and Operations, National Evaluation Systems.

THE NTE AND STANDARDS

Over the past 15 years, state-mandated use of the National Teacher Examination (NTE) often involved the establishment of a passing score by administrative decision. The procedure was not empirical, nor did it result in a cut score that bore systematic relationship to successful job performance. This pattern led to legal challenge in some states. Continued use of the NTE in this manner was not allowed by law in these cases: *United States v. North Carolina* (1975), *Baker v. Columbus Municipal Separate School District* (1971), and *Georgia Association of Educators v. Jack P. Nix* (1976). When the cutoff score determines those candidates who are qualified or unqualified, the test user must give sufficient proof that the cutoff was not established in a capricious or arbitrary manner.

In South Carolina in 1977, use of the NTE had an adverse impact against blacks. The state, however, decided to investigate the test, validate it in South Carolina, and set cut scores in a systematic, empirical fashion. The result was that some of the NTE tests were validated and approved for use in South Carolina.

Standard-Setting Approaches

Most standard-setting methods used derive from the procedures designed by Nedelsky (1954) and Angoff (1971). These procedures have been variously modified, consolidated, lengthened, and abbreviated for use in several states.

NEDELSKY

Nedelsky (1954) has outlined a procedure as it would be used with multiple-choice items to set a standard for a classroom test. A description of the Nedelsky procedure follows.

Description of the Technique

Letter grades *F, D, C, B,* and *A* used in this article have the conventional meaning of failure (*F*), barely passing (*D*), etc.

The proposed technique for arriving at the minimum passing score of an objective test, each item of which has a *single* correct response, is as follows:

Directions to Instructors

Before the test is given, the instructors in the course are given copies of the test, and the following directions:

> In each item of the test, cross out those responses which the lowest *D*-student should be able to reject as incorrect. To the left of the item write the reciprocal of the number of the remaining responses. Thus if you cross out one out of five responses, write ¼.
> *Example.* (The example should preferably be one of the items of the test in question.)
>
> Light has wave characteristics. Which of the following is the best experimental evidence for this statement?
>
> A. Light can be reflected by a mirror.
> B. Light forms dark and light bands on passing through a small opening.
> C. A beam of white light can be broken into its component colors by a prism.
> ¼ D. Light carries energy.
> E. Light operates a photoelectric cell.

Preliminary Agreement on Standards

After the instructors have marked some five or six items following the directions above, it is recommended that they hold a brief conference to compare and discuss the standards they have used. It may also well be that at this time they agree on a tentative value of constant k (see section on The Minimum Passing Score). After such a conference, the instructors should proceed independently.

Terminology

In describing the method of computing the score corresponding to the lowest D, the following terminology is convenient:

a. Responses which the lowest D-student should be able to reject as incorrect, and which therefore should be primarily attractive to F-students, are called F-responses. In the example above, response E was the only F-response in the opinion of the instructor who marked the item.

b. Students who possess just enough knowledge to reject F-responses and must choose among the remaining responses at random are called F-D students, to suggest borderline knowledge between F and D.

c. The most probable mean score of the F-D students on a test is called the F-D guess score and is denoted by M_{FD}. As will be shown later, M_{FD} is equal to the sum of the reciprocals of the numbers of responses other than F-responses. (In the example above, the reciprocal is $\frac{1}{4}$.)

d. The most probable value of the standard deviation corresponding to M_{FD} is denoted by σ_{FD}.

It should be clear that "F-D students" is a statistical abstraction. The student who can reject the F-responses for every item of a test and yet will choose at random among the rest of the responses probably does not exist; rather, scores equal to M_{FD} will be obtained by students whose patterns of responses vary widely.

The Minimum Passing Score

The score corresponding to the lowest D is set equal to $\overline{M}_{FD} + k\sigma_{FD}$, where $\overline{M}_{FD}$ is the mean of the M_{FD} obtained by various instructors, and k is a constant whose value is determined by several considerations. The F-D students are characterized not so much by the positive knowledge they possess as by being able to avoid certain misjudgments. Most instructors who have used the F-D guess score technique have felt that this "absence of ignorance" standard is a mild one, and that therefore the minimum passing score should be such as to fail the majority of F-D students. Assigning to k values -1, 0 ,1, and 2 will (on the average) fail respectively 16 percent, 50 percent, 84 percent, and 98 percent of the F-D students. An informed final decision on the value of k can be reached after the instructors have chosen the F-responses, for at that time they are in a better position to estimate the rigor of the standards they have been using. In keeping within the spirit of absolute standards, however, the value of k should be agreed on before the values of M_{FD} are computed and certainly before the students' scores are known.

It is the essence of the proposed technique that the standard of achievement is arrived at by a detailed consideration of individual items of the test. Only minor adjustments should be effected by varying the value of k. The reason for introducing constant k, with the attendant flexibility and ambiguity, is that F-responses in most examinations vary between two extremes; the very wrong, the choice of which indicates gross ignorance, and the moderately wrong, the rejection of which indicates passing knowledge. If a particular test has predominantly the first kind of F-responses, this *peculiarity of the test* can be corrected for by giving k a high value. Similarly, a low value of k will correct for the predominance of the second kind of F-responses. It is expected that in the majority of cases a change of not more than $\pm.5$ in the tentative value of k agreed upon during the preliminary conference should introduce the necessary correction. It would be difficult to find a theoretical justification for values of k as high as two; for most tests the value of $k = 0$ is probably too low. This suggests a rather narrow working range of values, say between .5 and 1.5 with the value $k = 1$ as a good starting point.

If a part A of a given test consists of N_A items, each of which has s_A non F-responses (one of these being the right response), the F-D guess score for each item, i.e., the probability that an F-D student will get the right answer in any one item, is $p_A = 1/s_A$.

The most probable values of the mean and the square of the standard deviation on this part of the test are given by $M_A = p_A N_A$ and $\sigma^2_A = p_A (1 - p_A) N_A$. M_{FD} and σ_{FD} for the whole test are given by $M_{FD} = \Sigma_A M_A$ and $\sigma^2_{FD} = \Sigma_A \sigma^2_A$. The value of M_{FD} must be accurately computed for each test. σ_{FD}, however, may be given an approximate value. In a test of five-response items s may vary from one to five. If these five values are equally frequent, $\sigma_{FD} = .41\sqrt{N}$. If, on the other hand, the extreme values, $s = 1$ and $s = 5$, are less frequent than the other three values, as seems likely to be true for most tests, $.41\sqrt{N} < \sigma_{FD} < .50\sqrt{N}$. Since $k\,\sigma_{FD}$ is usually much smaller than M_{FD}, approximations are in order. With $k = 1$ and $\sigma_{FD} = .45\sqrt{N}$, the equation, Minimum Passing Score $= \overline{M}_{FD} + .45\sqrt{N}$, should work out fairly well in the majority of cases and is therefore recommended as a starting point in experimenting with the proposed technique.

Refinements of the Technique

The definition of the F-response given above has an element of ambiguity. The lowest D-student may be expected to reject a given response on its own merits as clearly incorrect or because it is clearly less correct than some of the other responses. In the example given under "Directions to Instructors" response E cites evidence *against* the wave theory of light and thus is an F-response on its own merits; other responses are consistent with the theory and may be considered non F-responses. It may be argued, however, that even a D-student should see that response D constitutes less cogent evidence than some of the other responses, and that therefore it is an F-response. Judging a response in comparison with other responses is theoretically sound, for it probably more closely corresponds to the mental processes of the student. To make a proper judgment of this kind requires time and considerable pedagogical and test-wise sophistication; with responses more heterogeneous than in the example cited a reliable judgment may be impossible. Experimentation with both definitions of the F-response is certainly in order, but at least in the beginning, the simpler version, i.e., judging each response on its own merit, is to be preferred.

Some instructors find it difficult in a good number of cases to decide whether a response is an *F*-response. There is no theoretical reason against assigning to such a response half the statistical value of an *F*-response. (If, in the example cited, response *D* has been assigned the value of ½, the item would have had 1.5 *F*-responses and 3.5 non *F*-responses. Consequently the value of *p* for the item would have been $1/3.5$ rather than ¼.) If methodically and conscientiously pursued, such a procedure may result in a better agreement among the instructors. It is not recommended as a substitute for clear and hard thinking about the degree of correctness of a response.

In theory, the proposed technique can be extended to assigning minimum scores corresponding to grades *C, B,* and *A*. The author has few data bearing on such an extension; they indicate fairly clearly, however, that a very thorough discussion of the meaning of the grades of *C, B,* and *A* among the participating instructors must precede actual marking of the test. It seems fairly certain, moreover, that even if the instructors reach a really circumstantial verbal agreement on the meaning of these grades, modifications of the proposed technique are likely to be necessary. For, though an "absence of ignorance" standard may be adequate for identifying the barely passing students, more positive indications of achievement corresponding to higher grades seem desirable.

Perhaps a reasonable *D-C* guess score can be obtained by requiring the lowest *C*-students to reject responses that are in certain respects or to a certain degree inferior to other responses; the kind and the degree of inferiority must, of course, correspond to the instructors' definition of the meaning of the grade of *C*. To establish minimum scores corresponding to grades *B* or *A*, an instructor should probably focus his attention on the correct response and inspect the wrong responses primarily for their degree of deviation from the correct response; the allowable deviations for the lowest *B* or *A* will depend on the meanings assigned to these grades.

As the preceding paragraph suggests, the criteria used for determining the minimum scores corresponding to lowest *D, C,* and *B* or *A* may be qualitatively different; the method for computing these scores may be the same for all grades, e.g., lowest *C* score $= M_{DC} + k\sigma_{DC}$.

Directions to Instructors

a. In each item of the test, cross out, using a single pencil line, those responses which the lowest *D*-student should be able to reject as incorrect. To the left of the item, against the *D*-response, write the reciprocal of the number of the remaining responses. (Thus, if you cross out one out of five responses, write ¼.)

b. Of the remaining responses cross out, using a double line, those which the lowest *C*-student should be able to reject. Write the reciprocal of the number of responses that still remain to the left of the *C*-response. (Thus, if you had already crossed out one out of five possible responses, and now cross out two more, write ½.)

c. Repeat the procedure for the lowest *B*-student, using a triple line.

d. Repeat the procedure for the lowest *A*-student, using a cross.

Example: Light has wave characteristics. Which of the following is the best experimental evidence for this statement?

1 A̶. Light can be reflected by a mirror.

1 B. Light forms dark and light bands on passing through a small opening.

½ C̶. A beam of white light can be broken into its component colors by a prism.

¼ D̶. Light carries energy.

E̶. Light operates a photoelectric cell.

In the opinion of the instructor who marked the example above, response *E* should be rejected by the lowest *D*-student, responses *A* and *D* by the lowest *C*-student, and response *C* by the lowest *B*-student. Since the letters of the responses happen to correspond to the usual letter grades, it is convenient to record the reciprocal of the number of responses among which the lowest *D*-student is to choose against the *D*-response, etc. In the example above, the lowest *B*-student is expected to reject all but the correct response; the lowest *A*-student is of course expected to do just as well; hence number 1 is placed against both response *B* and response A.

It is possible to construct a test in such a way as to make the determination of the scores corresponding to lowest *D, C, B,* and *A* easier and more reliable. In such a test some responses would be designed to be attractive only to *F*-students, others to *F*-students and *D*-students, etc. By including predetermined numbers of such responses the test maker can prepare a test having any desired value for the minimum score corresponding to any letter grade. Whether or not absolute standards are to be used, a test of this kind is likely to have the advantage of being discriminating in the whole range from *F* to *A* (Nedelsky, 1954, pp. 4-10).

Glass (1978) and Zieky and Livingston (1977) adapted the original Nedelsky procedure for easier implementation. The Zieky and Livingston description includes a simplified case for only the minimum competence level, and the Glass description includes the consideration of groups of students at different competence levels.

ANGOFF

In the Angoff (1971) method, expert judges review a test item in its entirety and state the probability that a person with minimum competency can give the correct response. The Angoff procedure is easy to explain, easy to understand, and easy to administer. It is less time-consuming than Nedelsky's and can be used on open-ended items. In this procedure, judges are asked to:

> . . . state the *probability* that the 'minimally acceptable person' would answer each item correctly. In effect, the judges would think of a number of minimally acceptable persons, instead of only one such person, and would estimate the proportion of minimally acceptable persons who would answer each item correctly. The sum of these probabilities, or proportions, would then represent the minimally acceptable score (Angoff, 1971, p. 515).

JAEGER

Jaeger (1978) proposed a method for standard setting for student assessment that maximizes the involvement of educational constituencies. In a North Carolina application, for instance, 700 persons convened in groups of 50 to participate in the following standard-setting procedure.

Judges first took the exam they would later rate. For each item, judges were asked one of the following questions:

1. Should every high school graduate be able to answer this item correctly?

2. If a student does not answer this item, should he or she be denied a high school diploma?

Judges next received the results from the survey questions above as well as actual student performance data. With this information, judges reviewed and revised their initial judgments as they considered necessary.

The procedure then called for recalculation of the judges' ratings, redistribution of the new ratings, and another judgment. Judges next assessed information on the proportion of students who would have passed or failed on the basis of the recommended cutoff scores.

With this information, judges made a final statement on the "necessity" for each item on the test. Median scores were calculated for each group of judges participating in the process, and the passing score was then set at the minimum median score calculated for a group.

This process is technically straightforward, involves iterative reviews, and includes normative student data.

Procedures in Use

GEORGIA, ALABAMA

In 1977 Nassif (1978) employed a modified procedure that aimed at simplifying the Nedelsky procedure in two dimensions. Each item was to be reviewed in its entirety, rather than distractor by distractor, and one level of competence (minimum acceptable) was considered rather than several. The resulting procedure matches Angoff's conceptually. The operational steps are described below:

> Panels of expert judges reviewed items independently on an item-by-item basis. The following was asked about each valid item: "Should a person with minimum competency in the teaching field be able to answer this item correctly?" Each judge was asked to imagine the skills of a hypothetical candidate with minimum competency in the content of a teaching field. Within this frame of reference the item was examined as to whether it required too sophisticated a knowledge of the content or whether it required content knowledge of trivial or minor importance.
>
> Judges responded "yes" if the item was considered appropriate for measuring minimum competency or "no" if otherwise. The "I don't know" option was available for judges unfamiliar with the content of an item.
>
> The significance of agreement was determined by comparing the number of "yes" responses with probability tables for the binomial distribution. The ratings of "I don't know" were not considered for any item, so that dichotomous ratings with different numbers of judges were generated. If the probability of receiving a given number of "yes" ratings (i.e., appropriate for minimum competency) was less than a chance of 1 in 10, the item was classified as an appropriate requirement for minimum competency (Nassif, 1978, pp. 11-12).

This procedure has been used in both the Georgia and Alabama teacher certification programs.

SOUTH CAROLINA, OKLAHOMA

As mentioned earlier, South Carolina conducted a post hoc validation of the NTE in 1977. In the standard-setting portion of this procedure, judges used a modification of the Angoff procedure in which they selected from a seven-point scale the probability rather than provided the probability that minimally competent candidates should be able to answer an item correctly. Although this modification restricts a judge's choice of response, it eases data reduction and analysis.

In a subsequent teacher certification effort, South Carolina developed 10 criterion-referenced content area tests and a basic skills education entrance test. The Angoff procedure as described earlier was used for the content tests; the state employed the Jaeger approach for the basic skills test.

The Oklahoma Teacher Certification Program used the Angoff approach to determine the standards for its criterion-referenced teacher certification tests.

FLORIDA

The Florida Teacher Certification Exam program assesses candidates on competencies in four areas: math, reading, writing, and professional education. Each area forms a separate subtest that the candidate must pass, and each section has a separate cut score. The writing sample is scored holistically; the state board reviews performance data and the level of competence described by the score points on the performance range to set a passing score.

An advisory committee sets the cut scores on each of the three multiple-choice sections. The state commissioner then approves these scores. The procedures involve a review of performance data generated by a field test and an examination of sample items and their associated Rasch calibrations.

Advantages

Why are the Nedelsky, Angoff, and Jaeger approaches used predominantly, when the list of methods used to set standards for other competency testing programs includes several other models? (See Nassif, 1979, for a discussion of these models.)

1. These procedures are based on and permit an item by item review. This is a very important consideration since the tests are regenerated in part quite frequently because of test security demands and job analysis requirements.

2. The procedures permit the incorporation of performance data as additional information in the decision-making process.

3. These procedures allow the establishment of single or multiple cut scores as necessitated by the testing program. In the case of multiple cut scores, either compensatory or disjunctive scoring is possible.

4. These models are easy to understand, a factor that contributes to the reliability of judges' ratings and to the comprehensibility by constituent audiences.

5. The three approaches involve and rely on expert judges.

6. The resulting cut score bears a relationship to necessary job performance—a legal requirement. It allows all competent candidates to pass without restriction from quotas.

7. None of these procedures require information (statistical or demographic) not generally available.

8. These methods produce a cut score that can be adjusted easily by standard error of measurement to incorporate relevant employment factors.

9. These methods can be employed on a test with any number of items, although the original Nedelsky and Jaeger approaches can be time-consuming with long instruments.

Until recently, few studies compared the results of using different cut score models. In 1976, Andrew and Hecht found that different cut scores resulted from using the Nedelsky and the Ebel procedures. Skakun and Kling (1980) reviewed modified Ebel and Nedelsky procedures, along with their currently used normative approach. Although the magnitude of the differences in yielded cut scores varied across comparisons, Skakun and Kling found that "results indicate that different approaches for establishing a passing score on an examination produce different standards" (p. 233). Brennan and Lockwood (1979) found different cut scores produced by Nedelsky and Angoff procedures.

EQUATING[1]

Teacher certification testing programs generally provide the candidate with opportunities to retake an examination he or she has failed. If the same questions are used repeatedly, the examiner will not know if the candidate's knowledge of the subject matter or the candidate's memory is being assessed. Moreover, public scrutiny of certification exams may require dissemination of the test even after only a single administration. Repeated test administrations and public dissemination require a practical solution:

One response to these issues, and perhaps the most prevalent, has been an increased emphasis on development of parallel forms of tests. This response is understandable for three reasons. First, the availability of parallel forms reduces the problem of test security between administrations. Second, it answers political pressure to release the test after administration for use in diagnosis of candidates' weaknesses and tailoring of remedial services. Third, it ensures that an individual student may be retested on the same skills with different test items, minimizing the effects on performance of the prior administration.

The increasing need for alternate forms of tests in programs across the country has redoubled interest among researchers, educators, and policy-makers in how best to ensure that the score or pass-fail decision for a given student not depend on "which form" the student took or "when" the student participated. The statistical problem of test form equivalence takes two primary forms. The first is maximizing the likelihood that a student would receive the *same score* on two different forms of a test. The second is a more simplified task of minimizing errors of classification—that is, maximizing the likelihood that a student will receive the same classification (pass or fail), although not necessarily the same score, on two alternate forms. The former is most appropriate when the purpose of testing and the prescribed use of test results is to analyze a student's level of functioning and compare it from administration to administration. The latter is most typical of minimum competency testing programs that are directed primarily at determining a student's status simply with respect to a cut score (Nassif, Pinsky, & Rubinstein, 1980).

APPROACHES

In practical terms there are two basic approaches to accomplishing statistical equivalence of alternate forms. One is to "equate tests" by selecting items with equivalent psychometric characteristics; for example, the p-value method (Nassif, Pinsky, & Rubinstein, 1979) or one of several item response theory models (Wright, 1977), among others. The other is to "equate scores" by paying relatively less attention to the psychometric characteristics of individual items (except in the normal course of screening for psychometric adequacy) and solving the statistical problem by scaling the test (or subtest) scores produced, for example, the linear and equipercentile methods (Angoff, 1971).

A comprehensive technical analysis of equating methods, factors, and consequences is well beyond the intent of this chapter. Angoff (1971), Jaeger (1980), Kolen (1981), and Wright (1977), to name a few, have presented research on various aspects of this topic. The goal here is to provide the practitioner with information on some aspects of this complex process. In addition, the reader should know that numerous avenues for assistance exist for solving these technical issues, which so directly affect teacher certification testing.

Following are brief citations of the linear equating technique, the p-value item substitution method, and the Rasch model (representing the item response theory family).

LINEAR EQUATING (ANGOFF, 1971)

In the linear equating model, raw scores are converted to scale scores so that the emphasis is on correct score conversion. Scores are calibrated to adjust for variations in test difficulty and dispersion by using a set of items common to both forms of the test. This common item section establishes a statistical link between the two test forms. Through this link, scores on the one form can be calibrated to the scale of the other form (cf. Angoff, 1971, Design IV).

We assume that in two test administrations in a program, the two different groups are equivalent random samples from the same population. The two groups are taking tests x and y, with a common anchor (u) given to both groups (e.g., Group A takes x and u; Group B takes y and u). Statistical assumptions are applied to estimate

$$\hat{\bar{X}}_t \qquad \hat{s}_{x_t}$$

for each test, if it were given to

$$\hat{\bar{Y}}_t \qquad \hat{s}_{y_t}$$

the total group (T = A + B).

The goal is to transform raw scores on y (the new form) to the scale of x (the original form). Given the estimated parameters, the conversion equation is defined as:

$$X_i = aY_i + b$$

Where $a = \dfrac{s_{x_t}}{s_{y_t}}$ and $b = \hat{\bar{X}}_t - a\hat{\bar{Y}}_t$

The Tucker model of linear equating is used when the two groups do not differ widely in ability as measured by performance on u. The Levine method is used when the two groups do differ. Forms of the National Teacher Examination, administered several times a year, are equated by linear or equipercentile methods (Angoff, 1971).

The Alabama and Georgia Teacher Certification Testing Programs currently use the Tucker linear equating method. The anchor tests in these programs are the subset of items that are repeated across (are common to) two successive administrations. The anchor tests contain the same distribution of items by content area as each total test and comprise 70-80% of each total test. New items replace previously used items matched on the basis of content and difficulty. After analysis of the test data, items with the best statistical properties representing maximum content coverage constitute the scorable items on the new main form. The scorable items are equated to the same number of scorable items on the form previously administered. The data are reported on a converted scale that allows the same reported cut score across different test forms or fields and multiple administrations.

The advantage of linear equating is that equivalence of scoring is ensured. Moreover, field testing items before actual administration is not strictly necessary. A disadvantage in the teacher certification environment occurs, however, in those teaching fjelds with too few examinees for equating. In low incidence fields the p-value approach, described later, may be more appropriate.

It should be noted that linear equating is appropriate only when the relationship between the raw scores and transformed scores is, in fact, linear. Because this approach equates a new test form with an old form with considerable overlap in items, there is no reason to expect severe departures from linearity in this relationship.

P-VALUE AND POINT-BISERIAL TEST EQUATING

This approach requires the construction of tests with equating, replaceable, and experimental (field test) sections. Each of these sections is a mini-test, a stratified sample of items from the entire test domain. (The pass-fail decision is based on the scorable equating and replaceable items; that is, the experimental items do not contribute to the examinee's score.) The movement of experimental items into the scorable section for subsequent administrations occurs within an objective for items of the same difficulty and of comparable point-biserial (item-total test discrimination) as determined from their "experimental" testing session. The item substitution plan preserves the content validity of the test as well as the statistical difficulty of the test. When items cannot be matched exactly on p-value within an objective, one averages the differences over clusters of objectives within the same content subarea (Nassif, Pinsky, & Rubinstein, 1979).

This method was used successfully in the past in the Georgia Teacher Certification Program.

RASCH MODEL

A variety of approaches exist within the umbrella of item response theory. These different models share certain fundamental characteristics, but they differ in terms of the number of parameters they estimate. The one-parameter (Rasch) model has been used more commonly in the teacher licensing environment. A complete technical discussion is beyond the scope of this chapter. According to Wright (1968) the Rasch model calibrates test items independent of the ability level of the examinee sample used for calibration purposes. Further, the measurement of examinees occurs independently of the difficulty of the test form used.

The approach facilitates item banking since sample-free estimates of item difficulty with respect to a common score are obtained for all items. Developers can then create parallel forms of tests and ensure equivalence of scoring by using test forms of known difficulty and dispersion.

The Florida program and parts of the South Carolina Teacher Certification Testing Program rely on the Rasch model for creating equated tests across successive administrations. Items from previous administrations are seeded onto subsequent test forms to track shifts in values. These seeded items also provide a link back to the item bank.

Why Are These Methods Used?

Each approach has its benefits and limitations in the credentialing context.

1. Linear equating is a straightforward procedure that accommodates varying amounts of item overlap from one administration to the next. Generally, it is advised that at least 25% of the test be anchored from one administration to the next.

2. Different linear equating methods available accommodate varying statistical assumptions or effects (e.g., Tucker & Levine).

3. Linear equating does not require a separate field test of the new replacement items, assuming sufficient sample size.

4. All models allow for, but may not require, content mapping and difficulty and discrimination matching for replacement items.

5. The p-value approach for creating new forms accommodates teaching fields with low numbers of applicants since data are pooled over several administrations until an adequate data base has accumulated.

6. The Rasch model facilitates the creation and maintenance of an item bank from which test forms of known difficulty and dispersion may be generated.

When Do Test Forms Need to be Changed?

If there is reason to believe that there has been a security break on the test, developers should prepare a new test form. After a test form has been administered several times and there is reason to believe that performance on the test can be significantly affected by multiple retakes of the same exam, a new exam should be developed. And clearly, if the content domain or job definition changes, the test should reflect corresponding changes.

In an environment of restricted resources, no educational administration wants to develop more tests than are necessary. In teaching fields with few examinees, multiple administrations of the same exam are justified for the purpose of test statistical data collection. In larger fields the test form may be changed after it has been administered to a predetermined minimum number of examinees (say, 250). This generally occurs at least once a year in these more populated fields.

Summary

The technical aspects of teacher certification program design need careful attention. Several states, notably Georgia, Florida, South Carolina, Oklahoma, and Alabama, have addressed the issues of validity, job analysis, standard setting, and test equating in their various developmental efforts. Their work toward design solutions can inform program planning in newer teacher certification testing programs. Resources are available to the administrative and policy decision makers who must address matters of legal and technical consequence. Progress is being made even in a context of practical, political, and financial limitations.

Footnotes

1. The author wishes to acknowledge the contributions to this section of the chapter by Dr. Steven Lang-Gunn, Director of Data Processing, National Evaluation Systems.

References

Andrew, B. J., & Hecht, J. T. (1976). A preliminary investigation of two procedures for setting examination standards. *Educational and Psychological Measurement, 36,* 45-50.

Angoff, W. H. (1971). Scales, norms, and equivalent scores. In R. L. Thorndike (Ed.), *Educational measurement* (2nd ed.)(pp. 508-600). Washington, DC: American Council on Education.

Baker v. Columbus Municipal Separate School District, 329 F. Supp. 706 (1971).

Brennan, R. L., & Lockwood, R. E. (1979, April). *A comparison of two cutting score procedures using generalizability theory.* Paper presented at the annual meeting of the National Council on Measurement in Education, San Francisco, CA.

Ebel, R. L. (1972). *Essentials of educational measurement.* Englewood Cliffs, NJ: Prentice-Hall.

Georgia Association of Educators v. Jack P. Nix, 407 F. Supp. 1102 (1976).

Glass, G. (1978). Standards and criteria. *Journal of Educational Measurement, 15,* 237-261.

Hambleton, R. K., & Eignor, D. R. (1978). *Competency test development, validation, and standard-setting* (Research Rep. No. 84, Laboratory of Psychometric and Evaluation Research). Amherst: University of Massachusetts, School of Education.

Jaeger, R. M. (1978). *A proposal for setting a standard on the North Carolina High School Competency Test.* Paper presented at the meeting of the North Carolina Association for Research in Education, Chapel Hill, NC.

Jaeger, R. M. (1980, April). *Some exploratory indices for selection of a test equating method.* Paper presented at the annual meeting of the American Educational Research Association, Boston, MA.

Koffler, S. L. (1980). A comparison of approaches for setting proficiency standards. *Journal of Educational Measurement, 17*(3), 167-178.

Kolen, M. J. (1981). Comparison of traditional and item response theory methods for equating tests. *Journal of Educational Measurement, 18*(1), 1-11.

Nassif, P. M. (1978, March). *Standard-setting for criterion-referenced teacher licensing tests.* Paper presented at the annual meeting of the National Council on Measurement in Education, Toronto.

Nassif, P. M. (1979, December). Setting standards. In *Final Program Development Resource Document:* A Study of Minimum Competency Testing Programs, National Institute of Education, 93-120.

Nassif, P. M., Pinsky, P. D., & Rubinstein, S. A. (1979, April). *Generating parallel test forms for minimum competency exams.* Paper presented at the annual meeting of the National Council on Measurement in Education, San Francisco, CA.

Nassif, P. M., Pinsky, P. D., & Rubinstein, S. A. (1980, April). *Further work developing parallel tests by p-value substitution.* Paper presented at the annual meeting of the National Council on Measurement in Education, Boston, MA.

Nedelsky, L. (1954). Absolute grading standards for objective tests. *Educational and Psychological Measurement, 14,* 3-19.

Skakun, E. N., & Kling, S. (1980). Comparability of methods for setting standards. *Journal of Educational Measurement, 17,* 229-235.

United States v. North Carolina, 400 F. Supp. 343 (E.D. N.C. 1975), 425 F. Supp. 789 (E.D. S.C. 1977).

Wright, B. H. (1968). Sample-free test calibration and person measurement. *Proceedings of the 1967 Invitational Conference on Testing Problems.* Princeton, NJ, Educational Testing Service.

Wright, B. H. (1977). Solving measurement problems with the Rasch model. *Journal of Educational Measurement, 14,* 97-116.

Zieky, M. J., & Livingston, S. A. (1977). *Manual for setting standards on the basic skills assessment tests.* Princeton, NJ: Educational Testing Service.

Teacher Certification Testing Technical Challenges: Part II

JOB ANALYSIS

Any instrument designed for certification or licensing, as in teacher certification testing, must be shown to be job related. That is, it must measure the content knowledge relevant to the job as performed by job incumbents. Determining the job relatedness of content selected for tests is both recommended in the *APA Principles for the Validation and Use of Personnel Selection Procedures* (1980) and required by the *Equal Employment Opportunity Commission Guidelines* (1978). The EEOC Guidelines require that the criteria used as a basis for certification must bear an empirical and logical relationship to successful job performance. For teacher certification purposes, this suggests that test content should reflect the content knowledge or pedagogical skills required for teaching. Although there are a number of ways of empirically identifying this domain of knowledge (cf. Popham, 1980), a systematic job analysis is recommended.

Job Analysis Approaches

Job analysis is a process of systematic data collection for the elements of a job. Although job analysis has been used routinely in personnel areas for close to a century, only within the past few decades has it been employed in personnel testing.

Scott Elliot is Director of the Division of Licensing and Certification, National Evaluation Systems.

A variety of approaches to assessing the work situation are available. Regardless of the selected method, however, most approaches include some determination of the critical and frequently performed elements of the job. Importance (criticality or essentiality) and frequency of performance (time spent. or percentage of time consumed) are the two key dimensions underlying most job analyses. Within the teacher certification arena, this translates to the important and frequently applied teaching skills or content knowledge in the instructional setting.

Job analysis approaches vary in a number of dimensions; Levine, Ash, Hall, and Sistrunk (1981) have delineated three important dimensions: (a) the type of descriptor or element used to describe the job; (b) the source of job information; and (c) the data collection methodology.

Descriptors include tasks, activities, skills, knowledge, and personal characteristics. A number of sources of job information are potentially available, including job incumbents, supervisors, trained job analysts, and written documents. Data collection methods include questionnaires, interviews, observation, diaries, and actual job performance. Despite this range of possibilities, the application of job analysis methodology to teacher certification testing has been somewhat limited. This chapter first addresses current applications and then focuses on other potentially beneficial approaches.

Job Analysis Applications

Several states, including Texas, Georgia, Alabama, Oklahoma, and West Virginia, have employed job analysis in the development and content validation of teacher certification tests. In all four cases a survey approach was used. A sample of educators within the state responded to a survey instrument that had them rate, on a Likert-type scale, a series of content objectives developed by panels of content experts. The educators rated the objectives according to the amount of time spent teaching or using the objectives and according to the extent to which the objectives were essential or important to the field. Separate surveys were conducted in each content area. After the survey results were obtained, those objectives found to be most job related were included in the content of the examinations. In some cases an interview procedure was used with a sample of educators to supplement the quantitative ratings and gather further information about job content.

Similar procedures were used in the preparation of the Florida Teacher Certification Examination. A panel of teacher educators developed teacher competencies (objectives). The competencies were then sent to a sample of educators who rated the competencies in terms of their perceived importance to the field; in this case no ratings of "frequency of use" or "time spent using" were collected.

More process-oriented assessment measures, written for teacher certification, have used similar procedures. The Texas Professional Development Examination, which assesses knowledge of instructional skills, relied on job analysis to determine the content for the test. A sample group of educators across teaching fields rated the importance of a series of instructional skills and the frequency with which they were used. Likewise, the content of South Carolina's Performance Observation Instrument was defined through a job analysis procedure. Again, using a survey approach, a sample of South Carolina educators rated the importance and frequency of use (as well as observability and relevance) of a series of teaching skills and behaviors.

The development of the current National Teacher Examination (NTE) did not involve job analysis; however, a form of job analysis is being used to define content for a revised version of the NTE. This will not be implemented, however, until 1987.

Job Analysis Alternatives

Although job analyses for current teacher certification tests have been limited almost exclusively to survey questionnaires requesting ratings of proposed test content in terms of importance and frequency of use, alternatives are available. Recommendations for alternatives in the teacher certification environment reflect different (a) sources of job information and (b) data collection methodologies.

SOURCES OF INFORMATION

Teacher certification test development efforts have relied on the collection of job information from a cross section of job incumbents in a specific teaching area. Alternatives include the collection of job information from supervisors or solely from superior performers on the job. Previous research comparing the job information obtained from job incumbents and other observers conflicts. Although the information obtained from incumbents and other observers is consistent in some job settings, Levine, Ash, Hall, & Sistrunk (1981) have found that in other settings there are discrepancies across sources. These studies do not cover teaching per se, and the accuracy of teacher- or educator-supplied information remains to be explored. Future job analysis efforts within the realm of teacher certification should consider obtaining information from teacher supervisors or outside observers as well as from teachers for purposes of comparison.

Similarly, little work has been done comparing the job information obtained from teachers judged as superior performers to information obtained from educators judged as poor performers. Although Levine et al. (1981) suggest that there are few differences in the information obtained from superior and less capable performers in a variety of job settings, this finding remains to be verified in the instructional setting. Again, future efforts in job analysis for teacher certification should investigate this issue. It must be noted, however, that the validity of teacher certification tests based on job content defined solely by superior performers may be in question since these measures are generally designed as minimum competency assessments.

DATA COLLECTION

Alternative data collection methods for teacher certification job analysis efforts include (a) observation, (b) critical incident technique (Flanagan, 1954), (c) document review, and (d) group discussion.

Observation: Observational methods rely on trained individuals observing the performance of job incumbents, that is, the classroom behavior of teachers or other instructional personnel. Although observation has the appeal of directness, its feasibility is questionable because of its obtrusiveness and the time and, hence, money it requires. These limitations particularly affect content knowledge examinations; repeated observations of many teachers over an extended period of time would be required to provide an accurate assessment of the content actually taught on the job.

Critical incident: The critical incident approach (Flanagan, 1954) identifies job events that have resulted in either inferior or superior performance. A large number of incidents are collected from job incumbents (through diaries, interviews, etc.) and are used to determine what behaviors are necessary to be effective on the job. This approach is potentially useful for the development of measures of teacher performance or pedagogical skills; however, the critical incident technique appears to have little application to measures that are content knowledge oriented. Levine et al. (1981) report that this approach was not favored by experienced job analysts for use in personnel selection.

Document review and discussion: The final two data collection approaches with potential application to teacher certification are document review and group discussion. The former uses available literature (e.g., job descriptions) to determine necessary job content. In fact, the review of documents is typically carried out as an initial step in the definition of content knowledge or skills to be included on job analysis survey instruments used in existing teacher certification test development projects. Similarly, the latter method—group discussion—has been used in the development of existing teacher certification tests. For instance, in Georgia, Texas, Alabama, West Virginia, and Oklahoma, panels of experts in the specified content areas met to generate content for inclusion on the job analysis survey instrument. The group discussion approach could include supervisors and incumbents in the content areas who would formally rate the importance of the knowledges and skills; this step is recommended by Primoff (1975).

Whether the information gained from these approaches warrants the additional expenditure of resources is uncertain. Additional research is necessary to determine the effectiveness of current job analysis approaches used in teacher certification programs and to identify superior techniques.

VALIDITY

A primary concern in the teacher certification testing effort is validity. Validity is the ability of a measuring instrument to do what it is intended to do (Nunnally, 1978) or, more specifically, "the degree to which inferences from scores on tests or assessments are justified or supported by evidence" (APA Principles, 1980). In licensing, three aspects of validity are relevant: criterion-related validity (predictive and concurrent), content validity, and construct validity (APA Standards, 1974). Criterion-related validity concerns the inference, from a given test instrument, of an individual's performance on some other variable referred to as the criterion (e.g., classroom performance) (APA Standards, 1974; Nunnally, 1978). Content validity is important in estimating "how an individual performs in the universe of situations the test is intended to represent" (APA Standards, 1974). Construct validity references the extent to which a measurement tool is related to the various elements or underlying traits associated with the psychological construct it is purported to measure.

Validity is of particular concern in certification situations where one wishes to establish that a test indeed measures the aspects of job performance it is purported to measure. It is imperative to establish a relationship between teacher certification decisions based on a test and aspects of the job required for successful performance. Most of the validation efforts for teacher certification tests focus on content validity, that is, whether the tests reflect significant aspects of classroom teaching.

A discussion of the validation of teacher certification assessment measures follows, with the emphasis on content validity.

Content Validity

The content validity of a test is established by demonstrating that the test content represents a sample of the content or behavior in the performance domain. As applied to teacher certification, content validity generally has two components: (1) determining whether the test content reflects significant aspects of the educator's job and measures those aspects proportionally and (2) determining whether test items themselves accurately measure that job's content. The first component is often assessed through some form of job analysis, as discussed earlier. A discussion of item validation is presented in the following sections.

CONTENT VALIDATION APPROACHES

Methods available to assess content validity include (a) index of item-objective congruence, (b) rating scale approach, and (c) dichotomous judgment model. In each of these methods, a panel of judges evaluates individual examination items to determine if each is a valid measure of the domain (objective, item specification, topic) for which it was written.

In the item-objective congruence model, content experts assign ratings of +1 (measures the objective), 0 (undecided whether item measures the objective), and -1 (does not measure the objective) to each item. One then computes an index of item-objective congruence (ranging from 1 to -1) for each item and sets a "cutoff score" for classifying items as valid or invalid (Rovinelli and Hambleton, 1977).

In the rating scale approach (Hambleton, 1980), expert judges use a rating scale to assess each item as a measure of its intended objective. The mean or median score across judges is computed, and a cutoff score for accepting items as valid is set. Rating scale procedures and the index of item-objective congruence are described in more depth in Hambleton (1980).

In the dichotomous judgment model (Nassif, 1978), content experts indicate for each item whether they think the item is or is not a valid measure of the objective for which it was written. Item validity is defined as having four parts: accuracy, congruence with objective, significance, and lack of bias. One then compares the results from the evaluations for each item to the binomial distribution to determine the probability, by chance alone, of obtaining "x" valid responses for an item from a total of "N" raters. Items receiving ratings that meet statistical significance are treated as valid.

CONTENT VALIDATION APPLICATIONS

Content validation procedures have been employed in a variety of teacher certification testing efforts. The dichotomous judgment model has been widely used with content knowledge examinations. In Georgia, for instance, panels of approximately 15 content experts in each content field made dichotomous judgments about prospective test items. Items were categorized as valid if the probability of obtaining "x" valid responses from "N" raters because of chance was less than .10. Similar procedures were employed with content examinations in Alabama and Oklahoma and the basic skills examination (CONNCEPT) for individuals seeking admission to teacher education programs in Connecticut.

The content validation of the tests for the Florida program involved a review in the four subtest areas by two independent panels of experts. The panel review was based on supplied criteria (e.g., item-competency match, bias) and led to recommendations of acceptance, rejection, or revision of each item.

Several states have made post hoc efforts to establish the validity of the National Teacher Examination (NTE). In South Carolina a validation study involved panels of content experts in the various NTE teaching areas who judged whether the individual questions appearing on the examination were covered in the curriculum of South Carolina teacher education programs. This is similar to the dichotomous judgment model presented earlier. In this case, however, if 51% or more of the judges cited the item as congruent with the curriculum, the item was accepted as valid (rather than relying on comparisons to the binomial distribution). Similar validation efforts for the NTE are planned or have been conducted in several states including Arkansas, Kentucky, Virginia, and Tennessee.

Item validation for the South Carolina Teaching Area Examinations (in fields not covered by the NTE) relied on the rating scale approach. Panels of South Carolina educators in each area rated each item on a scale from 1 ("clearly valid") to 5 ("clearly not valid"). Items receiving mean ratings below 3.0 across judges were treated as valid.

There has been little effort to apply item-objective congruence models in teacher certification to date. The primary reason stems from feasibility; the approach is quite time-consuming and potentially quite costly to the consumer. For example, if there are 50 objectives and 100 test items, each participant must make 5,000 separate judgments.

The rating scale approach and dichotomous judgment model offer practical advantages. They are relatively simple to administer, and the analysis associated with them is straightforward. The dichotomous judgment model, when used in conjunction with the binomial distribution, offers the added advantage of preventing determinations of validity based on chance alone.

Content validity is clearly an important element in the development of teacher certification tests, but some measurement specialists have argued that it is an insufficient criterion for establishing the validity of a test. Messick (1975) and, more recently, Hambleton (1980) note that content validity does not provide evidence in regard to the uses of or inferences made from test scores. And despite the importance assigned to criterion-related validity and construct validity, few validation studies of these types have been conducted in the teacher certification field.

Criterion-Related Validity

Criterion-related validity "compares test scores, or predictions made from them, with an external variable (criterion) considered to provide a direct measure of the characteristic or behavior in question" (Cronbach, 1971, p. 444). In teacher certification testing, the relationship at issue is the relationship between a certification test and actual teacher performance on the job. A teacher certification test should accurately predict the aspect of teacher competency for which it was designed.

Two forms of criterion-related validation are generally discussed: (1) concurrent validity and (2) predictive validity (APA Standards, 1974). "Statements of concurrent validity indicate the extent to which the test may be used to estimate an individual's present standing on the criterion," whereas predictive validity refers to "the extent to which an individual's future level on a criterion can be predicted from a knowledge of prior test performance" (APA Standards, 1974). Concurrent validation, as applied to teacher certification testing, examines the relationship between the test scores of practicing educators (job incumbents) and current performance. Establishing the predictive validity of a teacher certification measure involves examining the relationship between the test scores of prospective teachers (job applicants) and future performance.

Although criterion-related validation has been held to be a necessary part of certification tests, a number of obstacles have prevented its implementation. Hecht (1976), though supporting the importance of criterion-related validation for licensing and certification tests, notes that criterion-related validation studies are "difficult to develop, time-consuming, impractical for numerous reasons, and expensive." Nassif, Gorth, and Rubinstein (1977) provide a more in-depth treatment of these issues as they relate specifically to teacher certification testing. These authors suggest that the following criteria are required to demonstrate the predictive validity of a teacher certification test:

1. Admission of *all* applicants for employment in the field.
2. Sufficient time lapse before observing the criterion variable.
3. Unexamined, unused results of the test (i.e., the predictor is stored until correlated with the criterion, which here is the retention or dismissal of a teacher because of subject-matter competence or incompetence).
4. A measurable criterion (i.e., a mechanism for accurately and reliably collecting the reasons for retention or dismissal of teachers that clearly separates content knowledge as one of those reasons).
5. Sufficient sample size.
6. Stability of the criterion.

These factors are simply not present in a certification program. Thus the practical constraints overwhelm the advantages to be gained by the approach.

Construct Validity

Construct validity deals with the question "Does the test measure the attribute it is said to measure?" (Cronbach, 1971). Construct validation is a process, rather than a single study, in which evidence is accumulated that relates test scores to the attributes of the construct the test is purported to measure. Cronbach (1971) notes that when one says that test scores reflect levels of a certain skill or knowledge, one is "constructing" an interpretation of these scores, and construct validation is necessary. The constructs underlying teacher certification measures (i.e., pedagogical skill or content knowledge) are somewhat simpler than those encountered in a more complex and abstract personality construct such as aggressiveness.

The construct validation of tests designed for teacher certification presents a number of problems, and there has been little effort in this area. Potential approaches to construct validation and problems inherent in construct validation studies in the teacher certification area are discussed below.

One of the primary methods for investigating the construct validity of a given measure is to establish a relationship between that measure and other measures of the same construct. For content knowledge tests in teacher certification, this implies a comparison of the tests with other assessments of the applicants' content knowledge. Attempts to construct validate teacher certification tests using alternative measures of the construct suffer from many of the problems noted earlier in the discussion of criterion-related validity, notably the location of a suitable criterion measure and the stability of that criterion. A "well-matched" criterion measure is often unavailable. Moreover, instructor or supervisor assessments of a candidate's proficiency are unsuitable as criterion measures because of their unreliability and questionable accuracy.

Despite these difficulties, Hambleton (1980) notes that construct validation should also aim at examining possible sources of error that reduce the validity of test scores. Among other factors, Hambleton suggests the effects of test administration procedures, examinee test-taking skills, and examinee motivation. Little formal investigation has dealt with the significance of these factors for teacher certification; they merit more attention.

Another approach to construct validation suggested by Hambleton involves the use of factor analysis to verify the domain structure of the test. One would expect the factor structure of the test results to correspond to the domain structure of the test design, with individual test items loading on a single factor that corresponds to the appropriate domain. This approach has been employed in the development of the teacher performance instruments in Georgia.

RELIABILITY

Reliability concerns the extent to which a measure consistently produces the same result under similar conditions (Nunnally, 1978). This is a major concern with teacher certification tests. Traditionally, reliability has been thought of as the internal consistency of a test or the stability of test scores across repeated administrations and parallel forms of the test. More recently, particularly in the area of certification, test developers have begun to examine reliability in terms of the dependability of classification decisions (e.g., pass-fail). Traditional and more recent approaches to the reliability of teacher certification tests are considered below along with current applications.

Approaches

Traditionally, there have been three approaches to determining test reliability: (1) stability, (2) equivalence, and (3) internal consistency. Stability refers to the consistency of the measurement over time; equivalence estimates are obtained to determine the consistency of measurement across two or more forms of the test. The internal consistency of a test refers to the consistency of items included within a single test form. The most common approach is internal consistency because of the need for only one test form and the ease with which these estimates can be obtained.

STABILITY AND EQUIVALENCE

The most common approach to assessing test stability is the test-retest method, in which the same test is administered to a single group of individuals at two different times. The correlation between the two sets of scores is an estimate of the test's reliability (Nunnally, 1978). Similarly, the reliability of two alternative forms—equivalence—can be determined by administering two forms of a test to a pool of examinees and computing the correlation between the two sets of scores as an estimate of test reliability (Nunnally, 1978). The equivalence approach has little application in teacher certification testing because only a single test form is employed in most certification programs.

INTERNAL CONSISTENCY

The techniques employed in internal consistency approaches estimate test reliability using a single test form. The two most common internal consistency approaches are split-half reliability and the Kuder-Richardson indices of item homogeneity (K-R20, K-R21; Nunnally, 1978). The former involves the splitting of a test into halves and correlating results from the two sets of items. The latter reflects the average of all possible split-half reliability coefficients. The Kuder-Richardson formulas are considered more accurate and are therefore employed more often.

CLASSIFICATION DECISIONS

More recently, a number of writers (cf. Huynh, 1976) have suggested that the reliability of tests in situations where a dichotomous decision is made (e.g., pass-fail) should be assessed on the basis of the consistency of those decisions across test administrations. This is particularly applicable in criterion-referenced testing in which the range of test scores may be restricted.

Although a number of decision-consistency approaches have emerged in recent years, only a sample of the more visible approaches applicable to teacher certification is presented here— Kappa reliability (Huynh, 1976; Subkoviak, 1980; Swaminathan, Hambleton, and Algina, 1974), generalizability analysis (Brennan, 1980), and the Livingston Reliability Coefficient (Livingston, 1972).

The Kappa reliability approach examines the consistency of classification decisions across test administrations. The extent of actual agreement across test administrations (computed by calculating the proportion of examinees consistently classified in a given mastery state on two administrations) is compared to the extent of agreement that could be expected by chance alone. These two figures are used to calculate a coefficient of decision consistency. Specific procedures for computing Kappa are described in Swaminathan et al. (1974). Huynh (1976) and Subkoviak (1980) discuss procedures for obtaining Kappa reliability estimates from a single test administration.

Generalizability theory employs estimates of the variance components attributable to the various elements in the assessment situation (e.g., items, persons). Reliability, then, is viewed as a function of the proportion of variance accounted for by the person variable.

The Livingston Reliability Coefficient (Livingston, 1972) is the internal reliability of the test with respect to the cut score. Whereas traditional reliability measures (e.g., K-R20) compute reliability with respect to the mean, Livingston's measure is centered on the more critical area of interest, the minimum passing score.

Applications

Although there are many techniques for examining test reliability, their applications to teacher certification testing have been somewhat limited. Traditional approaches to reliability, particularly internal consistency measures, appear most often. K-R20 reliability coefficients are routinely obtained for teacher certification tests administered in Georgia, Alabama, Oklahoma, and other statewide certification programs, as well as for the NTE. This is not surprising since these estimates are easy to obtain and provide a reasonable assessment of test reliability.

Because of increased criticism of more traditional reliability approaches, test developers in the area of teacher certification have begun to employ decision-consistency models and generalizability analysis with increased frequency.

References

American Psychological Association, Division of Industrial-Organizational Psychology. (1980). *Principles for the validation and use of personnel selection procedures* (2nd ed.). Berkeley, CA: Author.

American Psychological Association, American Educational Research Association, National Council on Research in Education. (1974). *Standards for educational and psychological tests.* Washington, DC: Author.

Brennan, R. L. (1980). Applications of generalizability theory. In R. A. Berk (Ed.), *Criterion-referenced testing: The state of the art* (pp. 186-232). Baltimore, MD: Johns Hopkins University Press.

Cronbach, L. J. (1971). Test validation. In R. L. Thorndike (Ed.), *Educational measurement* (pp. 443-507). Washington, DC: American Council on Education.

Equal Employment Opportunity Commission, Civil Service Commission, U.S. Department of Labor, & U.S. Department of Justice. (1978). Adoption by four agencies of uniform guidelines on employee selection procedures. *Federal Register, 43,* 38290-38315.

Flanagan, J. C. (1954). The Critical Incident Technique. *Psychological Bulletin, 51,* 327-358.

Hambleton, R. K. (1980). Test score validity and standard-setting methods. In R. A. Berk (Ed.), *Criterion referenced measurement: The state of the art* (pp. 80-123). Baltimore, MD: Johns Hopkins University Press.

Hecht, K. A. (1976). *Professional licensing and certification: Current status and methodological problems of validation.* Paper presented at the annual convention of NCME, San Francisco, CA.

Huynh, H. (1976). On the reliability of decisions in domain referenced testing. *Journal of Educational Measurement, 13,* 256-264.

Levine, E. L., Ash, R. A., Hall, H. L., & Sistrunk, F. (1981). *Evaluation of seven job analysis methods by experienced job analysts.* Unpublished research report, University of South Florida, Center for Evaluation Research, Tampa.

Livingston, S. A. (1972). Criterion-referenced applications of classical test theory. *Journal of Educational Measurement, 9,* 13-29.

Messick, S. H. (1975). The standard problem: Meaning and values in measurement and evaluation. *American Psychologist, 30,* 955-966.

Nassif, P. M. (1978, March). *Standard-setting for criterion-referenced teacher licensing tests.* Paper presented at the annual meeting of the National Council on Measurement in Education, Toronto.

Nassif, P. M., Gorth, W. P., and Rubinstein, S. A. (1977). *Developing and validating teacher certification tests according to federal guidelines.* Unpublished report, National Evaluation Systems.

Nunnally, J. C. (1978). *Psychometric theory.* New York: McGraw-Hill.

Popham, W. J. (1980). Domain specification strategies. In R. A. Berk (Ed.), *Criterion-referenced testing: The state of the art* (pp. 15-31). Baltimore, MD: Johns Hopkins University Press.

Primoff, E. S. (1975). *How to prepare and conduct job element examinations.* Washington, DC: U.S. Government Printing Office.

Rovinelli, R. J. & Hambleton, R. K. (1977). On the use of content specialists in the assessment of criterion-referenced test item validity, *Dutch Journal of Educational Research, 2,* 49-60.

Subkoviak, M. (1980). Decision-consistency approaches. In R. A. Berk (Ed.), *Criterion-referenced testing: The state of the art* (pp. 129-185). Baltimore, MD: Johns Hopkins University Press.

Swaminathan, H., Hambleton, R. K., & Algina, J. (1974). Reliability of criterion-referenced tests: A decision theoretic formulation. *Journal of Educational Measurement, 11,* 263-267.

Job Analysis in the Texas Educator Initial Certification Testing Program

Marvin Veselka
Nolan Wood
Barbara Clements
Pam Tackett
Cherry Kugle

INFORMATION SOURCES

In 1981 the 67th Texas Legislature, with the encouragement and support of state educators, passed and enacted Senate Bill 50 (S.B. 50). This bill provided for several reforms in teacher education programs in Texas. One portion of the bill required testing as a condition for initial certification of public school teachers and administrators. The state of Texas contracted National Evaluation Systems, Inc. (NES) to work with the Texas Education Agency (TEA) to develop these tests. Content tests, to be administered at the point of certification, will eventually be used in more than 60 fields.

A major concern in the development of tests that are part of a professional licensing process is the validity of the tests, which is the basis for their legal defensibility. In order to be legally defensible, tests of this nature must meet the Federal Equal Employment Opportunity Commission (EEOC) Guidelines (1978).

Marvin Veselka is Associate Commissioner for Professional Support, Texas Education Agency. Nolan Wood is Director of Teacher Competency Testing, Texas Education Agency. Pam Tackett is Program Director, Texas Education Agency. Barbara Clements is an Educational Specialist with the Texas Education Agency. Cherry Kugle is an Educational Specialist with the Texas Education Agency.

These guidelines require that all tests that influence employment have a direct relationship to job content and require that this relationship be demonstrated empirically. Traditionally, validation of teacher tests in the United States has been based on the content taught in teacher education programs—that is, what is learned before entering the profession. It is, in fact, more appropriate to base validation of licensing examinations on actual job duties as determined by a standard job analysis. This approach is not common, in part because the knowledge required by public school personnel derives from such a diversity of sources. As this chapter indicates, test validation activities in building the Texas program include an attempt to incorporate information that reflects this diversity.

Further legislation in Texas requires that information be provided that helps define the knowledge needed for successful teaching. House Bill 246, enacted in 1981, mandated the implementation of a basic curriculum for the state. The State Board of Education (SBOE) *Rules for Curriculum* (chapter 75) contain the essential elements of the curriculum that is taught in every public school in Texas. The rules include seven subject-matter areas to be mastered by students from prekindergarten through the 12th grade. The existence of a state-mandated curriculum is somewhat unusual and has provided an appropriate source for beginning the job analysis necessary for developing teacher certification tests in Texas.

Also used in this test development process are the SBOE *Rules for Teacher Education.* These are guidelines to be followed by teacher education institutions in training teachers and support personnel.

A third resource included in test content definition consists of educational materials in the form of public school textbooks and curriculum materials, as well as teacher education materials used in training preservice students.

The test development process, including the task of defining appropriate, job-related content for the tests, relies upon information obtained from these various sources. This chapter describes the general procedures used to systematically collect and integrate these data. It is both professionally and legally critical that test content reflects essential job characteristics and requirements. The Texas program has sought to expand the basis of information beyond that traditionally incorporated in teacher certification testing.

DEVELOPING TEST OBJECTIVES

The initial project activity was to assemble all the previously mentioned materials and to develop topic outlines and objectives tied to the content of the documents. In addition to the *Rules for Curriculum* and *Rules for Teacher Education* obtained from the state, NES acquired textbooks and other materials used in Texas from the TEA, textbook publishers, and other sources.

To create the objective outlines, the test development staff at NES reviewed all the materials and created an inclusive list of topics covered by or mentioned in the various books and documents. These topic outlines were then converted to organized sets of statements of learning objectives. After the initial development of the test objectives, the TEA convened more than 300 classroom teachers and teacher educators to serve on advisory committees to review and revise the objectives. These committees dealt only with the 31 certificate areas covered in Phase I of the development effort. A separate committee existed for each certificate area. Some of the objectives were fairly easily reviewed and revised; others, because of the complexity of the instructional delivery system, had to be revised extensively.

Although the committees invoked their expert judgment and knowledge to create final lists of objectives that reflect the content and emphasis in their individual certificate areas, further validation was required. That is, there are limitations on the credibility of the lists at this point in the process because of the relatively small number of individuals who have been involved in objective development and review.

JOB ANALYSIS INSTRUMENTS

When the review process was completed, NES developed job analysis survey forms based on the revised objectives. Forms were developed for each area of certification, as well as for three levels of professional development (elementary, secondary, and all-level). The instruments developed included ratings of the objectives as well as demographic information on the respondents.

In the survey, a series of ratings was collected for each objective. The rating dimensions requested for each objective varied across the different audiences from whom ratings were collected. It is this aspect of the job analysis that represents the expansion beyond what is traditionally done. Normally, only classroom teachers are involved in formal job analysis surveys. The Texas program, in contrast, included a multi-faceted review of objectives, including teachers, teacher educators, and students in teacher preparation programs.

MIRROR OF SOURCES OF INFORMATION

The selection of survey participants reflects the sources of information included in development of the original topic outlines and objective lists. As discussed previously, the outlines and lists derived from state board standards for both classroom instruction and teacher preparation as well as from actual classroom materials used in Texas. It seemed appropriate, therefore, that the job analysis surveys should include all three groups professionally and personally involved in the process: classroom teachers, preservice teachers, and university faculty involved in teacher preparation.

Incumbent Teachers

Individuals for the first group were randomly selected from those teaching in each of the 31 certificate areas covered in the first phase of test development. This initial group included more than 8,500 individuals. Superintendents of the school districts included in the sample were notified that the survey was being conducted and were requested to distribute the survey forms to the teachers in their district whose names had been generated in the selection process (using 1984 lists provided by the TEA).

Forms developed for the teacher group contained objectives (as revised by the committees) specific to the subject matter taught in the classroom. In the survey, respondents first stated if they were teaching the subject during the current year or had taught it the previous year. If the respondent was teaching or had taught the subject, he or she completed the rest of the form. For each objective listed, teachers addressed three issues:

1. Whether the content of the objective was used during the current or past school year (yes or no).
2. How much time was spent using the content of the objective (time rating—a scale of 1 to 5).
3. The extent to which the objective was essential to the content of the given area (essentiality rating—a scale of 1 to 5).

These last two dimensions, time and essentiality, constitute the basis of ranking the objectives in overall importance. The two scores are combined to create an overall ranking; typically the dimensions are highly correlated. Advisory committee members use these indices, along with their expert judgment, to select the objectives upon which to base test questions.

Preservice Teachers

The second group in the survey was composed of university seniors enrolled in approved teacher education programs. The deans' offices at individual institutions, following specific instructions from NES, selected respondents. Most of the students included in the survey were in the student teaching phase of their programs. The job analysis survey for this group required respondents to indicate whether they received instruction (either before college or as a part of their teacher preparation) in the content of each objective on the survey (extent of preparation rating—a scale of 1 to 5). Each content area sample included up to 100 respondents.

Whereas the results from classroom teachers indicate their actual practice with regard to each objective, this survey addresses the adequacy of preparation of preservice teachers. Traditionally, norm-referenced teacher certification examinations, such as the National Teacher Examination, were built solely on the basis of instruction provided in teacher preparation courses. The extent to which these curricula reflect what teachers actually do in the classroom is a question that can be addressed with the data collected in the Texas job analysis.

As noted previously, a fundamental reason behind the expanded job analysis in Texas is to bring multiple sets of data to bear on the same array of learning objectives within a certificate area. In addition, the results can serve the important educational function of comparing college preparation with classroom practices by correlating student and teacher survey results. One potential benefit of this kind of analysis is that individual teacher preparation institutions can review their curriculum in a particular content area in terms of what job incumbents say is actually essential in the field. This information then offers an opportunity to revise preparatory courses. Conversely, the job analysis allows the TEA to give feedback to teachers in the field that classroom practice may be placing too little emphasis on what are seen as fundamental elements of an academic discipline.

University Faculty

The third group surveyed consisted of up to 100 representatives in each content area from colleges and universities with approved teacher education programs. For each objective, selected respondents indicated (a) whether the objective was taught or whether students should already know the content of the objective (yes or no) and (b) the importance of the objective for public school teachers (essentiality rating—a scale of 1 to 5).

The potential benefits of these data go far beyond what is normally or minimally associated with the development of a certification test. Do perceptions of what is taught align with student perceptions on this issue? Do teacher preparation faculty members rate as essential to the discipline the same objectives that incumbent teachers rate as essential? Answers to these and similar questions can bring improvement to education programs in Texas above and beyond the contribution the answers will bring to the testing program alone. The TEA expects that gradually there will be more complete agreement between what preservice teachers are taught and what classroom teachers cover.

Results

Results from the surveys will yield two major types of information: (1) demographic characteristics of the respondents and (2) ratings for each of the objectives. All information will be computed and analyzed for each content area and for each respondent. The demographic information will provide a portrait of each population by field. The various analyses of the rating dimension scores constitute the next step in the test development process, that is, selecting the objectives NES will use to write test questions.

CONFIDENCE

In other criterion-referenced teacher certification testing programs, the job analysis surveys have included only classroom teachers. Their "votes" are the most important in building a legally defensible and job-related test. Texas elected to expand survey coverage to build additional confidence into the tests. In a state with formal standards for teacher preparation and public school instruction, it is advantageous to add the other two populations to the surveys.

ANALYSIS

The results from each sampled population in a content field will yield similar analyses. For all dichotomous response questions, the number and percent of answers will be compiled. The NES data analysis staff will compute the means and standard deviations for all the five-point rating scales (e.g., extent of preparation, essentiality). Scatterplots of the combined means for the time and essentiality dimensions for each objective rated by the classroom teachers will also be generated. Data reporting is deliberately clear and straightforward to facilitate committee review.

COMMITTEE DECISIONS

The advisory committees will review the survey results in their content fields and make recommendations with regard to the objectives that should be included in the tests. These recommendations will reflect a careful analysis of the data from the three surveyed populations. Only those objectives that are a part of state curricula, that are highly job related, and for which students have been provided adequate preparation will be recommended for final inclusion. This ensures that objectives for the test focus simultaneously on what the state has mandated as a basis of public school instruction and on what happens in the classroom.

TEST DEVELOPMENT

NES will then develop test items for each objective chosen. It is not surprising that much public attention is focused on the quality and difficulty of individual items in the tests themselves since it is the questions that the examinees experience. However, the actual item writing is the last step in a detailed process which is the key to the success of the testing program in Texas. Quite simply, if the tests are not based on objectives directly tied to on-the-job behaviors and state-required curricula, the quality of an individual item is irrelevant. Without the empirical links to those standards and to classroom practice, the tests are neither job related, legally defensible, nor fair to examinees. It was the TEA's desire to create a fair and legally defensible program that precluded the simple adoption of any existing set of content tests. The TEA believes that the process of defining test content is the characteristic that most distinguishes the Texas program.

The advisory committees will reconvene to review the test items for accuracy, appropriate level of difficulty, job relatedness, adequate preparation opportunity, and bias of various sorts (e.g., sex, ethnicity). It is likely that a small number of items will be dropped at this time and that others will require revisions to be acceptable. The primary criterion at this point will be the match of the item to the objective; that is, whether the question is a valid measure of the objective. The objectives are the foundation of the entire program.

Field Testing

Although the detailed procedures for field testing items are beyond the scope of this paper, it should be noted that the TEA is undertaking a major field-testing effort. Approximately 11,000 students will participate in a field test of items developed in the initial phase (31 content areas). NES project staff will generate summaries of field test results for committee action. The reports will provide basic psychometric data for each item (difficulty index, discrimination index, distribution of answers across response alternatives, etc.) plus various "whole test" reliability measures. Moreover, all items will be subject to a statistical review for potential adverse impact on any minority group.

Subsequently, the advisory committees will meet to review the results and determine if any items require revision. In addition, a separate minority review committee will be established to review items "flagged" for potential bias and to make suggestions for revisions. NES will use the recommendations of these committees to revise items where necessary. The combination of statistical analyses and expert judgment will provide some assurance of absence of bias in the tests.

Content Validation and Standard Setting

Once all item revisions are complete, the TEA will select a set of independent review panels mirroring the advisory committees in each field, to conduct a final validation of the objectives and test items for suitability, accuracy, job relatedness, and freedom from bias. These panels will also indicate whether the entire content field and all content subareas are adequately covered. Panel members will make passing score recommendations based on test items, specifications, and test objectives to the Commission on Standards for the Teaching Profession (CSTP). The CSTP will then make recommendations to the State Board of Education, which will determine the required passing score for each test. Initial teacher certification testing in Texas will begin in the spring of 1986.

SUMMARY

This paper has provided a brief overview of the test development process for the Texas Educator Initial Certification Testing Program. The emphasis has been on the expanded job analysis study that provided the empirical basis for content definition. The TEA considers the concentration on job relatedness and preservice training to be critical aspects of the program. An unprecedented amount of information from relevant populations is being gathered as a part of this effort.

Goals

The overall goals of the testing program are twofold. First, the TEA has an obligation, both in general and by imposed legislation, to ensure that newly certified personnel are well qualified for positions in public education. The expanded job analysis serves this regulatory goal by helping to create a program that is legally defensible, fair to all examinees, job related, and reflective of teacher training program content.

Without minimizing the regulatory aspect, we believe education in Texas is also well served by the testing program. Earlier, we mentioned the various research possibilities inherent in the survey data, such as the prospect of studying the relationship between what students say they are prepared for and what classroom teachers say they do. Information like this, over the long run, will exert pressure on training programs and bring them more in line with teaching practices. Influence will also come from the other direction as classroom behavior is adjusted to reflect state curricular requirements more fully. An educational system has many parts; the expanded job analysis provides data that we can use to bring the aspects of that system into balance.

References

Equal Employment Opportunity Commission, Civil Service Commission, U. S. Department of Labor, & U. S. Department of Justice. (1978). Adoption by four agencies of uniform guidelines on employee selection procedures. *Federal Register, 43,* 38290-38315.

State Board of Education (Texas). *State Board of Education Rules for Curriculum: Principles, Standards and Procedures for Accreditation of School Districts.* Austin, TX: Texas Education Agency.

Texas House Bill 246 (1981). *Texas Education Code* § 21.101.

Judgmental and Statistical Item Analyses of Teacher Certification Tests

Ronald A. Berk

At present, 29 states have mandated or implemented teacher certification testing programs, and 10 others are planning such programs (Bridgman, 1985). The tests measure basic, professional, academic, and on-the-job skills. Although the last category appears to be the most appropriate domain in certification or licensing, only 10 states require the assessment of on-the-job skills. Standard 11.1 in the *Standards for Educational and Psychological Testing* (AERA/APA/NCME Joint Committee, in press) states that "A rationale should be provided to support a claim that the knowledge or skills being assessed are required for competent performance in an occupation and are consistent with the purpose for which the licensing or certification program was instituted" (p. 11-3). Establishing this foundation by means of a comprehensive job analysis, the test developer proceeds to generate the test items. Subsequently, the items need to undergo review to identify structural flaws and to determine whether they function or "behave" consistently with the purposes for which they were constructed. This item analysis process is the subject of this paper.

If the certification test is criterion-referenced, then the item analysis process consists of four different phases:

1. A judgmental review to determine item-skill congruence and content bias.

2. Whole-item statistical analyses to evaluate the effectiveness of the items.

Ronald Berk is Professor of Education, Measurement, and Research, Johns Hopkins University.

3. A judgmental review of the statistical results to determine whether the items should be accepted, revised, or discarded.

4. Part-item statistical analyses to identify what part or parts of an item require revision or replacement.

Only brief descriptions of these phases are given in the succeeding sections. For further details, interested readers are referred to Berk (1984).

JUDGMENTAL REVIEW

Item-Skill Congruence

The most important item characteristic is item-skill congruence. Item-skill congruence is concerned with the extent to which an item measures the job-related skill it is intended to measure. Congruence is determined by a judgmental procedure in which the items are reviewed against the list of skills identified by the job analysis. As Standard 3.3 specifies, "Domain definitions and the test specifications should be sufficiently clear so that knowledgeable experts can judge the relations of items to the domains they represent" (AERA/APA/NCME Joint Committee, in press, p. 3-2). The review panel should include certified, experienced teachers who are the content experts to judge whether each item accurately measures its corresponding skill. The review can also take the form of independent ratings of congruence whereby the judges' input is elicited using survey methods. This approach tends to be more efficient and is not subject to the normative effects of a group discussion. Whether the panel or independent ratings format is employed, what counts ultimately is the degree of agreement among the judges on the congruence of each item-skill match. Various statistical indices have been proposed to quantify interjudge agreement (e.g., see Hambleton, 1984); the agreement found per item is a measure of congruence.

Once the judgments have been obtained and analyzed, attention should be directed to those items yielding low or unsatisfactory indices of congruence. Appropriate item revisions or replacements should be considered and must be completed. If it cannot be stated unequivocally that the items accurately measure the skill domain, then any other item characteristic becomes meaningless. Inferences of competent performance of skills measured by the test scores hinge on the congruence between the items and the skills. Congruence is a necessary but not, however, a solely sufficient condition for test score validity.

Content Bias

After it has been established that the items do measure their corresponding skills, each item should be examined for content bias. The *Standards* specify:

> When selecting the type and content of items for tests and inventories, test developers should consider the content and type in relation to cultural backgrounds and prior experiences of the variety of ethnic, cultural, age, and gender groups represented in the intended population of test takers. (AERA/APA/NCME Joint Committee, in press, p. 3-3)

Any language in an item that is stereotypic of a particular sex or of a racial or ethnic subpopulation should be removed. Also, words or phrases that are culture specific or offensive to a given group should be eliminated. Tittle (1982) has presented numerous review forms that have been employed by test publishers for this purpose as has Hambleton (1980). In addition, attention should be given to the characteristics of the persons and situations described in the items to assure fair representation in the work roles and life-styles of sex, racial, and ethnic groups, especially females and minorities.

These reviews should be conducted by panels of classroom teachers who are representative of the appropriate subpopulations (e.g., males, females, blacks, whites, Hispanics). The panel should carefully review the test items using a structured checklist (or some other set of guidelines) and make specific recommendations on the revision or elimination of those items judged to be questionable.

These procedures are consistent with the suggestion in the *Standards* for implementing Standard 3.5, stated previously: "Test developers might establish a review process using expert judges both to select item material and to eliminate material likely to be inappropriate or offensive for groups in the test-taking population" (3-3).

WHOLE-ITEM STATISTICAL ANALYSES

After the item reviews have been completed and a draft version of the test is ready, the test maker should plan a field test with one or more samples of teachers. The response data that are obtained can be used to evaluate the effectiveness of the items. The steps in the item evaluation process include selecting the samples, gathering informal teacher feedback, computing difficulty and discrimination indices, and conducting an item bias study.

Sample Selection

Since the purpose of the test is to certify those teachers who can demonstrate mastery of the skills required for successful classroom performance, it would be highly desirable to sample certified or "successful" teachers from the local school districts. The operational definition of "successful" is critical; therefore, explicit criteria must be specified. The samples should be stratified by grade level or subject area to assure representation of the populations for whom each certification test is designed. Comparable samples of uncertified teachers early in their training would also be useful in order to determine whether the items can discriminate between teachers who are known to be performing successfully and those who should not be able to perform successfully. These sampling recommendations are simply an application of the "known-groups" criterion validation model (see Hattie & Cooksey, 1984). The practicability of this model may be questionable in certain contexts.

Informal Teacher Feedback

Immediately following the administration of the items, informal feedback on the items can be obtained. The procedure entails conducting a discussion or individual interviews to elicit teacher reactions to the items and test structure. Much can be learned about test quality from this type of critique that would not be disclosed from a strictly quantitative analysis. Specific test weaknesses such as item ambiguity and cuing, miskeyed answers, inappropriate vocabulary, and unclear item and test directions can be revealed by asking leading questions pertinent to the item content and structure, test directions, and test format. Such questions may include the following:

1. Did any of the items seem confusing?
2. Did you find any item with no correct answer?
3. Did you find any item with more than one correct answer?
4. Were there any words in the items that were ambiguous?
5. Did you have any difficulty understanding what to do as you worked through the test?

Difficulty and Discrimination Indices

Standard 11.2 of the *Standards* states: "Any construct interpretations of tests used for licensure and certification should be made explicit, and the evidence and logical analyses supporting these interpretations should be reported" (AERA/APA/NCME Joint Committee, in press, p. 11-3). That is, "the claim that a particular skill is necessary for competent practice in a profession involves inferences that should be supported by evidence" (AERA/APA/NCME Joint Committee, in press, p. 11-3). Such evidence can take the form of item difficulty and discrimination indices. The difficulty index is the percentage of teachers who answer each item correctly and should be computed for the sample or samples for each item.

If two criterion samples were selected, it is also possible to compute a discrimination index that measures the performance differences between the samples. This type of item discrimination is consistent with the notion that a criterion-referenced test should maximize discrimination between groups and minimize discrimination among individuals within any one group (Glaser, 1963).

At present there are more than 17 statistics that have been recommended as discrimination indices for criterion-referenced tests. They range from the simple differences between criterion-group difficulties to the complex item information function based on the three-parameter logistic model.[1] To assist specialists in the selection of an index for a particular teacher certification test, "consumers' guide" tables, which indicate the advantages and disadvantages, have been prepared (Berk, 1984).

When this statistical information is gathered on successful and uncertified teachers, it is possible to assess whether the items are functioning properly. For example, difficulty indices should be high for the sample of successful teachers. Both the difficulty and discrimination indices provide evidence of item validity. The external criterion is successful-unsuccessful job performance.

Item Bias

Beyond the judgmental review of item content, there are statistical procedures that investigate item bias. Standard 3.10 of the *Standards* specifies:

> When previous research indicates the need for studies of item or test performance differences for a particular kind of test for members of age, ethnic, cultural, and gender groups in the population of test takers, such studies should be conducted as soon as is feasible. Such research should be designed to detect and eliminate aspects of test design, content, or format that might bias test scores for particular groups. (AERA/APA/NCME Joint Committee, in press, p. 3-4)

These procedures are appropriate for teacher certification tests constructed according to the mastery or domain-referenced model. Since extensive critiques of item bias statistics have been presented by Angoff (1982) and Ironson (1982), only a brief discussion of these statistics is given in this section.

An item is biased if individuals with the same ability have an unequal probability of answering the item correctly as a function of their group membership (cf. Pine, 1977; Scheuneman, 1979). Operationally, bias is inferred from differences in performance between groups. The focus of an item bias study is to detect discrepancies in item performance between specific groups (e.g., males and females, Hispanics and whites) while controlling for ability differences.

STRATEGIES

There are three major alternative strategies a test maker can use to search for bias: (1) plan a study using a true experimental design with a statistic such as analysis of variance or analysis of covariance (see Schmeiser, 1982); (2) plan a study using a quasi-experimental design with matched groups or pseudogroups and a statistic such as analysis of variance (item-by-item group interaction), arc-sine differences, delta-decrement analysis, delta-plot method, item difficulty performance differences, or item-group correlation (see Angoff, 1982); (3) plan a study with a statistical method that accounts for ability differences such as a chi-square type technique, contingency table analysis (e.g., log-linear model), or one- or three-parameter logistic model (see Ironson, 1982). The first two strategies control the variable of ability differences in the design; the third strategy adjusts for it statistically.

Research evidence clearly indicates that the different statistics yield different results (Burrill, 1982). The choice of a particular strategy and statistic should balance a need for precision with practical constraints. The recommendations of Angoff (1982) and Ironson (1982) can help guide these decisions.

GOLDEN RULE CASE

In addition to the aforementioned approaches to studying item bias, a recent out-of-court settlement between the Golden Rule Insurance Company (the plaintiffs) and the director of the Illinois Department of Insurance and the Educational Testing Service (the defendants) required another procedure to minimize differences in item performance between blacks and whites. The lawsuit of the *Golden Rule Insurance Co. et al. v. Washburn et al.* (1984) charged that the insurance licensing examination was racially biased. The settlement stipulated that the test items be selected on the basis of "least discriminatory impact." This meant the following:

    a. ETS shall classify all items as:

        1. Type I—those items for which (a) the correct-answer rates [item difficulties] of Black *(sic)* examinees, white examinees, and all examinees are not lower than forty percent at the .05 level of statistical significance, and (b) the correct-answer rates of Black *(sic)* examinees and white examinees differ by no more than fifteen (15) percentage points at the .05 level of statistical significance; or

        2. Type II—all other items.

    b. ETS shall assemble the test forms by selecting items according to the following guidelines:

        1. Type I Items shall be used exclusively so long as they are available in sufficient numbers.

        2. Those Type I Items for which the correct-answer rates of Black *(sic)* examinees and white examinees differ least shall be used first.

        3. Type II Items may be used, and shall be used before any new items. . .may be used, to the extent Type I Items are not available in sufficient numbers.

        4. To the extent it is necessary to use Type II Items, those Type II Items for which the correct-answer rates of black examinees and white examinees differ least shall be used first (p. 11).

For example, the most acceptable items (Type I) would be those with difficulty indices for blacks ($DIFF_B$) and for whites ($DIFF_W$) such as:

Item	$DIFF_W$	$DIFF_B$	Difference
1	80	80	0
2	75	60	15
3	67	65	2
o	o	o	o
o	o	o	o
o	o	o	o

Less acceptable items (Type II) would be those with difficulties such as:

Item	$DIFF_W$	$DIFF_B$	Difference
14	80	60	20
15	75	50	25
16	50	37	13
o	o	o	o
o	o	o	o
o	o	o	o

Item 16 is unacceptable because less than 40% of the black examinees answered the item correctly.

The key issue in regard to these item selections is the test's content validity. It is normally unadvisable to choose items only according to their statistical characteristics. As Robert Linn pointed out, if items are discarded on the basis of differences in item difficulties between blacks and whites, it is possible that those items not used will eliminate some of the knowledge domain the test is designed to measure (Cordes, 1985).

Despite the fact that the preceding item selection procedures will be used with one licensing examination, several questions remain unanswered:

1. Will the item selection method minimize or eliminate racial item bias?

2. Will the method negatively affect the test's content validity? If so, to what degree?

3. Will the method increase, decrease, or not affect the validity of the test for predicting the job performance of both blacks and whites?

The answers to these questions could have profound implications for the developers of licensing and certification tests in numerous occupations and professions.

JUDGMENTAL REVIEW OF STATISTICAL RESULTS

All of the preceding data gathering and analyses are conducted for one reason—to determine the quality or effectiveness of the test items. The characteristics that have been described must now be used to decide whether the items function consistently with the purposes for which they were constructed. The decision concerning an item may take three forms: (1) accept the item for inclusion in the final test, (2) revise the item before including it, or (3) discard the item and replace it. Criteria for assigning the items to these mutually exclusive categories have been proposed by Berk (1984). They are intended to guide the judgmental analysis of the statistical results.

Item Selection Criteria

The difficulty and discrimination indices for the items should satisfy the following criteria:

1. *Difficulty:* An item should be relatively easy for successful teachers (e.g., 70 to 100%) and difficult for uncertified teachers (e.g., 0 to 50%).

2. *Discrimination:* An item should yield high, positive discrimination between the criterion groups. The magnitude of the index will depend on the specific statistic used. For items calibrated according to the one- or three-parameter logistic model, the criteria suggested by van der Linden (1981) are appropriate.

In general, an item that produces indices within the ranges indicated should be accepted. When an item does not meet one or both of the criteria, however, should it be retained, revised, or discarded?

Item Revision or Elimination

The most conspicuous "flag" of a faulty item is a *negative discrimination index*. It may indicate ambiguity, two "correct" answers, or ineffective distractors. An examination of the internal structure of the item coupled with the information from the teachers' reviews will often reveal the part or parts that should be revised. When the item is in multiple-choice format, a quantitative analysis of each response choice (as described in the next section) should be considered.

An item that possesses no visible flaws yet fails to yield statistical indices that are acceptable should be discarded and a new item written to replace it. This procedure, however, should be viewed as a last resort. It is generally much easier to revise an item than to construct a new one, and the new item will also be "untested." It is imperative that an eliminated item be replaced. If it is not, the measurement of the corresponding skill as well as the overall content validity of the test are weakened.

PART-ITEM STATISTICAL ANALYSES

All of the reviews described thus far have been based on whole-item statistics, such as difficulty and discrimination indices. In order to provide specific directions for item revision and other types of analysis, it is necessary to break down an item into its component parts. For multiple-choice items, the response patterns of different groups of teachers can be especially informative. Patterns of responses to the correct answer and to the distractors are valuable (a) to guide the revision of faulty items and (b) to discern whether item bias is present and, if it is, to identify the distractors that may be the source of that bias.

Item Revision or Elimination

When informal teacher feedback or statistical analyses suggest that a multiple-choice item is faulty, an analysis of its internal structure can provide insight into what needs to be revised. The most common problems are often detected by the teachers and others who review the items. In order to identify flaws that may not be readily apparent, a more rigorous analysis, based on performance data, is required. This analysis is particularly appropriate for items yielding low positive, zero, or negative discrimination indices.

The analysis involves the visual inspection of the teachers' responses to each response alternative. Both criterion groups are employed to determine whether the distractors are functioning properly. The evaluation criteria are as follows:

1. Each distractor should be selected by more teachers in the uncertified group than in the successful group.

2. At least a few uncertified teachers (5-10%) should choose each distractor.

3. No distractor should receive as many responses by the successful group as the correct answer.

If any of these patterns is not observed, it is likely that particular distractors are ambiguous or implausible. Depending upon the nature of the error or errors, either revision or replacement of the specific part is generally indicated. The amount of modification may also dictate that a completely new item be written. Data would then have to be gathered on the new item to assure that it functions properly.

The analysis of response patterns of multiple-choice items is illustrated here for successful-uncertified teacher samples with item data from a teacher certification test. These data, given in Table 1, represent the performances of 95 certified teachers who were judged by their principals or supervisors to be successful teachers and of 47 uncertified teachers in a teacher training program at a nearby university.

Table 1

Illustrative Successful-Uncertified Teacher Groups Item Data for Choice Response Analysis

Item	Group	Response Choice					Omits	Total
		A*	B	C	D	E		
56	Successful	88	3	0	4	0	0	95
	Uncertified	29	8	1	6	3	0	47
	Total	117	11	1	10	3	0	142

* Correct Answer

The item has a discrimination index of $+.31$ and difficulty indices of 93% and 62% for the successful and uncertified groups, respectively. Distractors (C) and (E) are clearly ineffective for the uncertified teachers. One or both distractors should be replaced with plausible ones. Although better distractors probably will not markedly affect the responses of the successful teachers, it is inefficient and psychometrically unsound to use nonfunctioning choices in an item. Depending on the structural quality of the revised item, a decision can then be made to retain or discard it. The current item statistics point toward including the item in the final version of the test.

A Posteriori Analysis for Bias

As a follow-up analysis to an item bias study, it is necessary to examine each item detected by the statistical procedure. The statistical methods suggested previously can flag items that exhibit performance discrepancies between the sexes or between racial or ethnic subgroups. Further scrutiny is required to answer these questions: What contributed to the performance discrepancy? Why did the discrepancy occur? Is the item or some part of it truly biased against one group, or was the discrepancy in performance a statistical artifact? Can the source of the bias be eliminated?

These questions indicate that bias can only be inferred from the statistical results and a subsequent judgmental or logical analysis of the items. Bias is not an objectively measured component of an item. Scheuneman (1982) has hypothesized four features of items or tests that can produce performance discrepancies in an item bias study: "(1) flaws that may result from inadequacies or ambiguities of the test instructions, the item stem, the keyed response, or one of the distractors; (2) flaws that cause one or more of the options of an item (correct or incorrect) to be differentially attractive to members of different groups; (3) item features that reflect real differences between groups other than ethnicity; and (4) item features that directly reflect group differences in cultural characteristics or values" (p. 195).

The first category of flaws was addressed earlier in the item analysis process by eliciting teacher feedback on the items and test structure and by the choice response analysis to guide item revision. The second category, however, is derived from a different data base, the choice responses of the sexes or of ethnic subgroups, not of the criterion teacher groups. A distractor analysis using groups of, for example, blacks and whites, can reveal whether one group is attracted to a particular distractor while another group is drawn to other distractors.

Several statistical procedures for the analysis of distractors have been proposed in an attempt to identify not only biased items, but also the source of the bias, so that the item may be revised instead of discarded. Since the procedures have been described in detail by Scheuneman (1982), only one method, recommended by Veale and Foreman (1983), is presented here (see Table 2).

Table 2

Illustrative Racial Group Item Data (percentage form) for Distractor Analysis of Bias*

		Response Choice(%)				
Item	Group	A	B	C	D[+]	DIFF
17 (unbiased)[a]	black	11	14	75	-	45
	white	13	7	80	-	60
32 (biased)[b]	black	21	61	18	-	33
	white	40	57	3	-	70

* Adapted from Scheuneman (1982, p. 190, Table 7.2).
+ Correct answer
[a] $x^2 = 4.92$ (*n.s.*)
[b] $x^2 = 28.73$ ($p < .01$)

For the two items in Table 2, choice response frequencies were tallied for each group, a chi-square test of significance was computed for the group X response choice (2 X 3) contingency table, and then the frequencies were expressed as percentages of individuals choosing each wrong answer.

The results for item 17 indicate relatively consistent distractor attractiveness for both blacks and whites, which is confirmed by a nonsignificant chi-square. In contrast are the differing patterns of distractor attractiveness in item 32. These patterns yielded a significant chi-square. Distractor (C) seems to be considerably more attractive to blacks than to whites, although distractor (B) is pulling more blacks away from the correct answer (D). An examination of these choices in conjunction with correct responses should suggest the specific type of item revision needed.

The other item features mentioned by Scheuneman (1982) that can reflect group differences can be identified only by a carefully planned, systematic item review. She even cautions against too great a reliance on distractor data because they *can* be misleading. The complex and time-consuming tasks involved in an a posteriori analysis should not be underestimated. Scheuneman's (1982) nuts-and-bolts description of one phase of the analysis illustrates this complexity:

> Examine the items, singly or in groups, looking for item flaws and clues suggesting plausible explanations for the differences found and using the conventional item statistics where they may be helpful. Try to find patterns of differences that may support or disprove some of the possible explanations or that may suggest new hypotheses concerning the differences. Do not expect to find an explanation or hypothesis concerning the differences. Do not expect to find an explanation or hypothesis to account for all items. Remember that it is almost certain that some items have been incorrectly classified as biased, and the proportion of such items can be quite high depending on sample size and the decision rules used for selecting biased items (p. 196).

RECOMMENDATIONS

The framework for executing an item analysis for a teacher certification test consists of four phases: (1) a judgmental review, (2) whole-item statistical analyses, (3) a judgmental review of statistical results, and (4) part-item statistical analyses. The specific procedures in each phase may differ according to the particular test being developed and the decisions for which the scores will be used. The following is a summary of the recommended guidelines:

1. The judgmental reviews of the items for item-skill congruence and content bias should be performed by specially formed teacher panels.

    a. Appropriate content specialists should review the items in relation to the skill domain specifications to determine whether they are valid measures of those skills. Any discrepancies should be corrected.

b. Teachers who are representative of the different subpopulations (e.g., males, females, blacks, whites, Hispanics) should evaluate the items for content bias. Any language in an item that is stereotypic, culture specific, or offensive to a particular sex, race, or ethnic subpopulation should be removed. Attention should also be given to the characteristics of the persons and situations described in the items to assure fair representation in the work roles and life-styles of various groups, especially those of females and minorities.

2. Criterion successful and uncertified samples of teachers should be selected for the field test.

3. The test should be administered to both groups if possible. Immediately following the administration, teacher feedback on the items and test structure should be elicited.

4. Whole-item statistics such as difficulty and discrimination indices should be computed. An analysis of the results should indicate which items should be accepted, revised, or discarded.

5. An item bias study should be planned using a true experimental design, quasi-experimental design, or a statistical method that accounts for ability differences between groups.

6. Part-item statistical analysis should be considered for both criterion groups and for the sexes and the ethnic groups involved in the statistical item bias study. The analyses should focus on the revision or elimination of faulty and biased items.

7. The items that survive the scrutiny of the preceding six steps should be assembled into the final test. All improvements and changes undertaken as a result of the item validation should be incorporated into this version of the test.

Footnotes

1. If a teacher certification test is developed using either the one-parameter (Rasch) or the three-parameter logistic model, the special requirements for computing the discrimination indices, such as sample size, model assumptions, and computer program, suggest that this item analysis procedure should not be conducted in isolation. For example, test items that are calibrated on a Rasch scale should be evaluated statistically for characteristics other than discrimination power, especially sex and racial bias (see Ironson, 1982). A series of analyses of item difficulty, discrimination, and bias based on the same logistic model can serve to justify those requirements and the expenses involved, as well as provide useful data to evaluate item validity.

References

AERA/APA/NCME Joint Committee. (in press). *Standards for educational and psychological testing*. Washington, DC: American Psychological Association. (Quotations based on November 1, 1984 Final Report).

Angoff, W. H. (1982). Use of difficulty and discrimination indices for detecting item bias. In R. A. Berk (Ed.), *Handbook of methods for detecting test bias* (pp. 96-116). Baltimore, MD: Johns Hopkins University Press.

Berk, R. A. (1984). Conducting the item analysis. In R. A. Berk (Ed.), *A guide to criterion-referenced test construction* (pp. 97-143). Baltimore, MD: Johns Hopkins University Press.

Bridgman, A. (1985). States launching barrage of initiatives, survey finds. *Education Week, 4*(20), 1, 11-31.

Burrill, L. E. (1982). Comparative studies of item bias methods. In R. A. Berk (Ed.), *Handbook of methods for detecting test bias* (pp. 161-179). Baltimore, MD: Johns Hopkins University Press.

Cordes, C. (1985). ETS to reweigh test items' racial bias. *APA Monitor, 16*(2), 26, 28.

Glaser, R. (1963). Instructional technology and the measurement of learning outcomes: Some questions. *American Psychologist, 18*, 519-521.

Golden Rule Insurance Co. et al. v. Washburn, et al. (1984, November). 419-76 (7th Cir., Ill.), out-of-court settlement.

Hambleton, R. K. (1980, April). *Review methods for criterion-referenced test items*. Paper presented at the annual meeting of the American Educational Research Association, Boston, MA.

Hambleton, R. K. (1984). Validating the test scores. In R. A. Berk (Ed.), *A guide to criterion-referenced test construction* (pp. 199-230). Baltimore, MD: Johns Hopkins University Press.

Hattie, J., & Cooksey, R. W. (1984). Procedures for assessing the validities of tests using the "known-groups" method. *Applied Psychological Measurement, 8,* 295-305.

Ironson, G. H. (1982). Use of chi-square and latent trait approaches for detecting item bias. In R. A. Berk (Ed.), *Handbook of methods for detecting test bias* (pp. 117-160). Baltimore, MD: Johns Hopkins University Press.

Pine, S. M. (1977, March). Applications of item characteristic curve theory to the problem of test bias. In D. J. Weiss (Ed.), *Applications of computerized adaptive testing* (RR 77-1, pp. 37-43). Minneapolis: University of Minnesota, Department of Psychology, Psychometric Methods Program.

Scheuneman, J. D. (1979). A new method of assessing bias in test items. *Journal of Educational Measurement, 16,* 143-152.

Scheuneman, J. D. (1982). A posteriori analyses of biased items. In R. A. Berk (Ed.), *Handbook of methods for detecting test bias* (pp. 80-98). Baltimore, MD: Johns Hopkins University Press.

Schmeiser, C. B. (1982). Use of experimental design in statistical item bias studies. In R. A. Berk (Ed.), *Handbook of methods for detecting test bias* (pp. 64-95). Baltimore, MD: Johns Hopkins University Press.

Tittle, C. K. (1982). Use of judgmental methods in item bias studies. In R. A. Berk (Ed.), *Handbook of methods for detecting test bias* (pp. 31-63). Baltimore, MD: Johns Hopkins University Press.

van der Linden, W. J. (1981). A latent trait look at pretest-posttest validation of criterion-referenced test items. *Review of Educational Research, 51,* 379-402.

Veale, J. R., & Foreman, D. I. (1983). Assessing cultural bias using foil response data: Cultural variation. *Journal of Educational Measurement, 20,* 249-258.

Policy Issues in Standard Setting for Professional Licensing Tests

Richard M. Jaeger

The call for increased reliance on formal assessment methods in the certification of beginning teachers is a common theme of the reports produced by recent commissions on the so-called crisis in education. Reports include those of the National Commission on Excellence in Education (1983), the Carnegie Foundation for the Advancement of Teaching (Boyer, 1983), and the Education Commission of the States' Task Force on Education for Economic Growth (1983). As an example, the report of the Education Commission of the States, in Action Recommendation 6, implores the various states to "provide quality assurance in education," and more specifically recommends that:

> boards of education and higher education in each state—in cooperation with teachers and school adminis-trators—put in place, as soon as possible, systems for fairly and objectively measuring the effectiveness of teachers and rewarding outstanding performance. We recommend that the states . . . improve the process by which teachers and administrators are certified to teach and manage in the schools. They must establish higher standards to ensure that only individuals who are competent and well-qualified are licensed to teach and manage in the schools (p. 39).

The authors of the various commission reports were able to base their recommendations on a disturbingly rich storehouse of

Richard Jaeger is Professor of Education and Director of the Center for Educational Research and Evaluation, University of North Carolina at Greensboro.

supporting data. Weaver (1979) reported that students who majored in education, on the average, scored well below students in other majors on various measures of scholastic aptitude; he added fuel to the fire by concluding that there is little evidence to suggest that "education faculties sort out the academically weak students prior to student teaching or graduation" (p. 31). The 20-point decline in mean National Teacher Examination (NTE) scores over the five years from 1969-70 to 1974-75 was consistent with Weaver's assertion.

Giving prospective teachers a competency test is also appealing to the general public. A recent Gallup Poll (1979) indicated that 87% of parents of public school students believe that before prospective teachers are hired they should be required to pass a state board examination to demonstrate their knowledge of the subjects they will teach.

Testing for teacher certification is not a new idea. Indeed, the National Teacher Examination (NTE) program has been in operation since 1940, and Virginia used the NTE as a competency test for teacher certification as early as 1961 (Vlaanderin, 1982). However, the use of standardized tests for preservice and in-service assessment of teachers is growing in both frequency and complexity. Many more states use the NTE tests or the kinds of tailored criterion-referenced tests developed by National Evaluation Systems than did so a decade ago. In fact, over half the states that use tests in making teacher certification decisions began to do so during the 1980s (Rubinstein, McDonough, & Allan, 1982; Vlaanderin, 1982).

Many more states have installed multistage assessment procedures for screening would-be classroom teachers. The Teacher Quality Assessment Program developed by North Carolina is representative of these latter movements. To become eligible for renewable certification as a public school teacher in North Carolina, a college sophomore must jump three assessment hurdles. First, to enter a state-approved teacher education program, the student must earn passing scores on the General Knowledge and Communication Skills tests of the NTE. Second, to gain provisional two-year certification as a beginning teacher, the recent teacher education graduate must earn passing scores on the Professional Knowledge test and an Area test of the NTE. Finally, to become eligible for renewable certification, the beginning teacher must be judged competent in classroom practice by a group of outside observers.

Every use of an assessment procedure, whether for selecting students for teacher education programs, selecting graduates of teacher education programs for initial certification, or selecting beginning teachers for renewable certification, requires the establishment of a minimum standard of acceptable performance. The use of multistage screening procedures lends greater urgency than ever before to the need to choose standards rationally and defensibly. This chapter discusses some policy issues that affect these critical choices.

Because it is sometimes useful to consider the types of information one would have and the types of actions one would take in an ideal setting, this chapter first addresses those possibilities. Second, it reviews some of the real-world consequences of setting standards on teacher certification tests and the sorts of adaptive behaviors that might be necessary to cope with these consequences. Third, it suggests some desirable properties of standard-setting methods and the type of standard-setting procedures those properties imply. It should be stated at the outset that there is less than universal agreement on the properties of a good standard-setting procedure and even less agreement on the implications of those properties for effective practice.

Certification and licensing examinations serve a multiplicity of purposes. At best they protect an unsuspecting public from people who lack the fundamental knowledge or skills required to provide competent service. Certification and licensing examinations also protect prospective employers from people whose lack of knowledge or skill would preclude their effective on-the-job performance. And these examinations provide a tangible benefit to successful examinees; satisfactory performance conveys to prospective employers or to the public the ability to provide adequate professional service.

All of these benefits depend in equal measure on the adequacy of professional licensing examinations as predictors of future examinee capability and on the reasonableness of standards used to discriminate between those certified as competent and those deemed incompetent. If the examination is lacking in validity or the standards are inappropriate, the potential benefits of certification will likely be lost.

Standard Setting
In the Ideal World

If we were operating in an ideal world, we would have full information on the relationships between prospective teachers' performances on a certification examination and their later effectiveness as teachers. Teacher effectiveness would be operationally defined, more likely as a multidimensional than as a unidimensional quality. We would have identified one or more valued dimensions of student behavior, clearly related those dimensions to teacher effectiveness, and then constructed some utility function on the valued student behavior. An overly simple example might help to clarify this model. Suppose that growth in student performance on a particular achievement test completely defined valued student behavior and that growth could be represented on an interval scale—the sort of scale that results from what Benjamin Wright (1984) calls "fundamental measurement." In that case, it might be possible to secure agreement from the consumers of education (taxpayers, parents, perhaps students themselves) on the smallest acceptable growth in student performance over the course of a school year.

Next in the ideal world, imagine that we could state, either with assurance or in terms of a probability function, the relationship between student growth and the levels of certain behaviors exhibited by the students' teachers. We could then use that relationship to compute the lowest acceptable levels of various teacher behaviors. Finally, if our ideal world permitted us to relate prospective teachers' scores on a certification test to their in-class behaviors, again either with certainty or through a known probability function, we could compute the lowest level of acceptable performance on the certification test. The two sets of relationships could be combined to produce a function that characterized the relationship between teacher performance on the certification test and student growth on the achievement test.

Even in the ideal world, one would expect a probabilistic, rather than a deterministic, relationship between teachers' scores on the certification test and students' growth on the achievement test. Using the bivariate distribution of these variables, it would be possible to determine standards of teacher performance on the competency test that would result in any tolerable proportion of the distribution of students with growth below the lowest acceptable standard—from 0 to, say, 25%. The lower the tolerable proportion, the higher the required standard for teachers.

ARBITRARY STANDARDS

All methods of setting standards on competency tests have been judged to be arbitrary. Indeed, a distinguished committee of the National Academy of Education concluded that setting standards is "basically unworkable, exceeds the present measurement arts of the teaching profession, and will certainly create more social problems than it can conceivably solve" (National Academy of Education, 1978, p. iv). In large measure, the judgment of arbitrariness stems from the virtual impossibility of validating the reasonableness of a standard through any criterion that is independent of the standard-setting process itself.

Although it might appear that in describing the ideal world of standard setting, one arbitrary standard (the minimum acceptable level of student growth) has been substituted for another (the minimum acceptable level of teacher performance on a certification test), the ideal world would allow us to validate a student growth standard, and thereby eliminate arbitrariness. Economics would be the key to external validation.

VALIDATION OF STANDARDS THROUGH ECONOMICS

Market data could be used to determine the cost, in salaries and benefits, of attracting and retaining teachers with various levels of performance on the certification test. It is reasonable to expect a monotonically increasing relationship between teachers' test performances and the cost of attracting and retaining them. Research findings reported by Phillip Schlechty (1983) several years ago were consistent with this supposition. Schlechty investigated the relationship between North Carolina teachers' Scholastic Aptitude Test (SAT) scores and their longevity as teachers. He found a significantly negative correlation and concluded that teachers who earned the highest SAT scores were quickly attracted to more lucrative occupations.

By knowing the total enrollment of the schools and having data on the annual turnover of teachers in the state where the certification test was to be used, it would be possible to determine the total demand for beginning teachers each year. Since we have assumed a monotonically increasing relationship between the costs of attracting and retaining new teachers and their average score on the teacher certification test, the implied minimum teacher certification test standard could be used, together with these data, to project the total annual cost of attracting new teachers. This total cost could be compared to the total funds budgeted by the state and by local educational agencies for hiring and supporting beginning teachers.

Consistency between the cost implied by the certification test standard and the amount budgeted for employing beginning teachers would validate that standard and, in turn, would validate the standard set for student growth. If the costs associated with the teacher competency test standard were substantially higher than the amount budgeted to employ new teachers, the public's demands for student achievement growth would be inconsistent with its willingness to bear the related costs. Either more funds would have to be appropriated, or the student achievement growth standard (and the associated teacher competency test standard) would have to be lowered.

The ideal world of standard setting would allow the development of an explicit utility function, in dollars, for student achievement growth. By dividing the total cost of employing beginning teachers with a given mean certification test score by the number of students who would be instructed by those teachers, the cost per student of maintaining a given standard of achievement growth would be computable. The public would know what it was buying with its education dollars and could reconcile its demands on the schools with its willingness to bear their cost.

THE ROLE OF JUDGMENT

It is worthwhile to note that judgment would still be required to set a certification test standard in the ideal world as postulated. The principal advantage of the ideal world would be an economic feedback loop that reduced or eliminated the arbitrariness of the standard. In the ideal world of standard setting, one would have a simple, unidimensional definition of valued outcomes of education, and would know how inputs and outputs were related. Under those conditions, setting a standard on a teacher certification test would boil down to the old adage, "you get what you pay for."

Implications for Standard Setting in the Real World

Although things are not so tidy in the real world, the ideal-world model of standard setting can still be instructive. The adage on return to investment is still true, but the functional relationship is far more complex and, except in general terms, is largely unknown. Nonetheless, some useful observations can be made.

From the flawed analyses of the original Survey on Equality of Educational Opportunity (Coleman et al., 1966) to the work of the Far West Laboratory, the wealth of available evidence shows that the quality of teachers is the most potent determiner of the outcome of instruction. To be effective, certification testing programs must result in employing teachers who are more capable. In the absence of other actions, it is doubtful that setting higher employment standards will achieve this end. We must entertain the possibility that as a unitary action, setting higher employment standards will result in the opposite. If we provide no greater rewards for teachers, yet increase the cost and difficulty of entering the profession, we might well expect the best of potential teachers to seek more attractive alternatives. Sufficiently high standards without commensurate rewards will seriously upset the balance of teacher supply and demand. We have seen this happen already in secondary-level mathematics and in the sciences. Even in the real world, where we can't easily specify what we want from the schools, and the relationships between investment and return are barely understood, the realities of economics might reveal the inconsistency, and thus the arbitrariness, of test standards. In an attempt to gain better beginning teachers, we might raise the costs of entering the profession to the point where we have defeated our purpose.

TENTATIVE STANDARDS

As a practical matter, this possibility can be addressed by setting certification test standards tentatively and monitoring their effects on the size of the teacher education applicant pool and the size and quality of the pool of applicants for teacher certification.

One can expect market realities to force occasional adjustment of standards, and it might even be necessary to use different standards for some secondary certification areas, depending on the availability of candidates.

These ideas have been applied in other sectors of society, such as the armed forces. In the depths of the last recession, all branches of the military met their enlistment quotas easily and raised their standards accordingly. In recent years it has been virtually impossible for non-high school graduates to enlist in any branch of service other than the army. And even in the army, over 90% of enlistees last year had high school diplomas.

The Impact on Minorities

A second important policy issue associated with setting standards on teacher certification tests concerns the shockingly disparate impact of such tests on racial minorities. Cross, Impara, Frary, & Jaeger (1984) reported last year that more than 50% of the graduates of Virginia's five historically black colleges who applied for teacher certification since 1982 would have failed at least one of the three NTE Core Battery tests at the standards set by Virginia's State Board of Education. The corresponding failure rate for graduates of historically white institutions in Virginia was 3.1 percent.

In 1983, the Educational Testing Service administered the Professional Knowledge and Communication Skills tests of the NTE to sophomores and juniors in the 44 North Carolina colleges and universities that offer teacher education programs. The testing program was part of a standard-setting and validation study that was supported by the State Board of Education in North Carolina. The study led to the adoption of standards on both of these tests that have been applied to applicants for admission to North Carolina teacher education programs since July 1984. When the test performances of examinees in the validation study who identified their ethnic group membership as "black or Afro-American" were compared to the performances of those who identified their ethnic group membership as "white or Caucasian," it was found that 41.3% of the former group and only 1.7% of the latter group would have failed at least one of the NTE Core Battery tests. At the higher standards to be used by the North Carolina State Board of Education beginning in July 1986, 56.8% of black examinees and only 4.2% of white examinees would have failed at least one of the tests.

Findings such as these have profound social and legal implications. Although 30.4% of the students enrolled in the North Carolina public schools during the 1983-84 school year were black, black teachers accounted for only 20.4% of the public school teachers employed by the state that year. In all likelihood the disproportionate representation of black students and black teachers will grow substantially in North Carolina as the Teacher Quality Assurance Program, with its three-stage testing of those seeking teacher certification, becomes fully installed.

Although research evidence on the academic benefits to black students of having black teachers is decidedly mixed, there is clear and consistent evidence on the benefits of having strong and successful black role models. Since the schools provide the principal focus of such role models for students during their early, formative years, the sociological costs of greatly reducing the number of black teachers in the public schools are obvious, if not explicitly calculable.

LEGAL CONSEQUENCES

The legal issues associated with teacher certification testing are addressed elsewhere in this volume, and this chapter will merely mention a series of articles by Pullin (1982), Citron (1983a, 1983b), and Melvin (1983) that cite the legal consequences of selection tests having disparate racial impact. According to these authors, disparate failure rates by race provide sufficient basis for the courts to apply "strict scrutiny" principles in reviewing the state's use of any testing program as a criterion for admission to any education or employment program. Under such principles the primary obligation rests with the state, rather than with a plaintiff alleging racial discrimination, to show that use of the tests is valid, relevant, and free from racial bias in effect as well as intent.

How best to cope with test standards that have substantial racial impact is not clear. None of the obvious remedies is appealing, and some might even be viewed as racist. The practices of graduate professional schools notwithstanding, it is difficult to imagine a state adopting separate test standards for teacher certification applicants by ethnic group. Such a practice could ensure any desired ethnic distribution in the teacher workforce but would leave the state vulnerable to all manner of equity disputes.

Another approach would be to modify the certification test rather than the standards. The "golden rule agreement" recently reached by the Educational Testing Service and the Illinois State Licensing Bureau on the composition of the Illinois insurance licensing examination provides one model for reducing the disparate racial impact of a competency test. It remains to be seen whether it is possible to construct certification examinations that minimize differences in performance by race, without attendant losses in test validity. It is difficult enough to write test items that are job related, measure important competencies, and have acceptable psychometric properties, without adding the requirement that they have small differential difficulties across ethnic groups.

Some Desirable Properties of Standard-Setting Methods

It already has been noted that there is little agreement among measurement theorists on the most desirable properties of a standard-setting method. Both Glass (1978) and Shepard (1979, 1980) have asserted that competence is almost always more sensibly regarded as a continuous rather than a binary variable. Setting a cutoff score that supposedly divides examinees into two distinct categories—the competent and the incompetent—is therefore unrealistic and illogical. Shepard suggests that several standard-setting methods be used in every application, and Glass would have us abandon competency testing altogether.

Although they cannot agree on the relative merits of various standard-setting methods, measurement specialists do agree that standard setting is a judgmental process. Many contributors to the literature on standard setting have endorsed the conclusion reached by Jaeger (1976) that:

> All standard setting is judgmental. No amount of data collection, data analysis, and model building can replace the ultimate judgmental act of deciding which

performances are meritorious or acceptable and which are unacceptable or inadequate. All that varies is the proximity of the judgment-determining data to the original performance (p. 22).

Recognition of standard setting as a judgmental process stimulates several important and interrelated questions: Who should make judgments? How should judgments be elicited? Should judgments be based on information about tests, test items, performances of examinees, or a combination of these factors? These questions have motivated an extensive set of research studies in recent years. Many questions have not yet been answered conclusively, but the literature is informative nevertheless.

THERE IS NO "RIGHT ANSWER"

A great amount of early work on standard setting was based on the often unstated assumption that determining a test standard parallels estimation of a population parameter—there is a "right answer" and it is the task of standard setting to find it. Yet the observations of Glass (1978), Shepard (1979, 1980), and Linn, Madaus, & Pedulla (1982) clearly refute this view. If competence is a matter of degree rather than kind, there is no point on the continuum that will separate examinees into the "competent" and the "incompetent." A "right answer" to the standard-setting question does not exist, except perhaps in the minds of those providing judgments. This recognition underscores the importance of the questions listed above.

BEST POSSIBLE JUDGMENT SITUATION

What would the best possible judgment situation look like? Here are some descriptors: All persons who had a legitimate stake in the outcome of certification testing would be asked to make judgments on appropriate standards. Each judge would be fully informed on the nature of the certification test, the distribution of abilities of the population of examinees, the decisions to be reached on the basis of test scores, and the costs and benefits associated with failing or passing examinees with various levels of ability. The resulting standard would not be *the* right answer to the standard-setting question. But it could be regarded as the best obtainable answer, given the necessity of setting a standard by resorting to judgment. One could view the standard resulting from this best possible situation as a parameter to be estimated using a realistic standard-setting procedure. This conception might provide a basis for judging the relative desirability of various standard-setting methods, at least theoretically, if not empirically.

THE ANGOFF PROCEDURES

The standard-setting method that would probably come out first in a retrospective analysis of popularity was suggested by William Angoff (1971) in his classic chapter on scaling, norming, and test equating. However, Angoff has attributed the idea to Ledyard Tucker. In the last decade Angoff's procedure has been applied to countless competency tests, licensure examinations, and certification tests, usually in some modified form. A growing body of empirical research has suggested that the method produces reasonably stable test standards, at least in comparison with those resulting from popular alternatives. In addition, modifications of Angoff's method often result in standards that are politically palatable.

A PREFERRED MODIFICATION

The modification that I would advocate, based on the proposed properties of an ideal standard-setting procedure, my own research, and the research of others, would have the following characteristics:

1. Several types of judges would be asked to review a certification test item by item, after first having taken the test themselves.

2. The judges would be asked to choose, from among uniformly spaced values, the proportion of minimally competent examinees who would answer each test item correctly.

3. Reasonably large samples of judges who represent various interested and informed populations (e.g., experienced teachers and teacher educators) would be asked to provide judgments.

4. Judges would be given an opportunity to modify their initial judgments, after being provided with data on the actual test performances of a representative sample of the population of intended examinees.

5. As part of a well-controlled data-collection process, judges who provide both high and low estimates for an item would be asked to explain the basis of their recommendations.

6. Before computing a recommended test standard, judgment data would be edited to remove the recommendations of judges whose patterns of recommendations were inconsistent with actual examinee performance data.

A standard-setting procedure that had all of these characteristics would still be arbitrary, and the standard it produced might not be "right." But the standard would be based on the informed judgments of professionals who had several perspectives on the characteristics of a competent examinee and who had carefully considered the content of the certification test, the actual test performances of examinees, their own initial judgments, and the reasoning underlying the initial judgments of their colleagues. Perhaps in the real world of imperfect and incomplete information, this is the most we can expect.

References

Angoff, W. H. (1971). Scales, norms, and equivalent scores. In R. L. Thorndike (Ed.), *Educational measurement,* 2nd ed. (pp. 508-600). Washington, DC: American Council on Education.

Boyer, E. L. (1983). *High school: A report on secondary education in America.* New York: Carnegie Foundation for the Advancement of Teaching.

Citron, C. H. (1983a). Courts provide insight on content validity requirements. *Educational Measurement: Issues and Practice, 2*(4), 67.

Citron, C. H. (1983b). *Legal rules for student competency testing* (Issuegram No. 36). Denver, CO: Education Commission of the States.

Coleman, J. E., Campbell, E., Hobson, C., McPartland, J., Mood, A., Weinfeld, D., & York, R. (1966). *Equality of educational opportunity.* Washington, DC: U.S. Government Printing Office.

Cross, L. H., Impara, J. C., Frary, R. B., & Jaeger, R. M. (1984). A comparison of three methods for establishing standards on the National Teacher Examinations. *Journal of Educational Measurement, 21,* 113-130.

Education Commission of the States. (1983). *Action for excellence* (Report of the Education Commission of the States' Task Force on Education for Economic Growth). Boulder, CO: Author.

Glass, G. V. (1978). Standards and criteria. *Journal of Educational Measurement, 15,* 237-261.

Jaeger, R. M. (1976). Measurement consequences of selected standard-setting models. *Florida Journal of Educational Research, 18,* 22-27.

Linn, R. L., Madaus, G., & Pedulla, J. (1982). Minimum competency testing: Cautions on the state of the art. *American Journal of Education, 91*(1), 1-35.

Melvin, L. D. (1983). Legal aspects of pupil evaluation. In T. N. Jones & D. P. Semfer (Eds.), *School law update—1982* (pp. 89-116). Topeka, KS: National Organization on Legal Problems of Education.

National Academy of Education. (1978). *Improving educational achievement* (Report of the National Academy of Education Committee on Testing and Basic Skills to the Assistant Secretary of Education). Washington, DC: Author.

National Commission on Excellence in Education. (1983). *A nation at risk: The imperative for educational reform.* Washington, DC: U.S. Government Printing Office.

Pullin, D. (1982). *Minimum competency testing, the denied diploma and the pursuit of educational opportunity and educational adequacy* (CSE Report R-180). Los Angeles: University of California, Center for the Study of Evaluation.

Rubinstein, S., McDonough, M., & Allan, R. (1982). *The changing nature of teacher certification programs.* Paper presented at the annual meeting of the National Council on Measurement in Education, New York.

Schlechty, P. C. & Vance, V. S. (1983). Institutional responses to the quality/quantity issue in teacher training. *Phi Delta Kappan, 65,* 94-101.

Shepard, L. A. (1979). Setting standards. In M. A. Bunda & J. R. Sanders (Eds.), *Practices and problems in competency-based measurement* (pp. 59-71). Washington, DC: National Council on Measurement in Education.

Shepard, L. A. (1980). Technical issues in minimum competency testing. In D. C. Berliner (Ed.), *Review of research in education* (Vol. 8, pp.30-82). Washington, DC: American Educational Research Association.

Vlaanderin, R. B. (1982). Teacher competency testing: Status report. *Educational Measurement: Issues and Practice, 1*(2), 17-20, 27.

Weaver, W. T. (1979). In search of quality: The need for talent in teaching. *Phi Delta Kappan, 61,* 29-32.

Wright, B. D. (1984). Despair and hope for educational measurement. *Contemporary Education Review, 3*(1), 281-288.

Applications of Item Response Theoretic Methods in Low-Incidence Testing Fields

Hariharan Swaminathan

In any testing situation, whether it be achievement testing, aptitude testing, competency testing, or certification testing, the procedures for constructing the test, determining the proficiency level of examinees, equating test forms, and assessing item bias must be based on sound measurement principles. Classical test theory provides a general and well-established set of procedures for carrying out the various phases of testing. However, procedures based on classical test theory have several drawbacks in spite of their generality and wide utility. To understand the applicability of methods based on item response theory, it is first necessary to describe the basic features and shortcomings of the procedures based on classical test theory.

CLASSICAL PROCEDURES AND THEIR DRAWBACKS

The primary quantities of interest in a testing context are item indices that characterize the items that make up the test and indices that characterize the proficiency levels of the examinees. The item indices should facilitate the selection of items to be included in a test. Ideally, the item index for one item should not be influenced by the characteristics of other items in the test; if this happens,

Hariharan Swaminathan is Professor of Education and Psychology, University of Massachusetts at Amherst.

the inclusion or exclusion of an item will alter the characteristics of the other items, and it may not be possible to study the effect an item has on the test. Similarly, the index that characterizes the proficiency level of an examinee should be independent·of the set of items administered and also independent of the performance of the other examinees taking the test.

These requirements seem reasonable enough. Nevertheless, the item and proficiency-level indices obtained using classical procedures do not possess these qualities. The basic classical item index—the difficulty level of an item, or the p-value—is determined by the proportion of examinees in a group who respond correctly to the item. Clearly, the p-value depends upon the proficiency level of the group of examinees who take the test. The p-value will be high for a highly proficient group and low if the proficiency level of the group is low. The other widely used item statistic is the discrimination index, defined as the correlation between the item score and the total test score. A correlation coefficient, this index is affected by the composition of the group. The index will be low if the group is homogeneous with respect to proficiency level and high if the group is heterogeneous. Standard test construction procedures require that items included in the test be based on the p-values and the item-discrimination indices. The group-dependent nature of these indices makes this practice somewhat questionable.

Similar problems arise in the assessment of proficiency levels of examinees. Typically, the number correct score, or some linear transform of it, is used as an indicator of the proficiency level. This value clearly depends on the set of items included in the test. If easy items with high p-values are included in the test, the proficiency level will be estimated as being high. The opposite conclusion will be drawn if difficult items are included. This relationship between p-values and proficiency-level values does not present a major problem if a comparison of examinees is required. This is not the case in certification or competency testing, where accurate assessment of the proficiency level of the examinees is needed. In addition, this assessment must be comparable over years. If the same test is not used, comparability of the test must be ensured. Comparability is ensured if the tests are parallel (Lord & Novick, 1968), a concept that is difficult to implement in practice.

The precision with which proficiency level is measured is indicated by the standard error of measurement. Proficiency is measured with greater accuracy when the standard error is small than when the standard error is large. The importance of the index of the precision of measurement becomes apparent if the issue of certifying or not certifying is based on the proficiency level. It can be shown (Hambleton & Swaminathan, 1984) that the standard error of measurement is dependent upon the reliability of the test. If the reliability is high, the standard error of measurement is small, and vice versa. Unfortunately, the reliability of the test, being defined as a correlation coefficient, is dependent upon the composition of the group of examinees. Moreover, the standard error of measurement is an aggregate index over the range of proficiency levels. Since the error of measurement is different at different levels of proficiency, the aggregate index is not appropriate when it is necessary to assess the accuracy with which examinees at a given proficiency level are measured.

The index of reliability described above is a central concept in classical test theory. It is important that a test be highly reliable, partly because it provides an indication of the precision of measurement. Unfortunately, the extent to which each item that is included in the test affects the reliability of the test cannot be determined exactly. Hence, the decision to include or to exclude an item from the test may have an unknown effect on the reliability of the test.

These drawbacks—the sample-dependent nature of the item indices and the item-dependent nature of the measurement of proficiency, together with the sample-dependent nature of the measurement of its precision—make the classical procedures less than optimal. Procedures based on item response theory (IRT), on the other hand, remove these problems, but not without exacting a price.

ITEM RESPONSE THEORY

Item response theory (IRT) is based on the premise that the response of an examinee to an item is dependent upon the "ability" or the proficiency of the examinee. This relationship is formally expressed by the probability with which a randomly chosen examinee responds to an item; an examinee with a high proficiency level has a higher probability of responding correctly to the item than an examinee with a lower proficiency level. There is, thus, a monotonically increasing relationship between the probability of a correct response and the proficiency level. It is possible for the proficiency level to be multidimensional (i.e., to be made up of subcomponents, each reflective of skills that are needed to respond correctly to an item). Such multidimensional models have not been fully developed and, therefore, a basic assumption in IRT is that the proficiency level is unidimensional.

The next step is to formulate or specify the mathematical relationship between the probability of a correct response, the proficiency level, and the characteristics of an item. The mathematical function chosen to represent this relationship is based on convenience as well as appropriateness. For example, as proficiency level increases, the probability of a correct response must approach one. Similarly, for a very low proficiency level, the probability must approach zero. Thus the function must take on values between zero and one. If it is required that the function be "smooth," then a convenient mathematical function with the characteristics desired is the logistic function defined as

$$P = \exp(x)/[1 + \exp(x)]$$

where P is the probability of a correct response and $\exp(x)$ is the exponential function of x. Other functions for the probability are available (Hambleton & Swaminathan, 1984), but the logistic function given above is the most commonly used.

In order to complete the specification, it is necessary to relate the probability to the proficiency level, denoted by θ, and the characteristics of the item. An item can be described in terms of one, two, or three characteristics or parameters. The number of parameters used to describe the items indicates the nature of the item response models. If each item is described in terms of one parameter, difficulty level b, the item response model is known as the one-parameter model, or the Rasch model, named after the Danish mathematician who first developed it. The one-parameter model has the form

$$P = \exp(\theta-b)/[1 + \exp(\theta-b)].$$

Since exp(0) = 1, the probability of a correct response is 0.5 when $\theta = b$. Therefore an examinee with a proficiency level equal to b has an even chance of responding correctly to the item. If b is larger, then a higher proficiency level is necessary. Thus b can be referred to as the "difficulty level" of the item. For a difficult item, b is high, and for an easy item, b is low. Since each item has to be characterized by one parameter, the item response functions for the set of items are parallel as indicated in Figure 1 (a).

Characterizing each item using the difficulty parameter as well as another parameter known as the discrimination parameter results in the two-parameter item response model. This is given as

$$P = \exp a(\theta-b)/[1 + \exp a(\theta-b)].$$

The parameter a is an indication of the slope of the curve at the point $\theta = b$. A high value for a indicates that the probability of a correct response when the proficiency level exceeds b is very high; it is low if the proficiency level does not exceed b. Since examinees are discriminated sharply at the point $\theta = b$, the parameter a is named appropriately. Each item can have different a and b values and therefore the item response functions will cross each other (see Figure 1, b), unlike the situation with the one-parameter model.

It has been argued that with multiple choice items, examinees, particularly those with low proficiency levels, may respond to the item correctly by guessing. The probability of a correct response at low proficiency levels may be a value c and not zero. This parameter c is named the chance-level parameter and the item response function is given by

$$P = c + (1-c)[\exp a (\theta-b)]/[1 + \exp a (\theta-b)]$$

and graphed in Figure 1 (c). This item response model is known as the three-parameter model. It should be noted that when $\theta = b$, the probability of a correct response is $\frac{1}{2} + \frac{1}{2}c$ and not $\frac{1}{2}$ as with the one- and the two-parameter models.

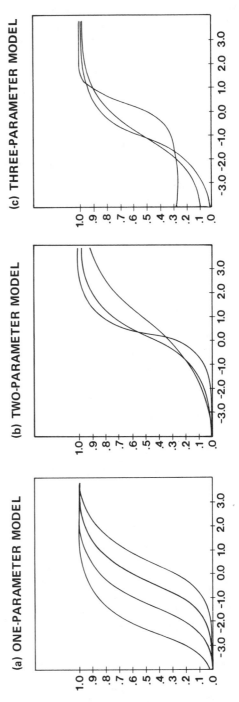

FIGURE 1

ITEM CHARACTERISTIC CURVES FOR THE THREE
ITEM PARAMETER MODELS

Features of the Item Response Models

In item response models, the quantity that is modéled is the probability of a correct response to an item. Once the proficiency level and the item parameters are specified, the function can be determined and the probability calculated. It is obvious that once specified, the values of *a, b,* and *c* for a given item are fixed and remain the same at every value of the proficiency level. In this sense, the item-parameter values are independent of the proficiency level of the group that takes the test. It can be argued along the same lines that the probability of a correct response can be calculated for each item and from this the proficiency level can be calculated. Once the item parameters are known, different items can be administered to different examinees and proficiency levels computed. This important property—the possibility of computing the proficiency levels according to the set of items administered to each examinee—makes the determination of proficiency level "item free." Construction of equivalent forms of the test for comparing the performance of examinees across different administrations is obviated.

The invariance of item parameters across different groups of examinees and the ability to determine proficiency levels that can be compared across examinees without requiring that all items be administered to all examinees are the two most attractive features of the IRT. The invariance of item parameters makes the study of item bias possible and the equating of test forms straightforward. Details may be found in Hambleton and Swaminathan (1984).

The Proficiency-Level Scale

As indicated in Figure 1, the proficiency level ranges from positive values to negative values. Although this is not a problem mathematically, the interpretation or the reporting of a negative proficiency level may raise problems. The proficiency scale, however, can be linearly transformed to eliminate the negative values. Alternately, the probability of a correct response can be calculated for each examinee. The average of the probabilities for each examinee results in a score that ranges in value from zero to one (except in the case of the three-parameter model where the lower score is the average of the chance-level parameter values). Multiplying this by 100 yields a score that can be interpreted as the percent correct "true score," or "true mastery score." Mastery or nonmastery decisions can be made by comparing this with a preestablished cut score. The interesting aspect of this is that the proficiency level of an examinee can be determined from one set of items. If the item-parameter values for one set of items are known, the probabilities of correct response to these items can be calculated and the percent mastery score on a second set of items can be computed, even though the examinee was not given this second set of items. Using this procedure, it is possible, if the need arises, to compute proficiency levels of examinees on tests given over a period of years for the purpose of making comparisons.

The Information Function

The issue of determining or estimating the proficiency level given the responses of an examinee to a set of items is clearly an important one. Given the statistical nature of this issue, it will not be dealt with in detail here. However, the precision with which proficiency level is estimated plays an important role in IRT and has implications for test development.

The standard error of the estimate of the proficiency level is clearly important in its own right. Once the standard error is determined, confidence bands can be placed around the proficiency level of an examinee. For example, the 95% confidence band is given as the estimate plus or minus twice the standard error. If the standard error is large, the confidence band is wide and is indicative of poor determination of proficiency level. If the standard error is small, the proficiency level estimated can be taken to be close to the true proficiency level θ. The width of the confidence band provides an alternate assessment of the accuracy of estimation of θ.

The reciprocal of the square of the standard error is an easier quantity to work with than the standard error. This quantity is known as the information function and denoted as $I(\theta)$. Recall that the standard error of measurement obtained with classical procedures is a quantity that is aggregated over the entire proficiency-score range and is group dependent. In contrast, the standard error or equivalently the information function in IRT is appropriate at each value of the proficiency level. The information function is therefore specific to each examinee and also not group dependent.

The information function can be plotted for each item. These curves are shown in Figure 2 for a set of three items. Each curve peaks at a different value of θ. Since the standard error is the reciprocal of the square root of the information function, a large value of the information function corresponds to precise estimation of proficiency level. This implies that proficiency levels are measured with varying precision along the θ continuum. An important consequence of this is that if the cut score for classifying examinees into masters and nonmasters is set at a particular value of θ, items that have information curves peaking around this value are the optimal items to be included in the test. Reasonably precise classification can be obtained using this procedure.

The item information functions can be added up to yield the test information function. The test information function indicates the precision of estimation obtained using the entire test. The important feature is that the contribution of each item information to the test information can be determined immediately because of the additive nature of the item information functions. This differs from the classical procedure where the contribution of each item to the reliability of the test and, therefore, to the precision of measurement cannot be determined directly.

The concept of test information function plays a key role in test construction. Based upon the nature of the decisions that have to be made and the degree of precision with which proficiency level is to be estimated, a target information curve can be constructed. Test information functions using different items are constructed, and the set of items that yields a curve that is closest to the target information curve can be taken to yield the desired test.

Assumptions Underlying IRT

The advantages of using IRT-based procedures over classical procedures have been noted in the previous sections. These advantages are the result of making strong assumptions. The two

FIGURE 2

**GRAPHICAL REPRESENTATION OF THREE
INFORMATION FUNCTIONS**

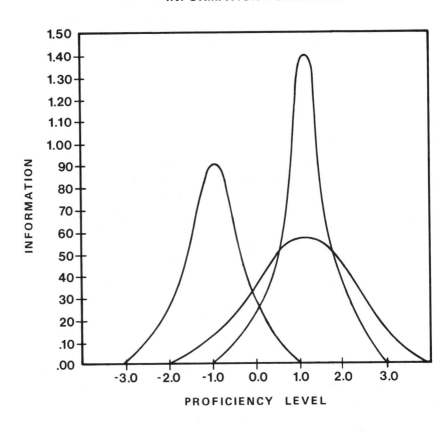

basic assumptions of IRT are: (1) For a given proficiency level θ, the responses to items are independent and (2) The item response function defined is appropriate for the data.

The first assumption—the independence of responses to items at a given proficiency level—is a strong assumption. It also implies in the present context that proficiency is unidimensional. It may happen in some cases that the response to one item depends upon the response to another, as in a reading comprehension test. The assumption of independence may be violated in such cases. Procedures based on item response theory are clearly not appropriate under such circumstances. The assumption of a particular form for the item response function may also present a problem, although this is slightly less critical than the assumption of independence. The appropriate procedure is to test the assumptions once the data become available.

There are several procedures currently available for testing the assumptions of IRT. Unfortunately, none of these procedures is totally satisfactory. Together, however, they may provide indications of the appropriateness of IRT (for details, see Hambleton and Swaminathan, 1984). In general, the methodology for implementing IRT-based procedures may be outlined as follows:

1. Construct a test using classical procedures as rough guidelines.

2. Administer the test to a well-chosen sample of examinees.

3. Fit the one-, two-, and three-parameter models. This is done by estimating the item parameters and, if necessary, the proficiency-level parameters.

4. Assess the goodness of fit of the models to the data.

The problem that needs to be addressed in implementing this sequence is the estimation of parameters.

ESTIMATION AND RELATED PROBLEMS IN CERTIFICATION TESTING

Once a particular item response model is chosen, the item and proficiency-level parameters have to be estimated before almost all applications. The problems associated with estimation are documented by Swaminathan (1983) and Hambleton and Swaminathan (1984) and will not be described here. Only the particular issues that have a bearing on certification testing are discussed in this section.

The basic problem in any statistical estimation problem is that of the sample size. In IRT, sample size refers not only to the number of examinees but also to the number of items in the test being administered.

The estimation procedure developed by Birnbaum (1968) is implemented in the LOGIST computer program (Wingersky, 1983). This is a commonly used program for estimation of parameters in the one-, two-, and three-parameter models. In the special case of the one-parameter model, a more appropriate computer program is BICAL developed by Wright and Mead (1976). The estimation procedure provided by these two programs is the joint maximum likelihood procedure.

The joint maximum likelihood procedure requires a large number of examinees and a reasonably large number of items. The procedure is used for estimating item parameters as well as proficiency-level parameters. Proficiency level is estimated well when a large number of items is available; item parameters are estimated well when a large number of examinees is available. With the three-parameter model, the number of examinees needed should be in excess of 1000, and the number of items should be at least as large as 50 (Swaminathan & Gifford, 1983). Lord (1983) has suggested that 200 examinees and 20 items favor the use of the one-parameter model.

The size of the samples indicated may prove to be a problem with certification testing programs. The number of items available for calibration may be large, but the number of examinees may not be proportionately large. The joint maximum likelihood procedure will not be effective in this situation unless the one-parameter model is chosen. Even with the one-parameter model a problem arises when the number of examinees is small in comparison to the number of items.

The alternatives available are (a) the conditional maximum likelihood procedure for the one-parameter model (Gustafsson, 1980), (b) the marginal maximum likelihood procedure (Mislevy & Bock, 1982), and (c) the Bayesian procedure (Swaminathan & Gifford, 1982, 1985, in press). The conditional and marginal procedures work reasonably effectively when there is a small number of items but a proportionately large number of examinees. The Bayesian procedure works reasonably well for the one- and two-parameter models with a small number of items and examinees. However, the Bayesian procedure requires specification of prior information on the items and examinees; this may not be feasible or acceptable in some situations. An alternate procedure is currently being investigated by this author. This approach involves a jackknife procedure that estimates a subset of item parameters and then uses the information to estimate the remaining parameters. The process is repeated until the estimates stabilize. Further results and research are required on this procedure before it can be implemented.

Another problem that arises in certification testing when the number of examinees available is small is that the performance of these examinees during pilot testing may not be reliable. Since nothing is at stake, it may be that the examinees do not take the testing situation seriously. This phenomenon may greatly affect the validity of the pilot test results.

CONCLUSION

In conclusion, it should be noted that item response theory holds great promise for a variety of measurement situations. It is clearly superior to the classical procedures when assumptions are met or are reasonable. However, in the case of low-incidence testing, as in teacher certification, the immediate application of IRT-based procedures may not be feasible. The classical test procedures are also not totally reliable in this situation, but since they do not involve strong assumptions as do IRT-based procedures, they may be more acceptable. The item response theory can be used when information is accumulated over a period of years. When this happens, item and proficiency-level parameters can be estimated and goodness of fit assessment can be carried out. Only under such circumstances can IRT-based methods be safely applied.

References

Birnbaum, A. (1968). Some latent trait models and their use in inferring an examinee's ability. In F. M. Lord, & M. R. Novick (Eds.), *Statistical theories of mental test scores* (pp. 397-479). Reading, MA: Addison-Wesley.

Gustafsson, J. E. (1980). A solution of the conditional estimation problem for long tests in the Rasch model for dichotomous items. *Educational and Psychological Measurement, 40,* 377-385.

Hambleton, R. K. (1983). Applications of item response models to criterion-referenced assessment. *Applied Psychological Measurement, 6,* 33-44.

Hambleton, R. K., & Swaminathan, H. (1984). *Item response theory: Principles and applications.* Boston, MA: Kluwer-Nijhoff Publishing Co.

Lord, F. M. (1980). *Applications of item response theory to practical testing problems.* Hillsdale, NJ: Erlbaum.

Lord, F. M. (1983). Small N justifies Rasch methods. In D. Weiss (Ed.), *New horizons in testing* (pp. 51-61). New York: Academic Press.

Lord, F. M., & Novick, M. R. (1968). *Statistical theories of mental test scores.* Reading, MA: Addison-Wesley.

Mislevy, R. J., & Bock, R. D. (1982). *BILOG: Maximum likelihood item analysis and test scoring with logistic models for binary items.* Chicago: International Educational Services.

Swaminathan, H. (1983). Parameter estimation in item-response models. In R. K. Hambleton (Ed.), *Application of item response theory* (pp. 24-44). Vancouver, BC: Educational Research Institute of British Columbia.

Swaminathan, H., & Gifford, J. A. (1982). Bayesian estimation in the Rasch model. *Journal of Educational Statistics, 7,* 175-192.

Swaminathan, H., & Gifford, J. A. (1983). Estimation of parameters in the three-parameter latent trait model. In D. Weiss (Ed.), *New horizons in testing* (pp. 13-30). New York: Academic Press.

Swaminathan, H., & Gifford, J. A. (1985). Bayesian estimation in the two-parameter logistic model. *Psychometrika,* in press.

Swaminathan, H., & Gifford, J. A. Estimation of parameters in the three-parameter latent trait model. *Psychometrika,* in press.

Wingersky, M. S. (1983). LOGIST: A program for computing maximum likelihood procedures for logistic test models. In R. K. Hambleton (Ed.), *Applications of item response theory* (pp. 45-56). Vancouver, BC: Educational Research Institute of British Columbia.

Wright, B. D., & Mead, R. J. (1976). *BICAL Calibrating rating scales with the Rasch model. Research Memorandum No. 23.* Chicago: Statistical Laboratory, Department of Education, University of Chicago.

Variations in Approaches to Assessment for Teacher Certification

Michael Priestley

Since the mid-1970s concerns about the quality of teaching in public schools have led to significant changes in the requirements for teacher certification throughout the country. An increasing number of states and school districts are looking at various methods of assessment that may help improve the efficacy of the certification process (Harris, 1981; Nothern, 1980). In some cases, state programs now incorporate competency-based, criterion-referenced tests and performance assessment for evaluating candidates seeking initial teacher certification. Dozens of other states have begun the process of exploring options and implementing similar changes; still others require candidates for initial certification to pass some component or components of the National Teacher Examination (NTE).

With a cry no less vocal than the call for teacher testing, some groups have protested that no examination can adequately measure the skills essential to competent teaching (NEA, 1982). This perspective seems to posit that most or all teacher competencies are intangibles—words that begin with capital letters such as *Patience* and *Enthusiasm*. Although it seems fairly apparent that no test composed of multiple-choice questions can suffice as the sole criterion for certification, it is also apparent that some form of content-based assessment is essential to ensure that candidates at least know the information they are supposed to impart in the classroom. Whether or not teachers can teach the content effectively becomes the subject of later assessment through different

Michael Priestley is the former Director of the Division of Technical Services, National Evaluation Systems.

procedures. Today, even the major professional organizations representing teachers, such as the American Federation of Teachers,
support the use of tests to assess the qualifications of candidates
for certification.

The goal should not be to eliminate assessment and leave
teacher training institutions on their own to monitor quality, but
rather to support the effort to maintain standards by improving
the tests and other assessment methods used to evaluate candidates
for certification. As a goal, this perspective raises some significant
conceptual issues that must be carefully considered.

CONCEPTUAL ISSUES

The first major issue to consider is when to assess teacher
candidates. Recently developed programs seem to indicate
agreement that prospective teachers should be assessed at at least
two of three different stages: before admission to a teacher training
program, upon completion of the program, and during on-the-
job performance in the classroom. A comprehensive program for
initial certification would provide assessment of teacher candidates
at all three of these stages.

The second major issue is how to assess teacher candidates
at each stage. On this issue alternatives abound, and agreement
founders.

In a comprehensive assessment program, the third major issue
to consider is how to conduct the assessment in a manner that is
technically and legally defensible. According to federal employment
guidelines, which also affect certification procedures, any
instrument used for licensing or selection must be a representative
measure of the actual domain of skills used on the job. An
instrument used for licensing or selection must also be able to be
validated for its actual or intended purpose (EEOC, 1978). In
addition, state and local laws that apply specifically to certain
programs or aspects of teacher certification must be heeded
judiciously. In many cases state legislation or a board of education
has provided the impetus for developing and implementing a
teacher certification program. For example, state laws requiring

competency tests have been passed in Florida, Oklahoma, South Carolina, and Texas; board of education mandates have been established in Alabama, Georgia, and New York.

The purpose of this chapter is to explore various approaches to assessment for initial teacher certification. Conceptual issues and the relative merits of each approach currently available are considered in relation to test design, assessment for entry to a teacher education program, exit certification, and classroom performance assessment.

ASSESSMENT DESIGN

Certification Areas

To a large extent, the first step in designing assessment instruments depends upon the structure of the state's certification program, that is, the definition of certification areas. One state may certify a teacher only in a general area called social studies, for example; another may certify teachers according to specialty: history, political science, economics, and so on. The definition of these areas will influence the number and type of assessment instruments required. In the example above, the first state would require only one general content-based test for the social studies certificate; the second would have to develop an umbrella test for social studies and/or a discrete test for each of six to eight specialty areas. The major reason for this is to ensure that each candidate is only held responsible for content essential to his or her field; for example, a person who would be certified only to teach economics should not be required to pass a test that includes sociology and geography.

The task of designing tests to measure a specific array of certification areas usually precedes, but often depends on, the determination of what to measure within each test. One important fact to keep in mind: tests should be developed or adapted to certification areas—not the other way around—in order to maintain the integrity of the state's own program design.

Domain Definition

Determining what to assess for admission, for initial certification, and for classroom performance involves defining domains of knowledge and skills for each assessment area. Assessing qualifications for admission to a teacher education program may involve an evaluation of the student's academic records or a test of basic skills, literacy, and communication. Exit requirements may involve another evaluation of the candidate's credentials, a test of content knowledge in a chosen teaching field, a test of pedagogy, or alternative assessments of various performance skills. Evaluating performance in the classroom may involve any of a large number of assessment strategies.

In the process of designing a comprehensive assessment program, the task of determining what to assess must precede or occur at the same time as choosing assessment methods. Basically there are two ways of determining what to assess.

INSTRUCTIONAL BASIS

One method of defining the domain is to identify the knowledge and skills taught at the college level. For example, a candidate for teacher certification could be tested on his or her knowledge of the curriculum required by the teacher education program. This can be a legally defensible method (*U.S. v. State of South Carolina Education Division,* 1977), according to the notions of "curriculum" and "instructional" validity, and it seems fair to test candidates on what they have been taught in teacher training. This approach may not be fair to students in the public school classroom, however, because it assumes that colleges train teachers in what they need to know in order to teach. What they need to know and what they are taught may not be the same.

JOB ANALYSIS

A second method of defining the domain—job analysis— solves this problem and lays the foundation for establishing that the test measures a representative sample of knowledge and skills required on the job, in accord with federal guidelines. In teacher certification programs job analysis has been used successfully in several states, including Georgia and Oklahoma.

Essentially, a job analysis—conducted by survey, observation, and/or interviews—generates empirical data describing what people do in their jobs, and thereby identifies the qualifications needed of a candidate who wants to be certified for that kind of job. In one approach to job analysis for teachers, skills and content knowledge are defined by behavioral objectives, which are rated by job incumbents (practicing teachers) in terms of job relatedness (i.e., time spent teaching or using the content of the objectives and the importance or essentiality of the objectives).

From the results of the ratings, the objectives can be ranked in an overall list or within subareas used to group the objectives in the teaching field. It is important to select the most job-related objectives in each subarea when selecting objectives for assessment. This ensures that the selected objectives reflect the proportional size of each subarea in relation to the size of the total job-related field. In turn, this proportionality provides an initial estimate of a blueprint or structure for the assessment instrument(s), which can be developed to reflect the relative importance of each subarea containing job-related objectives.

Using a job analysis to define assessment domains provides an empirical basis for developing the instruments. Nevertheless, a certification program in a given state should meet additional concerns. As the NEA (1982) points out, teachers must and should have considerable involvement in the assessment process. Among other roles, constituency groups can help to identify emerging fields that teachers may not teach now but may have to teach in the next year or the year after (e.g., metrics, the use of calculators); they can ensure that the assessment instruments serve the intended focus of education within the state; and they can ensure that the language and structure of the content is appropriate to the region (e.g., one state might teach the theory of evolution, while another might require a different approach).

Empirical information from a job analysis and expert judgments from teachers and other constituencies can provide the foundation for determining what to assess. The next step is to determine how to assess the competencies identified as essential for entry, initial certification, and classroom performance.

ASSESSMENT METHODS

Entry Tests

Assessment of qualifications for admission to a teacher education program usually occurs in the candidate's second year of college study, before entry into the program at the beginning of the third year. Traditional methods of assessing such qualifications have most often included teacher recommendations of the student and an examination of the student's academic record (grades, course requirements, etc.). However, programs in Connecticut and Alabama, for example, have abolished this essentially *pro forma* approach; instead, they require statewide entry tests to ensure that candidates have the basic skills (e.g., mathematics, communication skills, reading) required for some degree of success in the teacher education program. Another possibility for assessing admissions qualifications, recommended by Watts (1980), is to establish a professional standards board for admissions. This board would function independently of the training institutions, as similar boards now function in other professions such as engineering and architecture.

Of these three approaches, the most efficient means of assessing entry qualifications appears to be some form of entry test. Whether the qualifications are identified as general education (i.e., liberal arts) or literacy and basic skills, the entry test may involve assessment methods other than strictly multiple-choice, paper-and-pencil tests. The key is to decide what to test, then how to test it most effectively and efficiently. If entry qualifications include literacy skills of reading, writing, and listening, for example, then assessment methods must be capable of measuring the skills required.

Alabama has developed and implemented an entry exam called the English Language Proficiency Test, initially administered in November 1981. Its content, derived from a validation survey of practicing teachers in all fields, includes reading, writing, language skills, and listening. The chart below lists the methods used to assess these areas.

Alabama's English Language Proficiency Test	
Content Area	**Assessment Method**
Reading	— A cloze test of reading comprehension, using multiple-choice items with five choices.
Writing	— An essay test, scored by the holistic method.
Language Skills	— A multiple-choice test (four choices per item) of basic grammar, mechanics, and reference skills.
Listening	— A listening tape of passages read aloud, testing comprehension by multiple-choice items.

In addition to the state-developed programs, nationwide standardized tests are also available. One possibility is the Pre-Professional Skills Test, developed by Educational Testing Service, which includes sections on reading and math, plus an essay. This test is a norm-referenced instrument and does not provide diagnostic information to examinees or schools, but institutions may use it to assess basic skill areas for students entering teacher training programs.

Exit Tests

The next stage in the process involves an assessment of initial certification qualifications of an individual who has completed a teacher training program. Once the qualifications have been specified by job analysis or other method, a number of options exist for assessing these qualifications. Past certification procedures have been based largely on the candidate's completion of an accredited teacher preparation program (Hathaway, 1980). But this approach necessarily assumes adequate standards of competency enforced by each program and some relative comparability across programs in a given state. With the increasing concern for the actual competency level of teachers, fewer states are willing to assume the quality of teacher preparation programs; more and more states have implemented, or will implement, teacher competency tests for initial certification.

In most areas the essential competencies are content-based, and are therefore measurable by paper-and-pencil tests. For these areas states have the option of selecting and adopting an existing standardized test if it meets their needs, developing their own state-specific tests, or achieving some combination of the two approaches.

Basic or Professional Skills Tests

States often use exit tests to assess basic skills or professional skills common to all teaching areas. For example, Tennessee has used the California Achievement Test as an exit test of basic skills for all teacher candidates; many states have used one or more portions of the NTE Common Examination to measure general education or professional skills. In some states, colleges and universities develop and require their own tests of general education.

Other states, including Florida, Alabama, and Arizona, have developed their own instruments. Florida's Teacher Certification Examination, based on a list of 23 generic competencies, measures reading, writing, mathematics, and professional education. Assessment methods include a multiple-choice cloze test, an essay test scored holistically, and tests composed of multiple-choice items. Alabama requires that all teacher certification candidates pass a multiple-choice test of basic professional studies, which is based on a job analysis of practicing teachers in all fields. In addition to this test, candidates in Alabama must pass content knowledge tests specific to their teaching areas. In Arizona's program all teachers have to pass a multiple-choice test of general teaching knowledge and skills.

One important consideration in choosing assessment methods for professional education or pedagogy tests required of teacher candidates in all fields is to distinguish between content knowledge, which is measurable by paper-and-pencil tests, and classroom skills, which are not directly measurable by this technique. Professional skills required in the classroom should be measured during the performance assessment stage of the certification process.

TEACHING FIELD TESTS

States also use exit tests to measure content knowledge in the teaching field. Here again, states have several options for selecting or developing tests for this purpose. Choosing the NTE, which provides tests of some 28 specific areas, has its advantages and disadvantages. On the positive side, the NTE is relatively inexpensive compared with the cost of developing new tests. Also, it can be adopted and implemented in a relatively short time—an important factor if state law or mandate requires rapid implementation. On the negative side, adoption of the NTE can pose several potential problems. First, it has a pre-established set of teaching area tests available; therefore, a state must adapt its certification areas to the test and adopt some other method of certifying in areas not covered. Second, to conform to legal requirements, the NTE must usually be validated within the state in which it will be used (a process that can take up to three years). That is, the content of the tests must be compared and analyzed empirically in relation to state teacher preparation curriculum or to the results of a teacher job analysis. Thus, adoption is not as straightforward and unencumbered as it may seem. Third, the NTE provides norm-referenced scores comparing a student's performance to the performance of others or, in some modified programs, to standard scores determined within a state. The student receives a pass or fail and a numerical score, but (unless special modifications are made) no indication of strengths and weaknesses, information that could be extremely helpful both to the institutions and to the students who must retake the test.

An alternative to adopting available tests is to develop new tests, as several states have done, creating assessment programs to meet their own specific needs. Georgia began in 1975 and has since implemented tests in 31 different areas, all of them based on extensive job analysis and teacher involvement. Alabama has developed 45 area tests, which were administered for the first time in December 1981. Oklahoma has developed tests covering 79 different areas: 26 general tests for individual teaching fields; 8 umbrella tests for such fields as social studies, mathematics, and language arts; and 45 specific area tests, which must be taken along with the appropriate umbrella exam. Recently, Texas began work on what will eventually be 94 endorsement area tests.

Full-scale developmental efforts offer a number of advantages: the criterion-referenced tests are based on job analyses, the tests match the state's certification areas, tests can be empirically content-validated, and the test scores provide indications of strengths and weaknesses on specific domains within each test. In addition, teachers and administrators within the state participate in the development process, which ensures the relevance of the tests and helps instill grass-roots support for the testing program. The first disadvantage is cost: large-scale development projects can be expensive. The second, which only applies in some cases, is the time required for development. If done properly, programs of such magnitude and complexity require anywhere from one to three years for development, which may be a disadvantage if a mandate limits the time available.

Another alternative is to use existing tests for some certification areas and to develop tests for others. South Carolina used this approach, and other states are creating programs that reflect the unique configuration of their needs.

SPECIAL CONCERNS

Although these procedures for selecting or developing paper-and-pencil tests may seem relatively straightforward, a number of special concerns will arise during the process. The first, mentioned earlier, is the design of certification areas: general tests, special area tests, and so on. In a field such as special education, which has a number of specialization areas, this can be a critical and volatile issue. The second concern, also related to test design, is the need to provide subtest or domain scores. This provision requires careful design to ensure adequate measurement of knowledge and skills, not just within the test as a whole but also within each subtest or domain. The third special concern, related to assessment methods, deserves more detailed exploration at this point: multiple-choice, paper-and-pencil tests may not adequately cover the representative domain of content knowledge in some teaching fields. Although some special fields may be "low incidence" (i.e., only a few people are certified annually) and therefore relegated to local assessment programs, they must be considered first at the state level. Several examples here may be helpful.

The content knowledge required of a prospective teacher in music or a foreign language may only be partially covered by a paper-and-pencil test. Music teachers must also be able to listen to and recognize musical selections, proper articulation, misplayed notes, and so on. For this reason, both Georgia and Oklahoma have developed listening tests in music: examinees listen to tapes and then answer multiple-choice questions. Similarly, a foreign language teacher must be able to speak and understand the language; therefore, tests such as the NTE and those developed in Alabama, Georgia, and Oklahoma include language-tape tests. However, in most cases, speaking tests occur at the local rather than state level.

In vocational areas, on-the-job performance is often essential to the teacher candidate's preparation. The area commonly called "trades and industries" (T & I), for example, includes trades as diverse as cosmetology, tailoring, and diesel mechanics. Most states require a T & I teacher to be licensed and experienced within the trade he or she would teach; states may also require some amount of teacher training. Tests in the T & I field, as in South Carolina, for example, may include both a paper-and-pencil test of the generic skills taught in teacher training to all T & I candidates and an actual or simulated performance test of trade skills conducted by the colleges themselves.

In summary, these kinds of special concerns will undoubtedly arise in the development of a certification program. Efforts to accommodate them must consider the use of alternative assessment methods to measure skills that cannot be assessed adequately by strictly multiple-choice, paper-and-pencil tests; at the same time, efforts to accommodate special concerns must take into account the cost and practicality of alternative methods (Priestley, 1982).

Classroom Performance Assessment

The third and final stage of initial teacher certification involves the assessment of classroom performance, usually conducted while the candidate holds a temporary or "provisional" license or certificate. The goal of performance assessment is twofold: (a) to help the teacher improve his or her skills, and (b) to collect information on which to base an administrative decision about whether or not the candidate should receive full or "permanent" certification. Scriven (1981) distinguishes between the assessment methods appropriate to these two functions by identifying the requirements and benefits of formative and summative evaluation.

Achieving these goals demands that performance assessment be limited to competencies that teachers would be expected to possess as entry-level professionals, and it demands that the assessment methods provide fair, reliable measures of competencies determined to be essential. The first demand is a function of defining the domain of essential competencies, a process that may be based on teacher training curriculum or on job analysis (as stated earlier in relation to content-based tests). The second demand, for adequate assessment methods, requires a broader perspective.

As MacDonald (1973) reported, the state of the art of performance assessment technology was a "rather depressing picture" in 1973. Since then, however, considerable progress has been made as the demand for more effective methods has become more clamorous and persistent. Unlike assessment at the first two stages (entry and exit tests), assessment at this third stage does not include the option of standardized, off-the-shelf instruments. On the other hand, the methods available are numerous, and there are several potential models for performance assessment procedures. Most important at this stage is the development of an assessment that meets the specific needs of a state or local program, at the level at which actual evaluations will occur.

Medley (1978) constructively proposes six general alternative methods for assessing teacher performance, and Haefele (1980) critically reviews twelve (with considerable overlap among the alternatives presented). Millman (1981) examines a number of methods in depth, in relation to their use in teacher evaluation, and many of these methods can be adapted for use in assessment for initial certification.

Simply classified, the methods of assessment involve three basic types: observational ratings of the teacher (by students, peers, supervisors, principals, independent evaluators); training or simulation exercises; and testing of the teacher's classroom students (e.g., before and after instruction). Each of these categories includes a number of specific techniques, some more useful than others in measuring performance on specified competencies. For example, as Medley (1978) points out, Popham's suggested approach of the "teaching test" and related approaches involving pretests and posttests of the classroom students can really only yield overall averages and test scores. Although these kinds of data might be useful, they cannot be matched directly to specified teacher competencies. Similar to the situation with norm-referenced content tests, a total score on the "teaching test" (or students' scores) reflects how a teacher did but offers no formative feedback for improvement of specific aspects of classroom performance.

Programs designed to accomplish these purposes have been developed in several states. In Georgia, for instance, in addition to meeting the requirements of course credits and grades and passing a criterion-referenced teaching area test, the candidate undergoes performance assessment during the first year of teaching while holding a provisional certificate.

Georgia's teacher performance assessment instruments (Johnson, Ellett, & Capie, 1980) were developed to measure performance in relation to specific teaching skills which were identified through an extensive survey as both generic and essential to teaching in all fields. Five different instruments govern and provide for the assessment, as described in the chart on the next page. For each of the first four instruments, at least three trained data collectors (peers, supervisors, principals, independent evaluators) rate the teacher's performance on each indicator on the basis of a five-point scale.

It is important to note here that Georgia uses only the first three instruments for summative certification decisions; evaluators use the other two—student perceptions and professional standards instruments—in a formative manner to determine the need for in-service training and to create teacher performance profiles.

Instrument	Method of Assessment
1. Teaching Plans and Materials Instrument (TPM)	— A portfolio of instructional preparation rated by data collectors who also interview the teacher.
2. Classroom Procedures Instrument (CP)	— Direct classroom observation of teaching methods and practices.
3. Interpersonal Skills Instrument (IS)	— Direct classroom observation of the teacher's ability to create a sociable atmosphere and manage classroom interactions.
4. Professional Standards Instrument (PS)	— Interviews with the teacher, his or her colleagues, and supervisor to gather information on professional conduct (compliance with policies and procedures, participation in professional growth activities, etc.).
5. Student Perceptions Instrument (SP)	— A questionnaire filled out by students, composed of items parallel to those in the CP and IS instruments.

CONCLUSION

This chapter has explored a number of assessment options for initial teacher certification in relation to several conceptual issues. A basic tenet stated at the outset suggests that assessment should occur at three stages: before admission to a teacher training program, upon completion of the program, and during on-the-job performance in the classroom. Certification should be based on at least these three assessments and not on any one of them as the sole criterion.

Regarding the assessments themselves, the content or domain of what to assess should be defined carefully, preferably through job analysis and with extensive teacher involvement. Assessment instruments should then be designed and either selected or developed to measure the specified domains as effectively and efficiently as possible. Above all, since states' needs, teacher training programs, and qualifications for different teaching fields vary considerably, all assessment methods should be fitted to the specific requirements of a given situation. No all-encompassing solution exists for assessing competence in a profession of such importance, variation, and frequent change.

References

American Federation of Teachers. (1979). AFL-CIO *Convention resolutions.* Washington, DC: Author.

Equal Employment Opportunity Commission, Civil Service Commission, U. S. Department of Labor, & U. S. Department of Justice. (1978). Adoption by four agencies of uniform guidelines on employee selection procedures. *Federal Register, 43,* 38290-28315.

Haefele, D. L. (1980, January). How to evaluate thee, teacher—Let me count the ways. *Phi Delta Kappan, 61*(5), 349-352.

Harris, W. W. (1981). Teacher command of subject matter. In J. Millman (Ed.), *Handbook of teacher evaluation* (pp. 58-72). Beverly Hills, CA: Sage Publications.

Hathaway, W. W. (1980, April). Testing teachers to ensure competency: The state of the art. Paper presented at the annual AERA convention, Boston, MA.

Johnson, C., Ellett, C., & Capie, W. (1980). *An introduction to the teacher performance assessment instrument: Their uses and limitations.* Athens: University of Georgia, Teacher Assessment Project, College of Education.

MacDonald, F. J. (1973). The state of the art in performance assessment of teaching competence. Paper presented at the annual AERA convention, New Orleans, LA.

Medley, D. M. (1978, March-April). Alternative assessment strategies. *Journal of Teacher Education, 29* (2), 38-42.

Millman, J. (Ed.). (1981). *Handbook of teacher evaluation.* Beverly Hills, CA: Sage Publications.

National Education Association. (1982, January-February). A closer look at teacher competency testing. *NEA Reporter.*

Nothern, E. G. (1980, January). The trend toward competency testing of teachers. *Phi Delta Kappan, 61*(5), 359.

Priestley, M. (1982). *Performance assessment in education and training: Alternative techniques.* Englewood Cliffs, NJ: Educational Technology Publications.

Scriven, M. (1981). Summative teacher evaluation. In J. Millman (Ed.), *Handbook of teacher evaluation* (pp. 244-271). Beverly Hills, CA: Sage Publications.

United States v. State of South Carolina Education Division, U.S. District Court, Civil Action No. 75-1610, April 1977.

Watts, D. (1980, October). Admission standards for teacher preparatory programs: Time for a change. *Phi Delta Kappan, 62*(2), 120-122.

BEYOND REGULATION

On the surface, it is obvious that teacher certification tests serve to prevent certain unqualified individuals from entering the classroom. This is the regulatory function performed by such tests. In addition, however, many teacher certification testing programs provide a variety of benefits and support systems to individual examinees and to the educational programs of states as a whole. The three chapters in this section provide some evidence as to how a testing program can do far more than simply separate the examinee population into "pass" and "fail" categories.

Weaver's chapter describes the study guides that have been developed for the Oklahoma program and which are a fundamental part of the support system offered to examinees both before and subsequent to testing. The Baker & Fennell chapter speaks to how Alabama's English Language Proficiency program (used as a criterion for entry into teacher training programs) does far more than serve simply as a gatekeeper for individual students.

The Elliot & Stotz chapter discusses how test development and test results can be of major benefit in improving the quality of education in a given state. By providing diagnostic information to both examinees and the institutions that train them, the state can undertake a more widespread effort at educational reform, bringing teacher training programs into line with actual classroom activities.

Study Guides and
Their Effect on Programs

Joseph R. Weaver

One of the distinguishing features of the Oklahoma Teacher Certification Testing Program has been the ability to identify and find solutions to problems. Cooperation between the Oklahoma State Department of Education (SDE) and National Evaluation Systems (NES) has enhanced the development of creative solutions to the problems identified. An example of this cooperation is the development and implementation of study guides to help prepare examinees for teacher certification testing.

Program Goals

The intent of the SDE is that the Teacher Certification Testing Program (TCTP) do more than simply identify those teacher candidates who should be licensed and those who should not. One of the major program goals is that by preparing for and taking certification tests the candidates' knowledge of the content of their teaching fields will be strengthened. Another goal is that those who fail the teacher certification test (TCT) be provided feedback that contains useful information for remediation. The underlying perspective is that a failing score on an examination does not necessarily mean that candidates cannot become successful teachers, but that they should improve their knowledge of their chosen field before beginning teaching careers. That is, the candidates should review the subject matter and retake the test

Joseph Robert Weaver is Director of Teacher Education, Testing, and Staff Development, Oklahoma State Department of Education.

until they can meet the accepted standard established for a minimally competent teacher at entry level into the profession. Providing study guides for examinees helps attain the goal of strengthening the content knowledge of teacher candidates and is also consistent with the philosophy of providing useful information for remediation.

PURPOSES

The most important purpose of study guides is to help individual teacher candidates prepare for the Oklahoma Teacher Certification Tests. The guides are also used by faculty members and administrators of teacher education programs to assist examinees. Although these are the primary purposes of the study guides, experience has shown that they are serving other useful purposes. For example, students in teacher education programs are using them as guides to structure learning experiences in college course work before the certification testing process begins. Since the study guides were first published, students and college faculty members have had better access to information about the tests, particularly the test objectives. Incumbent teachers have also indicated an interest in the study guides as a method of validating the objectives of the courses they teach in the public schools.

Program Description

Development of the Teacher Certification Testing Program began in 1980 in compliance with the Teacher Reform Act of 1980, better known in Oklahoma as House Bill 1706. This law stipulates that a curriculum examination be developed in every area of teacher certification offered by the State Board of Education. Before being licensed, every person completing a teacher education program must pass the curriculum examination that covers the content of his or her teaching field.

The tests in the program cover 34 different certificate areas. "General tests" of 120 multiple-choice questions cover 26 of these certification areas. The remainder of the certificate areas involve a combination of an "umbrella test" and one or more "specific tests." The umbrella test measures general knowledge common to a broad field such as science and has 100 questions. The specific test measures knowledge of the content of a particular subject that is associated with the umbrella area, such as biology or chemistry, and has 80 questions.

Study Guides

Two types of study guides have been developed for the Oklahoma Teacher Certification Testing Program. The first is a generic guide that contains three sections. Section I provides general information about the testing program, Section II offers suggestions on how to study, and Section III gives tips for taking the tests.

The second type of study guide is more comprehensive than the one described above. A different guide has been developed for each of the 34 certificate areas. All of the guides of this type have the same format. The content of Section I is identical to the content of the entire generic study guide. Section II lists the learning objectives to be measured by the test or tests for a particular certification area. Section III provides one or more practice tests (depending on whether the guide is for a general test area or for an umbrella test area with the associated specific tests). The practice tests are identical in format to the actual tests and include an actual answer sheet. Following the practice test, an answer key is provided, identifying the particular objectives that each item on the practice test is designed to measure and presenting an analysis of why a particular response is correct. A sample study guide is appended to this chapter.

Background

The impetus for the development of study guides grew out of a concern about the pass rate of minority examinees, especially blacks. Following the publication of the first annual report of the Oklahoma Teacher Certification Testing Program (February 1983), the chairman of the Black Caucus of the Oklahoma Legislature contacted the office of the state superintendent and requested information about the test development process. A subsequent meeting between members of the Black Caucus, several black educators, and SDE staff members was held. This meeting focused on the relatively lower pass rate of blacks, and it was decided to search for ways to improve test performance. At a second meeting of this group, a representative of NES discussed the test development process, and issues related to possible adverse impact on minorities were considered.

An outgrowth of the discussions between the Black Caucus and the SDE was the appointment of a 21-member committee to study further the problem of minority test performance. Oklahoma educators, 16 of whom were black, comprised the committee. These individuals felt that, among other things, minorities had not had sufficient experience in taking the type of tests administered in the TCT program. Consequently, minorities lacked confidence as well as test-taking skill.

The committee established a set of objectives to address specific needs and concerns. One objective was to develop a study guide that would provide information about the tests, give some suggestions on how to prepare for the tests, and offer tips on how to take tests. The committee was concerned about providing as much help as possible to all examinees so that test scores would be indicative of one's subject matter knowledge and would not be affected adversely by lack of test-taking skills or lack of information about the tests.

Development

During the spring of 1983 the SDE staff communicated with the NES staff about the need for study guides. Together, NES and SDE developed an outline for the guides to be used across the 34 certificate areas.

During the summer of 1983 NES staff began writing the content of the guides. First, the material for the generic guide and Section I of the specific guides was written and approved by the SDE. The objectives for each test had been developed earlier in the testing program so they simply needed to be printed in the study guides.

The major task in the development of the study guides was writing the questions for the practice tests. When the preliminary writing was completed, the practice tests were presented to small committees of Oklahoma educators for their scrutiny. Individuals with expertise in the related certification area reviewed the content of each specific guide. Suggestions were made for changes in the practice test items and in the analysis given for correct answers.

Distribution

Following the approval of the practice test items, the NES staff formatted the guides and presented them to the SDE staff for final approval. After final approval by the SDE, 12,500 specific guides and 5,000 generic guides were printed in the fall of 1983. Offices of teacher education at state colleges and universities received the guides with instructions to distribute them to all teacher candidates who had registered to take the certification tests in December 1983. The SDE mailed guides to out-of-state registrants for the December administration.

Since this initial distribution, the SDE has continued to distribute guides to examinees through the institutions of higher education. The specific time and the procedure for this distribution are left to the discretion of each teacher education director. Out-of-state examinees receive study guides from the SDE at the time they register to take a test. College and university directors of teacher education are encouraged to provide a copy of a specific study guide to each faculty member responsible for instructing teacher education students in a particular field (e.g., a Mathematics Study Guide should be provided to instructors who have responsibilities in preparing mathematics teachers).

Directors of teacher education at state institutions indicate that faculty members are using the guides as resources in several ways. They use them to gain general knowledge about the tests, specific knowledge of the objectives to be measured by each test, and familiarity with the type of questions that appear on the tests. In this way faculty members are better able to assist teacher candidates in preparing to take the tests.

The popularity of the study guides has been such that a second printing in the fall of 1984 of almost 7,000 guides was necessary for some certificate areas. The SDE is distributing these guides upon request to colleges and universities as well as to individual out-of-state examinees. The cost of developing, printing, and distributing the study guides has been borne entirely by the state of Oklahoma. Examinees incur no cost for using the guides.

Effect

It is difficult to assess completely the effect the study guides have had on teacher education programs or on test performance by examinees. The information available consists of general impressions based upon observation of programs and anecdotal records from teacher educators.

From the SDE's standpoint, the greatest advantage of developing and distributing study guides may be the positive public relations that have resulted. The attitudes of both examinees and university instructors toward the teacher certification tests seem to be more positive since the study guides have been in use. Both groups view the guides not only as helpful for their own purposes but as reflective of an attempt by the SDE to provide as much assistance to examinees as possible. Several university professors and many examinees have expressed their gratitude in this respect.

Improvements in test performance as indicated by pass rates cannot be attributed with confidence to the use of study guides; many other variables clearly effect changes in test performance. It is a fact that the pass rate for examinees taking the tests for the first time remained constant at 80% for the first two years of the TCT program but increased to 82% during the third year of the program. The introduction of the study guides occurred approximately between the end of the second year and the beginning of the third year of the program.

In the three complete years of test administration the pass rate of teacher candidates from the one predominantly black institution in Oklahoma increased from 19% in 1982 to 70% in 1983 and to 80% in 1984. The 19% pass rate in 1982 is based on an extremely small number of examinees and is not an accurate indication of the quality of students at the school. Nevertheless, it is safe to say that there has been a marked improvement in test performance of examinees from this institution and that the use of the study guides contributed to the improved performance. Since the poor performance of blacks in general and of the candidates from the predominantly black institution in particular was the primary impetus for the development of the study guides, there is apparent reason to think that the effort and the expenditure of resources in developing the guides have been justified.

Conclusion

A generic study guide and specific guides in 34 certificate areas were developed in an attempt to address the problem of low pass rates for black examinees. The ultimate goal is that all examinees will be able to perform better as a result of using the study guides. Although research has not been done that would conclusively verify this judgment, it is reasonable to assume that the guides have helped improve test performance. The response to the guides by examinees and higher education personnel has been a positive outcome for the SDE.

References

National Evaluation Systems, Inc. (1984). *Oklahoma teacher certification testing program, annual report: 1983*. Amherst, MA: Author.

Appendix

A Word About the Study Guide

This Study Guide is designed to help you prepare for the Oklahoma Teacher Certification Tests. Education faculty and program administrators will also find the guide useful in assisting examinees to prepare for the tests.

This guide contains three sections:

Section I. Helpful Hints

Section II. Learning Objectives

Section III. Practice Test

Section I provides information about the testing program, suggestions on how to study for the tests, and tips for taking the tests. The second section provides a listing of all the learning objectives for the teaching field you have selected. The test measures a selected set of these objectives. Section III provides a practice test made up of questions similar to those which appear on the actual certification test, and it includes an explanation of the answer to each practice test question.

How to Use the Study Guide

To get the most out of this guide, you may want to follow these recommended steps:

Step 1.   Read the "Helpful Hints" section to help you prepare for and take the certification test.

Step 2.   Review the "learning objectives." You will want to study the material identified by all of the objectives to make sure you are prepared for the test. Reviewing the list of objectives first will help you identify those areas in which you may need to spend the most time.

Step 3.   Take the practice test, then review the answer key. The practice test questions are of the same type and format as the questions you can expect to see on the actual test. The answer key will help you understand the correct response to each question and how the question relates to a specific learning objective.

This Study Guide includes learning objectives and a practice test for the Mathematics, Algebra, Geometry, Trigonometry, Mathematical Analysis, and Calculus certification tests.

We hope you find it helpful for the test(s) you choose to take.

TABLE OF CONTENTS

SECTION I: HELPFUL HINTS

This first section provides background information about the testing program, suggestions on how to study for the tests, and tips for taking the tests.

About the Testing Program

In 1980 the Oklahoma legislature passed, and Governor George Nigh signed into law, House Bill 1706. The law stipulated that a curriculum examination be developed in every area of teacher certification offered by the State Board of Education. The purpose of the examination is to ensure that teachers know the subject matter of any area(s) in which they want to be licensed. Any person completing a teacher education program must pass the curriculum examination before being licensed.

About the Tests

All of the tests are criterion-referenced and competency-based. These terms mean that the tests measure the minimum content knowledge and skills defined by specific learning objectives. Your performance will be scored in relation to an established standard of competence required for teaching in Oklahoma; it will not be compared with the performance of any other group or examinee.

The program offers three types of tests covering 34 different content areas. Twenty-six of these certification areas, such as Journalism or Speech Pathology, are each covered by a single "general test" of 120 questions. The remainder of the content areas involve a combination of an "umbrella test" and one or more "specific area tests." The umbrella test measures general knowledge common to a number of related subjects, such as Mathematics or Language Arts, and has 100 questions. The specific area test measures knowledge of the content of a particular subject which is associated with the umbrella area, such as Algebra or American Literature, and is 80 questions in length.

How the Tests Were Developed

Each test area was defined by a set of learning objectives written on the basis of Oklahoma teacher education and certification standards and teacher education curriculum materials. Committees of Oklahoma educators reviewed the objectives for relevance to each certification area. Then 4,000 practicing Oklahoma educators participated in a job analysis survey to judge the importance of the objectives in each area, in relation to classroom practices in Oklahoma schools. Test questions were written on the basis of selected objectives using textbooks, curriculum guides, and teacher education and certification standards. Oklahoma educators reviewed the test questions, which were then field tested at Oklahoma colleges and universities before being included in the certification tests.

How the Tests Are Scored

Your performance on the test is evaluated against an established level of competence represented as the minimum passing score. Oklahoma educators established the passing score based on the minimum content knowledge required to perform successfully in Oklahoma schools. Score reports, which you receive about six weeks after you take the test, will tell you whether you passed or failed, how you performed on the test as a whole, and how you performed on each major content subarea included on the test.

Since the number of questions on different types of tests varies, all scores are converted to a scale ranging from 0 to 100, with 70 representing the minimum passing score. You must obtain a minimum overall score of 70 in order to pass the test.

If you take a general test or an umbrella test, you will also receive a score for each major content subarea included on the test. (There are no subareas on the specific area tests.) Subarea scores also range from 0 to 100, with 70 representing the standard for mastery of the content included in the subarea. You do not pass or fail a subarea; scores are provided for each subarea to give you an idea of your areas of strength and weakness for your use in preparing to retake the test or for further study.

Suggestions for How to Study

The most important thing you can do to prepare for the tests is to study. An effective study plan will help you do well on the tests. This section of the Study Guide suggests some specific ways to study for the tests.

Using the Objectives

The first step in studying for the certification test should be to review the learning objectives. Each certification area is defined by a set of learning objectives (see Section II); the examination in each area measures a selected portion of the objectives.

Each objective defines a "piece" of content you should know to teach in your field and the level at which you need to know it.

Example Objective: Identify methods of conserving natural resources

verb   content

As this example shows, an objective consists of two parts: most of the objective defines the content you need to know ("methods of conserving natural resources"), and the verb ("Identify") implies the level of complexity required. In this example, you would need to be able to spot different methods of conserving natural resources. You do not need to "invent" new methods or "evaluate" given methods to explain which would be most effective.

Read through the entire set of objectives first to get a general picture of the material that the test covers. For the general test areas and umbrella test areas, the objectives are grouped by major content subareas. The number of objectives under each subarea will give you a rough idea of the amount of emphasis given to each subarea. Subareas with greater numbers of objectives receive more emphasis on the test.

After you have a broad picture of what the test includes, read each objective carefully and determine what information you will be required to know and at what level you will need to know it. For each objective, make notes interpreting what the objective requires.

After you have familiarized yourself with the objectives, make a list of those subareas and objectives you feel you do not know much about. By identifying these "trouble spots" you will have a better sense of the areas you need to concentrate on most.

The best sources for studying for the tests are your textbooks and notes from your college courses in the test area. For those objectives which you do not have materials for studying, consult your faculty advisor or another representative from an Oklahoma teacher education program at a college or university in your area to find out what books and other materials are available to help you prepare.

Study Methods

There are many methods you can use to study for a test. You need to find the approach that works best for you. One of the most effective methods for studying is the "SQ3R" method. The SQ3R method has five steps: Survey, Question, Read, Recite, and Review. The best way to use this method is to divide the material you need to study into relatively small pieces, then study the pieces one at a time.

SQ3R

Step 1: Survey—Scan the material quickly before you actually read it, to get an overall sense of the content. Look at the title, headings, key topics, diagrams, and the like.

Step 2: Question—Formulate questions about the material you will be reading. Turn the title and headings into questions that can be answered by reading the material. Try to relate the questions to the learning objectives.

Step 3: Read—Read the material actively to find the answers to the questions you raised.

Step 4: Recite—After you have finished reading, recite aloud the information you have learned. Answer aloud the questions you asked.

Step 5: Review—Go back over your notes and the learning objectives, and recall the important points. Quiz yourself and see which areas you may need to restudy.

When you have finished studying one section in this way, move on to the next section.

Study Skills

No matter what method you use to study, there are specific skills you can use to help make your study time effective. Here are some suggestions.

- If you are reading material for the first time, you will remember it better if you preview the material—read the titles, subtitles, bold print, and the first sentence in each paragraph. By spending two to three minutes previewing, you will have a general idea of the topic you will be reading. You will have created questions in your mind about the material that the actual reading will help answer.

- To indicate important information, write out, underline, or highlight major points, definitions, and important details. Identify key words in each section to trigger recall of important points in the text. When reviewing material, you can use your highlighting and key words to see if you remember the information.

- One of the most important parts of studying is REVIEW. Review your notes on a regular basis. The greatest amount of forgetting occurs just after you read the material. By reviewing your notes soon after writing them, you will remember more.

- LEARN the material by being an active listener or reader so that the information becomes meaningful to you. This is the best way to retain information over long periods of time.

- After studying, summarize the material aloud, using your own words. You will remember the information better if you force yourself to summarize the main points and say them aloud.

- Invent memory devices (called mnemonics) or clues to remember information. For example, make unusual associations to help you remember facts—the definition of the word "olfactory" could be remembered by thinking of "old factory" and therefore "of the sense of smell." Compose rhymes—"Thirty days hath September, April, June, and November." Use acronyms—"FIES" might remind you of "Freud's Id, Ego, Superego." Use any devices you can to help your memory.

- When you know the test administration date, prepare a written study schedule for each week showing how much time you will spend studying the different content areas included on the tests. Schedule more time for those areas in which you feel you need more work.

- Be realistic in your study goals. Try to stick to the written schedule, but be aware that circumstances can interfere with your planned schedules. Try to reschedule any missed study times.

- Allow more study time than you think you'll need. You generally will use the extra time.

- Determine the time of day you study best, and plan your schedule to use this time. Study in blocks of time of not more than two hours; you will remember more if you space your studying over time rather than cramming all at once. Take a few minutes' break every 20 minutes or so to relax.

- Study in an area free of distractions, preferably the same place each time (so you come to associate the place with the task of studying). Have all necessary materials ready (books, dictionary, notes, pad, pencils). Make sure lighting is adequate and that you are comfortable, but not too comfortable.

- Reward yourself after studying. For example, you might decide that when you have learned the day's materials, you'll treat yourself to a dessert, a movie, dinner with a friend, etc.

Tips for Taking the Tests

If you use the study methods suggested in this guide, you should be familiar with the content included on the tests. However, factors other than your knowledge of the content may affect your performance; these factors have to do with your ability to take tests. This section of the guide provides several strategies to help you improve your test-taking ability.

Taking the Practice Test

One of the most effective ways to prepare for a test is to take a practice test. Taking the practice test will familiarize you with the format and the kinds of questions you can expect on the actual tests.

First, take a practice test for each area in which you will be taking a certification test. Work through each question and mark your answer choice on the answer sheet. As you work through the test, you should note, on a separate sheet of paper, the questions and answer choices about which you are unsure.

After you have worked through the practice test, check the answer key to see which questions you answered correctly. Analyze all those questions which you did not get correct and all those about which you were unsure. Read the explanation for each question and determine why you had trouble with any question you answered incorrectly. Evaluate the question carefully to see how you could have worked differently to arrive at the right answer. It may not be enough to understand what the answer is; you need to understand how to arrive at the correct response.

Test-Taking Skills

There are a number of skills that may help you improve your ability to take tests. Here are some tips.

- If you are prepared for the tests and you know the material, you should not be worried about the outcome. Be prepared. Study.

- Get a good night's rest before the test. Do not spend the night before cramming for the examination.

- The Oklahoma Teacher Certification Tests are designed to allow you as much time as you need to finish the tests. All testing sessions are three hours in length to provide you with plenty of time. If you plan to take more than one test during a testing session, you should budget your time more closely. Time announcements are made periodically by the test administrator, but you should plan to bring a watch to the test center. If you need more than three hours to finish the tests, special arrangements can be made for you before the testing session is over.

● You may need less than three hours to take the test, but you should be prepared to stay for the full three hours. You should not make any other commitments for this time period.

● Scan the entire test before beginning. Find out how many questions are on the test, and become familiar with the types of questions. This will give you a sense of the questions and how much time to devote to each question.

● Don't waste time preparing once the testing session has begun. Arrive at the test center on time so that you are rested and ready to begin the test when instructed to do so.

● Be familiar with the test directions read aloud and printed in the test booklet. If anything in the directions is not clear, ask the test administrator. You will have a few minutes to ask questions before the test begins.

● Pay careful attention to directions for specific questions. Read the directions closely so that you understand what they ask for. Do not skim the directions in an effort to save time; key words may be misread and lead you to select the wrong answer.

● Think through each question logically. Read each question word for word. Consider all of the answer choices. Do not choose the first answer which seems reasonable. Read and evaluate all choices to find the best answer to the question. Give careful consideration before going on to the next question, but do not spend too much time on any one question.

● When selecting the best answer to a question, do not read too much into the question. The questions are written to be clear and straightforward. They are not intended to be tricky or misleading. None of the tests include questions involving "all of the above" or "I, II, and IV only" kinds of questions.

● If, after considering all answer choices, the correct answer is not clear, eliminate the choices you know are incorrect and choose from the remaining answers. Mark these questions for review after you have completed the rest of the test.

● Always guess even if you cannot eliminate any of the possible responses. Every question will be scored right or wrong. Your test score is based on the number of questions answered correctly. You do not lose points for incorrect answers, so you will not be penalized for guessing.

● After you have finished the test, review your answers. If possible, check all responses. Do not be afraid to change your answer. However, before changing your answer, consider the reasons for your original answer.

● Check all answers to be sure that they are correctly recorded on the answer sheet. Be sure that your answers are recorded next to the number on the answer sheet corresponding to the question number.

If you use the suggestions in this Study Guide, you should be able to prepare yourself to take the Oklahoma Teacher Certification Tests. We wish you success on the tests and a rewarding career as an educator.

FIELD 27: MATHEMATICS OBJECTIVES

Subareas

General Mathematics
Geometry
Algebra
Advanced Mathematics

GENERAL MATHEMATICS

Identify prime, composite, cardinal, and/or ordinal numbers.

Determine the value of a given exponential number (including both integral and rational exponents).

Identify characteristics and/or examples of integers.

Perform one or more basic arithmetic operations involving integers.

Apply positives, negatives, and/or absolute values to solve a given problem.

Analyze the principles or uses of the commutative, associative, distributive, closure, inverse, or identity properties of integers.

Identify properties, characteristics, and/or examples of rational numbers.

Convert an improper fraction to a mixed number or vice versa.

Solve a given problem involving ratio and proportion (including standard and scientific notation).

Solve a given problem involving decimals and/or scientific notation.

Solve a given problem involving percents.

Solve a given problem involving English or metric linear measurement.

Solve a given problem involving English or metric area measurement.

Solve a given problem involving English or metric volume measurement.

Solve a given problem involving English or metric weight (mass) measurement.

Solve a given problem involving English or metric capacity measurement.

Identify a point on a graph given its coordinates, or the coordinate pairs of a given point.

Identify the X and Y axes and/or the quadrants of a given graph.

Interpret information from a line, bar, or pictograph.

GEOMETRY

Identify the undefined terms in geometry.

Analyze the use of sets and/or logic in the study of geometry.

Identify the sequence followed in doing a basic geometric construction.

Analyze procedures for constructing basic theorems or proofs.

Analyze the union/intersection relationships between a given set of points, lines, or planes.

Identify characteristics and properties of lines and/or line segments.

Identify sets and/or subsets of points, lines, or planes.

Identify units or techniques of angle measurement.

Classify a given angle according to its properties (e.g., acute, obtuse).

Identify characteristics and/or properties of congruent angles.

Analyze the relationship between a given pair of angles (e.g., adjacent, complementary).

Classify a given triangle according to its sides or angles.

Identify congruent or similar triangles.

Apply the Pythagorean theorem to solve a given problem.

Identify the characteristics of a given line related to a circle (e.g., tangents).

Calculate the measure of a given angle or segment related to a circle.

Calculate the area and/or circumference of a given circle.

Solve problems involving inscribed and/or circumscribed circles.

Classify a given polygon according to its sides or angles (e.g., concave, convex, pentagon, octagon).

Classify a given quadrilateral according to its sides or angles (e.g., parallelogram, rhombus, trapezoid).

Analyze the ratio and/or proportional relationships between given polygons.

Compute the area of a given polygon.

Classify a given geometric solid according to its characteristics and/or properties.

Compute the area and/or volume of a given geometric solid.

Identify the relationships between points, lines, and/or planes in a coordinate system.

Analyze a proof which demonstrates the coordinate method.

FIELD 27: MATHEMATICS PRACTICE TEST

1. $4\left[(-22) - (-23)\right] + (3)(-2) =$

   A. -106

   B. -10

   C. -2

   D. 10

2. If $\dfrac{x}{(7.28) \times (10^{-1})} = \dfrac{(5.0) \times (10^{-2})}{(9.1) \times (10^{-2})}$, then $x =$

   A. $(3.64) \times (10^{-2})$

   B. $(4.0) \times (10^{-2})$

   C. $(3.64) \times (10^{-1})$

   D. $(4.0) \times (10^{-1})$

3. $(6.3 + 0.832)(-5) =$

    A. -3.566×10^2

    B. -3.566×10^1

    C. -3.566×10^{-1}

    D. -3.566×10^{-2}

4. Use the graph below to answer the
    question that follows.

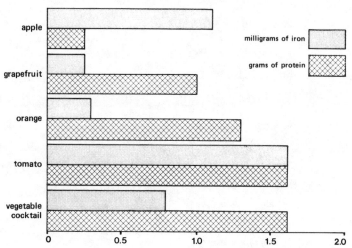

Nutritional Content per Six-Ounce Serving of Juice

Which juice contains the fewest
milligrams of iron in a 6-ounce
serving?

A. apple

B. grapefruit

C. orange

D. tomato

FIELD 27: MATHEMATICS PRACTICE TEST ANSWER KEY

1. Objective: Perform one or more
    basic arithmetic operations involving
    integers.

    Correct Response: $\underline{C}$.

    $4\left[(-22) - (-23)\right] + (3)(-2)$

    $= 4\left[(-22) + 23\right] + (-6)$

    $= 4(1) - 6$

    $= -2$

2. Objective: Solve a given problem
    involving ratio and proportion
    (including standard and scientific
    notation).

    Correct Response: $\underline{D}$. In a
    proportion, the product of the means
    equals the product of the extremes.

    $$\frac{x}{7.28 \times 10^{-1}} = \frac{5.0 \times 10^{-2}}{9.1 \times 10^{-2}}$$

    $(7.28 \times 10^{-1})(5.0 \times 10^{-2}) = (9.1 \times 10^{-2})\, x$

    $$x = \frac{3.64 \times 10^{-2}}{9.1 \times 10^{-2}}$$

    $x = 4.0 \times 10^{-1}$

3. Objective: Solve a given problem
    involving decimals and/or scientific
    notation.

    Correct Response: $\underline{B}$.
    $(6.3 + .832)(-5)\ =\ (7.132)(-5)$
    $= -35.66$
    $= -3.566 \times 10^{1}$

4. Objective: Interpret information from a line,
    bar, or pictograph.

    Correct Response: $\underline{B}$. Milligrams of iron are
    represented by the bars with the fine dots.
    Grapefruit juice contains the fewest milligrams
    of iron since its bar for that nutrient is the
    shortest.

The Alabama English Language Proficiency Test: A Criterion for Admission to Teacher Education Programs

C. C. Baker
Barbara Fennell

In 1972 the Alabama State Board of Education adopted a resolution that established provisions for improving the competence of those who teach by providing better opportunities and experiences in teaching at the preservice level. Following this action, in 1976 the board surveyed the state's practicing teachers in a study of teacher preparation programs. The survey results, along with other studies, were used to draft and recommend specific program admission, retention, and completion requirements at the undergraduate level for teacher education candidates. These requirements were subsequently adopted by the Alabama State Board of Education in March 1977 and became effective with freshmen beginning collegiate study as of June 1, 1977. For the first time a set of uniform, statewide minimum admission, retention, and completion criteria was adopted. In 1978 the board reaffirmed these criteria, creating an even more rigorous set of teacher education and certification standards.

Specifically, it had become mandatory that undergraduate teacher education candidates meet the following criteria before admission to a teacher education program:

1. A formal written application for admission to professional studies after completion of at least 60 semester hours or 90 quarter hours of work.

C. C. Baker is Assistant Superintendent for Professional Services, Alabama State Department of Education. Barbara Fennell is Teacher Testing Advisor for the Alabama State Department of Education.

2. A score of at least 16 on the American College Test (ACT) or 745 on the Scholastic Aptitude Test (SAT), the score not to be more than five years old.

3. A minimum grade point average of 1.2 on a 3-point scale or 2.2 on all college work attempted.

4. A passing score on an English language proficiency test approved by the State Board of Education.

5. Satisfactory interviews designed to provide information on the applicant's personality, interests, and aptitudes in regard to teaching.

6. Preprofessional experiences to facilitate a wise career choice.

Decision for a Uniform Test

In addition to the English language proficiency test, the standards also required an "exit examination," as it was called at that time. The selection of examinations or the decision to devise original tests was left to the discretion of each teacher education institution, but the selected tests were to be approved by the State Board of Education. It soon became apparent that wide variations in implementation existed for both the English proficiency requirement and the exit examinations. Teacher education institutions were clearly innovative in meeting the English proficiency requirement; implementation included everything from counting the examinations used in regular freshman English courses to the use of published standardized English tests. The approaches in implementing the required exit examinations were just as varied. It was within this environment that the board reached its decision to develop a single statewide testing program. The intent was to provide

- uniform, objective tests to eliminate the variation across teacher education institutions,
- tests that were specific to the previously adopted state standards, and
- tests that were developed with representative involvement of Alabama professional education personnel.

In January 1980 the board adopted a resolution giving approval for the Alabama State Department of Education to enter into a contractual agreement with National Evaluation Systems. This contractual agreement led to what is now the Alabama Initial Teacher Certification Testing Program. The major portion of the program involved the development and implementation of 35 teacher certification tests in content areas. The program also included the development of the Alabama English Language Proficiency Test as a criterion for admission to teacher education.

ENGLISH LANGUAGE PROFICIENCY TEST OVERVIEW

The English Language Proficiency Test (ELP) is criterion-referenced and measures specific competencies necessary for students' successful completion of course work in the academic and professional components of the teacher education program and for effective classroom teaching. It is diagnostic in nature, identifying the strengths as well as the weaknesses of the examinee. The test includes four sections: essay, listening, reading comprehension, and grammar skills.

Test Development and Validation

The Alabama English Language Proficiency Test was developed during the same time as the teacher certification tests and was developed using the same general procedures. The Alabama State Department of Education appointed a committee of educators whose specific task was to assist National Evaluation Systems and the department in the development of the test. The committee met first in October 1980 and was composed of seven individuals, representing classroom teachers, teacher education institutions (public and private), and the department of education.

The initial tasks of the committee were to review and refine a topic outline and an objective outline (prepared by National Evaluation Systems) related to English competencies needed for teaching. The committee was charged with the responsibility of changing, deleting, amplifying, reacting to, rewriting, and otherwise modifying the topics and the objectives presented in each outline. National Evaluation Systems provided the committee members with sets of criteria for their use in reviewing the topic outlines and the objective outlines.

JOB ANALYSIS SURVEY

To assess the job relatedness of the objectives, practicing Alabama educators were asked to participate in the job analysis surveys being conducted for the development of all Alabama teacher certification tests. In 1980 a stratified random sample of 200 educators in various teaching and instructional support fields received the English language proficiency objectives for review (other practicing educators responded to surveys developed for the certification field tests). Sampling factors included grade level, school size, and geographic area. Since the English Language Proficiency Test is not related to a specific certification area, the data were interpreted as a task analysis rather than as a job analysis, and the selected educators were asked to review the objectives in the context of a validation study. The data analysis was presented to the test committee in January 1981, at which time the final set of objectives was selected for item writing. Following the objective selection conference, National Evaluation Systems used item specifications and a test blueprint to begin the task of item writing.

ITEM REVIEW

A final conference to review the items occurred in March 1981 when the committee's task was to review and revise actual test items. Briefly, the committee evaluated the test items for congruence with their objective, for content accuracy, for measurement of a meaningful aspect of the objective, and for potential bias. National Evaluation Systems used the committee's reactions to each item to revise or replace any needed items.

VALIDATION AND STANDARD SETTING

The department of education then assembled a new and separate review committee, the Content Validation/Cut score Committee, to participate in a content validation and cut score process in August 1981. Members were selected for their expertise in the language arts area and were expected to apply their knowledge and skills to determine whether each item was a valid measure of a significant aspect of the knowledge or skill defined by its objective. The second function of the committee was to respond to each item for the purpose of deriving a preliminary minimum passing test score. The preliminary cut score data were applied to the examinees of the first test administration before the release of any score reports, allowing for needed adjustments in determining the final cut score.

NATURE OF THE TESTS

The test is divided into four sections: (1) essay, (2) listening, (3) reading comprehension, and (4) language skills. The total test consists of one essay question and approximately 150 multiple-choice items.

The essay section requires a sample of expository writing in response to a given essay prompt. The examinee has 40 minutes to write the essay, which is to be based on personal experiences and not on factual knowledge. The essay is written on lined pages within the test booklet, and there is no assigned length. Additional space is provided for the examinee to produce an outline before beginning the actual writing (the outline is not scored).

The listening section is 30 minutes long and requires the examinee to respond to a series of four or five multiple-choice questions related to each taped passage. The different forms of prose readings may include passages such as a play excerpt, an editorial message, a radio or television advertisement, and a newscast item. Professional media personnel record the taped passages for National Evaluation Systems. Examinees respond to the questions following each passage; they are not permitted to see the questions until after the passage presentation.

The reading comprehension section constitutes a series of ten to twelve cloze reading passages with several test items matched to each passage. Selections come from major published works and are about 200-300 words in length. For each blank left in the passage, the examinee is given a choice of five words. The passages are sequenced in order of ascending reading difficulty from Grade 10 through Grade 15.

The final test component, language skills, consists of fifty to sixty multiple-choice items related to grammar, vocabulary, study skills (such as using dictionaries, maps, and graphs), and life skills (such as analyzing advertisements or completing forms and applications).

TEST OBJECTIVES

Each teacher education institution has a copy of the test objectives. Colleges of education provide sets of the objectives to their students, or an examinee may request the objectives from the Alabama State Department of Education. Since the objectives on which test questions are based are readily available to the public, candidates can guide their preparation for the test.

Test Administration

The department offers the English Language Proficiency Test four times each academic year: in October, January, April, and July. Registration bulletins are available, and preregistration is required. Rules and regulations for the test are included in the bulletin. Examinees must submit the registration application and fee to National Evaluation Systems by the announced registration deadline; "walk-ins" on the test date are not accepted.

The 29 Alabama colleges and universities that train teachers administer the test on their campuses. Not all schools are test sites on each administration date, however. At least 10 examinees must register for a site before it is used, unless extenuating circumstances exist. For example, to accommodate the Saturday worship of a small Seventh-Day Adventist school, the test is given on the Friday preceding the regularly scheduled test date, regardless of the number of examinees. Otherwise, a school with fewer than 10 registered examinees may have its students assigned to another nearby campus.

The test is now scheduled on Saturday mornings for four hours. Originally, the teacher education institutions requested that the test be given on a weekday. The change to Saturday reflects several factors:

1. The chief test administrator, designated by the dean of education, is in the employ of the college or university. The administrator often had to make arrangements for his or her classes that were to meet during the test session hours.

2. Student examinees were also missing classes.

3. Institutions were concerned that they would be unable to find a chief test administrator and assistant test administrators willing to work on a Saturday. Remuneration of these individuals may have relieved that situation.

Test Scoring

As with registration, National Evaluation Systems scores the tests. The multiple-choice items are machine scored. Essays are holistically scored in Massachusetts by two readers with a third reader to resolve any score discrepancies. The readers are either qualified college-level instructors or certified high school English teachers. The holistic scale ranges from 0 (the essay is unintelligible or was omitted) to 4.

Of all sections of the test, examinees ask the most questions about the essay portion. In general the readers evaluate the essay for four overall qualities:

1. The topic has been addressed clearly and consistently.

2. The essay is organized into a logical sequence of ideas.

3. The essay contains complete sentences using the rules of Standard American English.

4. The examinee has shown an ability to select and use words appropriate to the ideas being conveyed.

Score Reports

National Evaluation Systems generates the examinee test score letters, the department of education score reports, and the college or university score reports within six weeks of the test administration.

Each examinee receives a score report letter stating that he or she has passed or failed the test. The letter states the overall minimum standard passing score and then gives the overall score of the examinee. Equal weight is given to each subarea in deriving the overall score. The score report letter also identifies the individual's score for each of the four subareas. The subarea scores give the examinee diagnostic information to identify his or her strengths and weaknesses, and are useful for remedial study if the examinee has failed the test. For examinees who fail the test, notification of the next test date and registration deadline is included. (See sample test score report letters in Appendix A.)

Each teacher education institution receives an alphabetized listing of examinees who requested that their score reports be sent to that particular school. The examinees are identified by name and social security number, and their total and subarea test scores are reported. The institution report also provides information related to the number of examinees in the institution and state and their passing and failing percentages. (See sample institution report in Appendix B.)

The department of education receives an alphabetical listing of examinees by institution, an alphabetical statewide roster of examinees with the total test and subarea information, a statewide summary score report, and the item analysis for each administration.

College and University
Use of Score Reports

The colleges and universities use the score reports in different ways. Some simply check the report to determine if applying teacher education candidates have met this criterion. Others undertake concerted efforts to help examinees prepare for the test. In most cases test score studies have been conducted on an informal basis. The following are representative of test score usage that occurs at some institutions:

1. Copies of the test scores are shared by the deans of education with chairpersons of English departments. Frequently, someone in the English department reviews the list of examinees to determine which students completed their freshman English courses at that school as opposed to students who transferred from another four-year institution or a junior college.

2. At one school, administrators studied aggregate student results over a number of test administrations. Information included comparisons between the school and the statewide pass or fail rates, a study of individuals who failed and their retake or nonretake performance, averages of the failed examinees by total test score and subareas, and the intended teacher education program of the failed examinees.

3. Test scores are often used by English laboratories on school campuses. The subarea scores are a basis for counseling and remedial work for retake purposes, although the examinee is often responsible for seeking assistance. Workshops are being included on test-taking skills and test anxiety as a part of the laboratory experience.

4. Using the test objectives, some schools are reviewing and amending course syllabuses to provide better coverage of all test objectives in the program of study for the teacher education student.

5. There is an increased emphasis on closer advisement of potential teacher education students. Schools are giving particular attention to reviewing an individual's previously earned English grades with the possibility of recommended remediation before the individual takes the test. At one teacher education institution administrators disseminate the registration bulletins with the test objectives included. A press-on label that names the English laboratory director and gives the phone number of the laboratory is affixed to the bulletin. A notice included with the objectives encourages the potential examinee to review the objectives and request assistance at the laboratory if the examinee feels there will be a problem with any one of the subareas.

6. The greatest concentration of remediation appears to be in the essay area. It also seems that schools have the most difficulty identifying and locating materials related to listening skills.

It should be emphasized that the list above reflects current test score use in a small sample of the state's teacher education institutions. Even in schools where there is little activity involving test scores, it would be unfair to assume a lack of interest. Rather, far greater emphasis has been placed on the study of the teacher certification test scores in Alabama because there is a distinct possibility that specific programs would be targeted for improvement.

Appendix A

ALABAMA ENGLISH LANGUAGE PROFICIENCY TEST
INDIVIDUAL TEST SCORE REPORT

Date Test Taken: November 18, 1981
Test Taken: English Language Proficiency Test

Examinee Number = _____

Congratulations! You have passed the English Language Proficiency Test which you took on November 18, 1981. Your score on the test was 83. The passing score is 70.

Questions on the test are grouped into major subareas. To assist you in further study, your performance in each subarea is presented.

Score	Subarea
85	Writing
75	Listening
90	Reading comprehension
80	Language skills

The results of this test have been forwarded to the college or university which you indicated at the time of registration.

ALABAMA ENGLISH LANGUAGE PROFICIENCY TEST
INDIVIDUAL TEST SCORE REPORT

Date Test Taken: November 18, 1981
Test Taken: English Language Proficiency Test

Examinee Number = _____

You have not passed the English Language Proficiency Test which you took on November 18, 1981. Your score on the test was 69. The passing score is 70.

The next test will be given on February 17, 1982. The deadline for registration for this test is January 13, 1982. Registration bulletins and objectives are available from schools of education at colleges and universities in Alabama or from the Alabama State Department of Education, Teacher Education Office, 347 State Office Building, Montgomery, AL 36130.

Questions on the test are grouped into major subareas. To assist you in further study or in preparation for retaking the test, your performance in each subarea is presented.

Score	Subarea
70	Writing
70	Listening
74	Reading comprehension
61	Language skills

The results of this test have been forwarded to the college or university which you indicated at the time of registration.

Appendix B

ALABAMA ENGLISH LANGUAGE PROFICIENCY TEST

TEST SCORE REPORT FOR STUDENTS APPLYING TO (COLLEGE NAME)

Date Test Taken: July 14, 1984

Questions on the test are grouped into major content subareas. The score for each examinee on each subarea is given.

The subareas on the test are as follows:

1 = Writing
2 = Listening
3 = Reading comprehension
4 = Language skills

Institution: 28 examinees took the test 20 passed (71%) 8 failed (29%)
Statewide: 651 examinees took the test 493 passed (76%) 158 failed (24%)

SSN	Examinee Name	Pass/ Fail	Total Test	Subarea 1	2	3	4
		Pass	85	80	75	99	88
		Fail	54	10	63	83	58
		Pass	78	80	70	91	72
		Pass	80	75	82	91	74
		Fail	66	70	62	69	64
		Pass	82	80	82	90	76
		Pass	80	70	82	97	74
		Pass	85	80	82	95	86
		Pass	95	90	99	99	94
		Pass	71	70	70	84	62
		Pass	79	80	82	91	64
		Pass	77	75	75	91	70
		Fail	60	70	36	73	64
		Pass	86	80	93	93	80
		Fail	68	70	62	83	58
		Pass	74	80	54	95	70
		Fail	55	10	82	67	64
		Fail	62	70	54	77	50
		Fail	67	75	49	79	68
		Pass	79	75	87	83	74
		Pass	79	70	65	97	86
		Pass	78	80	70	91	72
		Pass	75	70	70	97	66
		Pass	74	70	62	84	80
		Fail	53	10	65	79	58
		Pass	92	90	87	97	94
		Pass	70	70	70	80	62
		Pass	84	85	70	97	84
	Institution Average		75	69	72	88	72
	Statewide Average		75	71	72	86	72

Teacher Certification Testing: Beyond Regulation to Instructional Improvement

Scott M. Elliot
Joanna G. Stotz

More than 30 states now mandate some form of competency testing for initial teacher certification, and this trend shows little sign of waning. Although the regulatory function of testing in the teacher licensing process has been recognized, far less consideration has been given to the value of teacher certification testing in improving the quality of instruction. The purpose of this chapter is to describe how an ongoing statewide teacher certification testing program can contribute to instructional improvement.

Overview of Teacher Certification

Requiring candidates to meet an established set of criteria in order to teach is not a new phenomenon. In the early part of the nineteenth century, teachers were simply required to have basic proficiency in reading, writing, and arithmetic (Rubinstein, McDonough, & Allan, 1982). The advent of mass compulsory education in the late nineteenth century brought about an expansion of these criteria to include proficiency in pedagogy and other areas of professional technique as well as knowledge of the subject matter

Scott Elliot is Director of the Division of Licensing and Certification, National Evaluation Systems. Joanna Stotz is Manager of the Test Administration Department at National Evaluation Systems.

to be taught (Rubinstein et al., 1982). Although the emphasis, responsibilities, and methodologies for assessing prospective teachers have changed, these three elements of teacher assessment prevail.

Within the past decade there have been dramatic changes in teacher certification practices. With the increased demand for accountability in the educational system as a whole has come a growing concern over teacher competence. Hardly a day passes without an article in a major newspaper or periodical about teacher competence (cf. Maeroff, 1983; Traub, 1983). Perhaps the strongest voice is the widely publicized report issued by the National Commission on Excellence in Education (*A Nation at Risk: The Imperative for Educational Reform,* 1983). The report criticizes current educators, raises concern about prospective educators graduating from teacher training institutions, and calls for several reforms in teacher education including stepped-up assessment of prospective teachers.

Incumbent teachers and professional teacher organizations have been skeptical of increased assessment, citing problems elsewhere in the educational system (e.g., teacher salaries, school discipline). Yet teacher groups are increasingly supportive, with the American Federation of Teachers (AFT) and the National Education Association (NEA) coming out in support of a national teachers' test.

Regulation

This accountability movement has led to increased efforts to establish or redefine state-level programs for licensing teachers. Traditionally, the burden of ensuring the competency of prospective teachers has fallen on teacher training institutions; increasingly state government has come to play a role in this process through licensure. *Licensure* is the "process by which an agency of the government grants permission to an individual to engage in a given occupation upon finding that the applicant has attained the minimal degree of competency required to ensure that the public health, safety, and welfare will be reasonably well protected." (U. S. Department of Health, Education and Welfare, 1977). For teachers, the term *certification* is used to designate a license to teach. Although most states will continue to require candidates for licensure to successfully complete an approved teacher education program, more than 30 states are mandating some additional form of standardized assessment as part of the process (Education Commission of the States, 1984).

Tests may be administered at various points in the teacher certification process, typically at one or more of the following points:

1. Upon admission into a teacher education program.
2. Upon completion of a teacher education program.
3. During the first year of teaching.
4. During later years of teaching (renewal).

Although tests have been used to make competency decisions at all four points, most teacher licensing programs have focused on the first three points as part of the initial teacher certification process.

Teacher certification testing plays a major role in improving educational quality by ensuring that only those candidates who meet minimum established standards enter the classroom. However, the contributions of teacher certification testing to improved quality of instruction are certainly not limited to "screening out" not-yet-competent candidates.

Instructional Targets

Teacher certification testing provides one vehicle for improving the quality of teachers entering the classroom. The knowledge and skills, which are stated as the performance objectives or competencies identified during test development, serve as instructional "targets" for the preparation of prospective teachers. These targets can be used by individuals because diagnostic test results identify their strengths and weaknesses and help remediate the latter. They can also help teacher preparation programs focus on job-related skills.

Identifying Requisite Knowledge and Skills

In order to provide meaningful targets for teacher preparation, one must identify the specific knowledge and skills required for actual classroom teaching. These job requirements may include professional knowledge and skills (e.g., instructional planning, instructional methods, assessment); basic skills (e.g., reading, writing, computation); and knowledge of the specific content to be taught to students. Job requirements are unique to each state because of the various educational requirements mandated by the state boards of education. Regardless of the categories covered by the tests, classroom performance should be defined in terms of specific objectives or competencies that prospective teachers will be required to master. These initial performance objectives or competencies may be further refined through a systematic job analysis to determine the more critical aspects of the job. Several approaches for conducting job analyses are available including surveys, literature review (e.g., educational research, teacher education program standards), and classroom observation (Elliot, 1982; Levine, Hall, Ash, & Sistrunk, 1981). The job analysis helps define the critical elements of the job for which teacher candidates must be prepared.

The performance objectives and competencies found to be critical and frequently applied on the job are targets for preparing prospective teachers as well as the criteria upon which teachers will be evaluated before receiving a license to teach. The process of defining performance objectives provides a basis for establishing a clear link between actual job requirements, teacher preparation, and teacher evaluation that may not otherwise occur.

Instructional Support

A clear definition of classroom teaching requirements is useful largely because the identified performance objectives or competencies may be incorporated in teacher preparation. The use of performance objectives can occur in several ways. Their application in current teacher certification testing programs is described below.

Disseminating the Performance Objectives

The performance objectives may be disseminated to teacher training programs and prospective teachers enrolled in those programs. Through these objectives, prospective teachers become aware of what they need to know or do and the level at which they need to know or do it. The performance objectives provide a guide to individuals throughout their programs of study and ultimately help prepare them for the certification tests.

Assisting the Individual Candidate: Study Guides

Although the performance objectives are of considerable use to individuals and teacher education programs, they alone provide only partial direction as to how the objectives may be used. To assist prospective teachers in using the performance objectives, several teacher certification testing programs have developed study guides.

Study guides typically provide background information about the program, instruction on how to analyze and interpret the performance objectives, and tips on how to study for and take the certification tests. A single study guide may be developed to cover all the teaching fields in the program, or separate study guides may be prepared for each content area. These field-specific guides[1] contain sample test questions keyed to the performance objectives, the correct answers, and an explanation of each correct and incorrect answer.

Some programs have taken a somewhat different approach in the development of study guides. Rather than provide direction in how to interpret objectives and study for the certification tests, one program has elected to provide a list of resources for each test area (e.g., state-adopted textbooks, curriculum manuals) that can be consulted in preparation for each performance objective. This allows prospective teachers to focus their preparation on the curricula that are most relevant to the teaching jobs in their specific state.

Assisting Teacher Education Programs: Instructional Guides

Some states have prepared instructional guides to further assist teacher preparation programs in using the performance objectives. In addition to providing information to candidates, the instructional guide can assist teacher education programs by analyzing the performance objectives in relation to teacher preparation program curriculum. Moreover, the instructional guide can provide assistance in interpreting and using the test results to guide examinees and to review program curriculum. The sample "Objective-Curriculum Matching Chart" (see Figure 1) is one of the tools that has been included in an instructional guide to meet these goals.

Test Objective and Interpretation	Corresponding Curriculum	Curriculum Revisions
Distinguish between tragedy and comedy: Students must know the difference between tragedy and comedy.	Shakespeare's use of comedy in *A Midsummer Night's Dream* and of tragedy in *Macbeth* thoroughly explained in all lectures on those plays.	Explain comic and tragic elements in works by American playwrights such as Miller and Gardner in lectures on those works.
Analyze the function and elements of plot: Students must know parts of plot and how the parts function in literature.	Study questions that ask students to analyze what happens in each part of the plot are assigned for each literary work covered.	none
Identify the characteristics and uses of satire: Students must recognize satire and how it is used in literature.	none	Define satire and its elements such as irony, parody, and caricature; and explain its uses in the introductory lecture of the course.

Figure 1. Objective-Curriculum Matching Chart
Test Area: Language Arts
Subarea IV-Literature

Instructional Feedback

The contributions of teacher certification testing to teacher preparation are further enhanced through diagnostic score reporting. Diagnostic test results provided to individual examinees can be of use in remediating weaknesses or identifying areas for further study. Similarly, diagnostic test results provided to teacher preparation programs can be used both in assisting individual examinees and in reviewing teacher preparation programs. Diagnostic reporting at the individual examinee and institutional level are discussed below.

INDIVIDUAL TEST RESULTS

Following the administration of the tests, examinees receive a score report that provides information tied to the performance objectives assessed. To ensure the reliability of score reporting information, performance objectives may be grouped into major content subareas with results presented for each subarea. An example of this approach for a test of professional knowledge is provided in the following score report.

Subarea Score Report	
Score	Subarea
65	School Organization and Policies
84	Planning and Curriculum Development
61	Instructional Methods
70	Assessment and Evaluation

The score report can provide the examinee with valuable information for identifying strengths and weaknesses in professional knowledge. In the example above, the examinee did not score well in "School Organization and Policies" or "Instructional Methods," indicating that the examinee has not mastered the content in those subareas. (The question of standards for acceptable test performance is beyond the scope of this chapter.) This suggests that the examinee requires further preparation in the performance objectives included in these major content subareas.

Institutional Test Results

Test results, summarized across examinees from each teacher training institution, are another product of the administration of the tests. These reports are useful in targeting specific areas within the teacher preparation program that may require further emphasis. In the following example of an institution score report for a language arts test (see Figure 2), students as a whole did poorly in literature, suggesting that the institution may need to take additional measures to improve the curriculum associated with this area. The institutional test results can be reviewed against the Objective-Curriculum Matching Chart described earlier to provide a basis for determining specific actions to be taken.

Discussion

This chapter suggests that teacher certification testing programs can serve more than a regulatory function. They can contribute to more effective instruction through improved teacher preparation and diagnostic reporting of test results.

Requisite knowledge and skills should be defined in terms of specific performance objectives or competencies determined through a systematic job analysis. The objectives or competencies should be provided to prospective teachers and teacher education programs for use in preparing for the profession and as a basis for higher education institutions to evaluate their curricula. Assistance in interpreting and applying the established objectives or competencies may be offered through study and instructional guides.

Diagnostic reporting information following test administration can also assist in teacher preparation. Score reports to individual candidates can identify areas of strength and weakness in relation to the performance objectives. Moreover, score report information summarizing overall institutional performance in relation to specific performance objectives can identify areas of the curriculum that may require further emphasis.

The materials and procedures described throughout this chapter suggest that teacher certification testing programs are capable of going beyond the regulatory licensing function to facilitate the improvement of instruction. There is, at this time, little direct empirical evidence of the effectiveness of the measures described in this chapter. With several programs now well established and regulatory goals being met, research of this type should be initiated. This research will identify which measures are most effective and allow scarce state resources to be targeted to those with the most benefits.

INSTITUTION SCORE REPORT

Teacher Certification Testing Program

Test Score Report for _____

Date Test Taken: _____

Test Taken: Language Arts

Questions on the test are grouped into major content subareas.

The subareas on the test are as follows:

    1 = Writing Skills
    2 = Reading Skills
    3 = Research Skills
    4 = Literature
    5 = Additional Areas

Examinee Name	Pass/ Fail	Total Test	Subarea				
			1	2	3	4	5
Tina C.	Pass	77	83	83	71	82	64
Mitzi C.	Fail	65	66	69	93	35	70
Neida L.	Pass	76	77	83	65	76	76
Elizabeth L.	Pass	92	94	100	86	87	87
Philli A.	Pass	76	83	83	78	44	94
Nancy S.	Pass	72	77	78	60	55	94
Institution Average		76	80	83	76	63	81
Statewide Average		82	88	87	83	76	76

Figure 2. Institution Score Report

Footnotes

1. See chapter by Weaver in this volume.

References

Education Commission of the States. (1984, Fall). Newsletter.

Elliot, S. M. (1982). *Teacher certification testing: Technical challenges.* Paper presented at the annual meeting of the National Council on Measurement in Education, New York.

Levine, E. L., Ash, R. A., Hall, H. L., & Sistrunk. F. (1981). *Evaluation of seven job analysis methods by experienced job analysts.* Unpublished research report, University of South Florida, Center for Evaluation Research, Tampa.

Maeroff, G. (1983, April 12). Questions on teacher's skills fuel debate over quality of education. *New York Times,* 1, D22.

National Commission on Excellence in Education. (1983). *A national at risk: The imperative for educational reform.* Washington, DC: U. S. Government Printing Office.

Rubinstein, S. A., McDonough, M. W., & Allan, R. G. (1982). *The changing nature of teacher certification programs.* Paper presented at the annual meeting of the National Council of Measurement in Education, New York.

Traub, J. (1983, May). Principles in action. *Harpers,* 12-13, ff.

U. S. Department of Health, Education and Welfare, Public Health Services. (1977, July). *Credentialling Health Manpower* (DHEW Publication No. 05-77-55057). Washington, DC: Author.